Kashmir 'Face–Off' India's Quandary

Options for India

Books by the Author

Leadership & Leaders

LEADERS FROM THE BARRACKS

GENERALSHIP: ALL THAT REALLY MATTERS

Strategic and Regional Issues

KASHMIR: AN AFFAIR OF CONTINUED EXISTENCE

KASHMIR 'FACE OFF' INDIA'S QUANDARY- OPTIONS FOR INDIA

Professional Behavioural

MANAGING INNER CONFLICT IN PROFESSIONAL LIFE

Kashmir 'Face–Off' India's Quandary

Options for India

by

Brigadier Ashok Kumar Ganguly, SM, VSM (Retd)

Vij Books India Pvt Ltd
New Delhi (India)

Published by

Vij Books India Pvt Ltd
(Publishers, Distributors & Importers)
2/19, Ansari Road
Delhi – 110 002
Phones: 91-11-43596460, 91-11-47340674
M: 98110 94883
E-mail: contact@vijpublishing.com
Web : www.vijbooks.in

ISBN: 978-93-90439-45-4 (Hardback)

ISBN: 978-93-90439-53-9 (Paperback)

ISBN: 978-93-90439-61-4 (ebook)

The views expressed in this book are of the author in his personal capacity.

Contents

Preface   vii

Acknowledgement   xiii

Chapter - I   Backdrop   1

Chapter - II   Kashmir's Significance   26

Chapter - III Containment & Consolidation   50

Chapter - IV   Get Back Occupied Areas   106

Chapter – V   China and Reclamation   180

Epilogue   205

Index   209

Preface

"Deterioration, stagnation, and progress are the three aspects of the position. Those causes of human make which affect position are policy and impolicy (naya and apanaya); fortune and misfortune (aya and anaya) are providential causes. Causes, both human and providential, govern the world and its affairs"

- Chanakya

After the abrogation of the Article 370 and 35 A of the Indian Constitution on 5th August 2019, the special status to Jammu and Kashmir by the Indian Government got abrogated, this brought about certain changes in the geo-strategic sensitivity in reference to the State of Jammu and Kashmir, in terms of the separation of Regions/Divisions, governance, change of State laws, strategic revalidation vis-à-vis Pakistan and China, Pakistan's the proxy war theology (Operation Topac), associated ramification on the issue of demand for freedom by radicalised Kashmiri Muslims and its effects especially in the Kashmir Region.

With the abrogation came the division of the State of Jammu and Kashmir into two Union Territories of Jammu and Kashmir and Ladakh, thus furthering the geographical division of the regions into two parts. Kashmir and Jammu Regions got amalgamated as one entity and the mountainous region of Ladakh given a separate identity. State of Jammu and Kashmir was too large with a land area of about 222,236 Sq Kms, to be governed effectively; the concentrated population centres, therefore, got a better deal, as compared to the remote and sparsely populated areas due to the factors of accessibility and distance. Moreover, if one looks into history, the distance and remoteness were the main reason in the uneven development of the geographical regions; thus, Jammu and Srinagar became developed part of the state.

With the abrogation of Article 370 and 35A the exclusivity in having a separate constitution, separate flag for the state, independent assembly and judiciary, legal codes and separate citizenship rights, have got abolished. The Jammu and Kashmir State which had a separate penal code called Ranbir Penal Code or RPC, with its own judiciary and separate Constituent Assembly, without its concurrence the National Parliamentary directives and orders could get implemented. The people's perception of being independent of the Central dictate of the Indian Parliament was one of the causes of the 'Azadi,' i.e. freedom syndrome of the Muslim population of Kashmir; thus this Azadi has also got quashed along with the abrogation.

With the abrogation of Article 370 and 35A, the Constitution of India, which is relevant and applicable to the rest of India, has now become equally applicable in Jammu and Kashmir. The successful passage of the Jammu and Kashmir Reorganization Bill 2019 in the Rajya Sabah (The Upper House of the Indian Parliament) and Lok Sabah (The Lower House of the Indian Parliament) respectively has changed the dynamics and dimension of erstwhile State of Jammu and Kashmir. The Indian Penal Code, applicable to the whole of India, has come into force in both the Union Territories. Uniformity of law will be making difference in controlling the anti law and order syndicates of the militants /separatists /sympathisers and terrorist supported activities.

The autonomous status of the state of Jammu and Kashmir was therefore relinquished and the state was made to merge with the Republic of India without any discrimination or special status. The transition was peaceful, and the Kashmiri's have reconciled to an extent or one can say at present it is 'wait and watch' stage. The secular status was maintained in the division of the state, with Jammu and Kashmir Union Territory having population composition of Muslims, Hindus, Sikhs and other minority religious groups and Ladakh having population of Buddhists, Hindus and Muslims. The division of the state was thus based on geographical factors, contiguity and keeping the ethnic entity intact. NDA (National Democratic Alliance) Government in power at the Centre have maintained the constituent preamble of secularism of the Indian Constitution, by avoiding religious dominant segregation of the regions in the erstwhile State, under Regions or Divisions, with Kashmir Division having 98 percent Muslims and Jammu having about 62 percent Hindus.

In my book 'Kashmir: An Affair of Continued Existence' published in April 2019 by Vij Books India Private Limited, the historical perspective of the Kashmir, Kashmir issues, it's causes and reasons, prognosis and way out of the Kashmir problems have been covered and analysed. In the said book I have suggested that in order to stop the radicalisation of the Kashmiri Muslim, the War of Jihad in the Kashmir Region and the demand for Azadi (Freedom) by Muslim population was due to the Article 370 and 35 A. These must be abrogated, as it was getting exploited by people of Kashmir, Pakistan and was being made an instrument of political blackmail. Thus there was a need to merge the state with mainland India; this was only possible once the appeasement and special status under Article 370 and citizenship Article 35A were abrogated. Single Constitution, one National Flag and National Anthem as applicable to all other States of India, must be applicable to Jammu and Kashmir. The people of Jammu and Kashmir cannot consider themselves as separate from India. Discriminative provisions and demographic isolation of the people of India had made the syndrome of 'Jihad for Kashmir' and 'Azadi' of Kashmiri Muslim, tenable and which was getting used by Pakistan and Islamist fundamentalists. Whereas in the case of Pakistan and its apprehension of ethnic population of Jammu and Kashmir raising in arms in future and threat of plebiscite, it had changed the demographic equation of the occupied areas by population inversion and shift brought about Islamist radicalisation under the purview of declared Islamic Nation. The abrogation of the Article 370 and 35 A have definitely changed the dimension and dynamics of the perception of Azadi (freedom) by the Muslim population of Jammu and Kashmir, frustrated Pakistan as its interest and game plan has got disturbed and have put apprehensions in the minds of Chinese of forced occupation Aksai Chin and Shaksgam Valley which was ceded by Pakistan.

The quandary which has cropped up after abrogation of 370 and 35 A therefore remains. *Firstly,* the locus-standi of Pakistan Occupied and Disputed Jammu and Kashmir, the Map of India as proclaimed after division of the State into Union Territories (UT) of Jammu and Kashmir and Ladakh respectively and which has been authenticated in the Jammu and Kashmir Reorganization (Removal of Difficulties) Second Order, 2019, issued by the President of India. The UT Ladakh includes the areas of the districts of Gilgit, Wazarat, Chilhas and Tribal Territories of 1947, in addition to the remaining areas of Leh, Ladakh and the Kargil District which are part of India, in other words the UT Ladakh includes the whole of Northern Area (Gilgit-Baltistan) of Pakistan Occupied Jammu and Kashmir, part that had been ceded to China by Pakistan and Aksai Chin occupied after 1962 Indo-China War. Union Territory of Jammu and

Kashmir now includes whole of so called Azad Jammu and Kashmir of Pakistan Occupied Kashmir (POK), 10 districts of Jammu Region and 10 districts of Kashmir Region; the Union Territory extends from Greater Himalayan Range and the Valley of Kashmir in the north up till the Indian Punjab in the south. The occupied part of UT Jammu and Kashmir is the narrow strip of land of approximately 13,297 Sq Kms and is the buffer land between India and Pakistan to which Pakistan is highly sensitive. The map of Jammu and Kashmir after abrogation of the Article 370 and 35 A has been accepted by the world and except for Pakistan and China, no other nation has had any observations.

MAP OF UT OF JAMMU & KASHMIR AND UT OF LADAKH

**Map: Union Territory Jammu and Kashmir and Union Territory
Ladakh**

Secondly, it is the Pakistan Factor and its Proxy War which has been a cause of concern to India. By changing the geographical mapping of the state and sub dividing the state in two Union Territories, this has upset Pakistan's plans of amalgamation of Kashmir with Pakistan, based on the claims of the majority Muslim population. *Thirdly,* the radical elements of Jihad and terror organisations which are being nurtured in Pakistan occupied territories of Jammu and Kashmir and sponsoring of terrorism and militancy in hinterland of Indian Jammu and Kashmir, the propensity has not seen much shift and likely to continue till such time it loses the public support. The Indian secessionist and separatists groups in Kashmir Valley who are supporting Pakistan, after abrogation for precautionary measures were kept under arrest, even though presently their activates are suppressed but the apprehension of the reactions once released from custody remains, this is going to be a cause of concern and will require strong hand handling. *Fourthly,* the third estate i.e. the people of Jammu and Kashmir especially Kashmiri Muslims and their anti India stance within the Kashmir Valley and fringe areas, the silent simmering continues to exists as on date and when it gets impetus what will be the level of flare up or there will be reconciliation, is yet to be seen. *Fifthly* the Muslim dominated Political Parties within the state and their future course of action; and the anti BJP political parties of India will also be a cause of concern. *Sixthly* are the integration plans of the Government of India, in order to bring about overall socio-economic development and to convince the people of the seriousness of the approach to build the bridge with the mainland India, 'wait and watch' phase is in vogue and will depend how much time the people give to the Central Government. *Lastly,* the international and United Nations response and the issue of resolving the pending subject of the disputed territory under Pakistan's occupation which otherwise is part of India, possibility of UN or World Powers intervention on new terms as plebiscite declared in the resolution of 1948 is not valid anymore or will it be acceptable to Indian and Pakistan, is yet to be seen.

With the withdrawal of the special status and the strong hand handling of the state of affairs in the Jammu and Kashmir by the NDA Government (National Democratic Alliances of Bharatiya Janata Party), the real picture is yet to emerge; the stakes holders who were ruling the roost have been for the time being kept dormant but the question is, for how long? The issue of Kashmir is, presently still hanging in suspended animation, and the impasse which has been prevailing among the Kashmiri's cumulative psychological and perception build-up continues to be imbedded and is an issue of apprehension. Influence of events over the period since partition of India and Pakistan and signing of Instrument of Accession by the rulers of Jammu and Kashmir with India in Oct 1947, has kept changing the dynamics of the Kashmir embroil, as various players and stakeholders played their individual part to keep the issue of Kashmir in continued existence, this affected the perception, temperament and outlook of the common people who had to bear the hardships of insurgency and proxy war. Position in respect to the question of the 'Azadi' (freedom) of Kashmiri, in which Pakistan has been playing a domineering role since 1989 and the special status which was taken as exclusivity to separate the people from India since 1954 now stands abolished, and is going to have more changes in dynamics of strategies and geopolitical imperatives. It is against this back drop that certain scenarios are going to emerge, which will be having its various dimensions and their magnitudes which must be considered and need to be understood by the political bosses and the think tanks; this would help to contrivance approaches in addressing the possibilities arising after abrogation of article 370 and 35A. In order to understand what all had happened and what is going to happen, this book 'Kashmir Face Off: India's Quandary' tries to answer certain strategic and geo-political issues, as the lot of changes are anticipated and going to make difference in the subcontinent and the regional power equations.

Issues which I would be discussing and highlighting may be hypothetical, but certain issues are facts on ground and some are already under implementation or under planning by the think tanks of India. The possibilities must not be out rightly ruled out, as some of them can be developed to create position of advantage for India. The book must be read with this backdrop.

> *"Learn from the mistakes of others..... You can't live long enough to make them all yourselves"*
>
> ~ *Chanakya*

Acknowledgement

This book would not have been possible without support of my wife Keya, who had to bear with me and my late nights, forego weekends many a times and she silently went through the secession of the script proof reading and discussions. While writing this book I relived my days from young Second Lieutenant days, till my day of retirement, I am grateful to all my Regimental colleagues, Coursemates, Friends with whom I have served in Staff and Command and to my son who always believed in me. I am also grateful to my daughter Priya for going through the script, editing, downloading Maps and giving her frank opinion; which helped me in making the script and narratives more pragmatic. If I fail to mention my daughter Pritha who is physically challenged, great injustice will be done, she kept the logistic running even at very odd hours.

Chapter - I

Backdrop

"A person who is aware of future troubles, and fight against them with his intelligence will be always happy. And a person you remains inactive (without working) waiting for good days to come will destroy his own life."

~ Chanakya

It would be pertinent to understand the issue of Kashmir first, Kashmir was part of the kingdom of Jammu and Kashmir ruled by Hindu King, ironically the majority population was of Muslim, if one goes back to the history of Kashmir, it was very much part of Aryan settlement and if we go by religious evolutions, first to come into the region was Hinduism and as the reign kept changing gradually Islam became the majority following, however all religions co-existed and are still existing. Thus Jammu and Kashmir was part of Greater India as part of British India till partition in 1947.

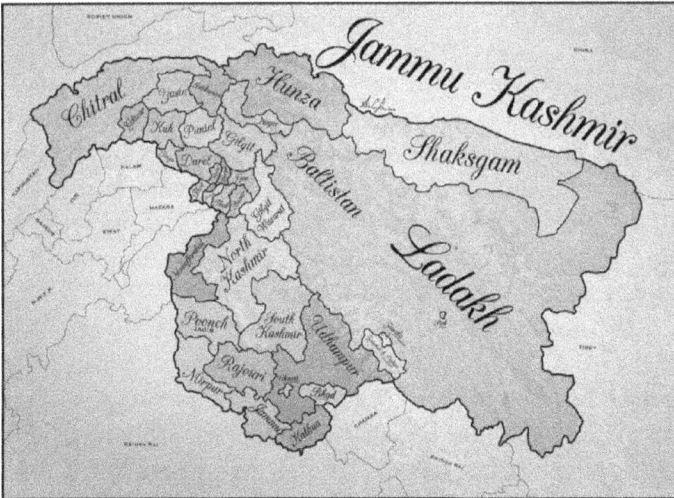

Map of Jammu and Kashmir during Dogra Hindu Rulers Times

The Muslim majority population, well before the partition had initiated the call of Azadi (freedom) during the Hindu rulers reign in 1930's and as the area was large and remote the control of Hindu Ruler was diminishing, call of freedom became more intense as the country was approaching the partition. The factor of majority did matter; especially in the areas of Kashmir Valley Region, Northern Area (areas of Chilas, Gilgit, Hunza, Skardu and Baltistan), the Kargil Region and Western Jammu Region which had high percentage of Muslim population. These areas were getting away from the Hindu Ruler's grip. The only State which was yet to commit to accession or merger after the partition and declaration of independence of India and Pakistan was Jammu and Kashmir. As per two-nation theory which was based more on religious and communal grounds of majority population, Jammu & Kashmir at that point of time was having majority population of Muslim 68 percent, Hindus 30 percent and Others 2 percent. As the State was bordering Pakistan, it was assumed that it would become part of Pakistan. Hindu ruler's reluctance to join either Pakistan or India became an issue of contention and matter of 'Face-off'.

Pakistan's higher command was very sure, that Jammu and Kashmir will be part of Islamic Pakistan based on three assumptions. *Firstly,* majority Muslim dominated areas in the State gives Pakistan the automatic accession. *Secondly,* internal political turbulence, especially by the Muslims who wanted to free itself from the yoke of the Hindu Ruler and the unrest/revolt against the rule of Maharaja by the Muslim population. *Lastly,* polarisation towards Pakistan of certain percentage of the Muslim population, especially in the Kashmir Valley, Punch and Rajouri Districts.

Maharaja Hari Singh with the view of forestalling military intervention by either country for forced accession/annexation, and in order to gain time to decide on the question of accession kept pending the issue. The Maharaja (King) of Jammu and Kashmir went in for Stand Still Agreement with both the countries, to which Pakistan became the signatory. Pakistan would have very much used its military, to bring a conclusive end to the Jammu & Kashmir issue. But as it had signed the Standstill Agreement with the Government of Jammu & Kashmir, it could not use its military forces. As the time passed and the interest which was shown by India, made Pakistan apprehensive, thus Pakistan launched a pre-emptive clandestine operation called 'Operation Gulmarg' and infiltrated tribesmen of Northern Frontiers under the command of Pakistan Army regulars. This changed the equation, the Maharaja fearing the collapse of the kingdom went in for accession with India in return of military intervention to drive out the raiders. Frankly speaking, Pakistan committed the greatest blunder, if not the whole Jammu and Kashmir, the possibility of Muslim majority areas going with Pakistan, was always there if negotiations had progressed under the British; in that case, Hindu and Buddhist part would have been with India.

Pakistan ventured into Jammu & Kashmir in Sep 1947 with the primary aim of annexing the State, with this premise that the Northern Area of Gilgit, Hunza, Skardu and Baltistan under the agreement with Pakistan Administered Kashmir was gifted by the British, who carried out coup to ouster the Maharaja's State Forces. The Pakistani assumption was that by capture of Srinagar the capital city, the whole of Jammu and Kashmir could be annexed, as the Muslims of the fringe areas of the Kashmir Valley would have joined the raiders by then and revolted. Thus Pakistan infiltrated both irregular militia from the Northern Province and regular troop under the garb of tribesmen, to capture Srinagar and the Kashmir Valley by force. There was a large scale desertion in the State Forces by Muslim troops, who went and joined the plunder. The State Forces deployed in various parts of Kashmir, after giving stiff resistance, gave way to the invaders onslaught and had to withdraw. On 26 October 1947, the Maharaja accepted the Indian accession and then Governor-General of India Lord Mountbatten endorsed the accession with his remark, "*it is my Government's wish that as soon as law and order have been restored in Jammu and Kashmir and her soil cleared of the invader, a reference to the people should settle the question of the State's accession*", however, the Maharaja Hari Singh did not ask for any referendum or plebiscite.

The Indian Army was able to evict the raiders and was on the verge of clearing the occupied areas West of Rajouri-Poonch-Uri-North of Neelam Valley line and West of Kargil in the Northern Area; the ceasefire was declared by Prime Minister of India by involving the United Nations and its intervention. There are many schools of thoughts on this subject why Prime Minister of India J L Nehru, went for the ceasefire at the nick of the time, when operations were going on for complete eviction and were on the verge of total recapture of the whole of Jammu and Kashmir. *Firstly,* on the advice of Lord Mountbatten, Prime Minister of India J L Nehru went to United Nations Organisation (UNO) with the request of ceasefire; it was basically to point out Pakistan as an aggressor, internationalise the accession issue as legal and assurance given by Lord Mountbatten of mitigating the issue in India's favour, as at that time Britain was one of the most powerful members of the United Nations Organisation. The irony was Britain took no interest to bring an end to the Kashmir issue and neither could UNO and its resolution of 1948 force Pakistan to vacate the occupied areas, thus denying the scope of plebiscite and people's choice. *Secondly*, some school of thought attribute the Indian Army's inability to evict the complete area, as it was becoming untenable to continue the war for over a year and winter was setting in, the war was becoming costly and lines of communication for support of the war effort was very large and cumbersome, moreover areas across the present Line of Control (LOC) was occupied by regular Pakistani Forces with strong defensive disposition. Thus force requirement was far more and it was not available at that point of time. Some attribute the slow progress due to faulty military leadership which Pakistan took advantage to reinforce their positions, as Pakistan did not want to lose the occupied part, it would have threatened the bordering strategic towns in depth. *Thirdly*, some are of the view that British purposefully brought the ceasefire to create buffer area between Pakistan and Indian Jammu and Kashmir, this argument does not hold much ground as the question of buffer in that case at that time was not restricted to Jammu and Kashmir only. On the contrary, the occupied areas were being exploited to give strategic depth to sensitive areas in Pakistan Punjab and North-West Frontier Province. Keeping aside all the arguments in respect of ceasefire, the point remains that the conditions of the UN resolutions were not fulfilled by Pakistan. Still as on date the Kashmir issue continues to remain in existence and is declared bilateral issue.

Question of the validity of Jammu & Kashmir accession to India is still contested by Pakistan, as it claims that under two-nation theory the majority Muslim population state rightfully belongs to Pakistan. Thus it has been asserting its rights over the whole of Jammu & Kashmir State. India's claim is based on the legality of the accession of Jammu & Kashmir to India, with unconditional and final consent of the Maharaja Hari Singh under his seal of office and seconded by the British Governor-General, now it is an uncontested legal document i.e. Instrument of Accession. On the other hand, Pakistan maintains that the accession was fraudulent and devious Indian political game. Both British and USA are also to be blamed who conjured the term Line of Control and disputed area, thus keeping the dispute in continued existence and giving credence to claims of both parties and terming it as a bilateral issue.

The legitimacy of Indian claim is put under doubts, with the word 'bilateral' put in between. Whereas there is no scope of word 'bilateral' existing, as accession was between Maharaja Hari Singh the Ruler of

Jammu and Kashmir and India, therefore the ambiguity which is made to prevail at the international level, in fact must not be there. It must be made clear to the world that Article 370 and 35 A were part of the Indian constitution and did not apply to the occupied territory of Jammu and Kashmir, nor it was an existing provision before the State accession. What has made Pakistan to oppose abrogation of the articles so vehemently, was the Kashmiri Card of self-governance which was part of Article 370, and citizenship exclusively for the State subjects under Article 35A, so that gradual Radical Islamisation of Jammu and Kashmir could be achieved by total Muslim occupation, thus forcing non Muslims to leave the State, as it happened in the case of Kashmiri Pundits. The Map of Jammu and Kashmir also gradually got formalised as Pakistan Occupied Jammu and Kashmir (POK) was being shown as Azad Jammu and Kashmir and Gilgit –Baltistan as disputed but part of Pakistan. Similarly, Jammu and Kashmir areas under China's occupation in 1962 (COK2) and Pakistan gifting part to China in 1963 (COK1), being shown as part of China when both the territories are disputed. What rightfully belonged to India as a whole now got divided in the maps between Pakistan, China and India as occupied territories? Thus there was the need to make the world aware about the facts which have been ignored since 1963.

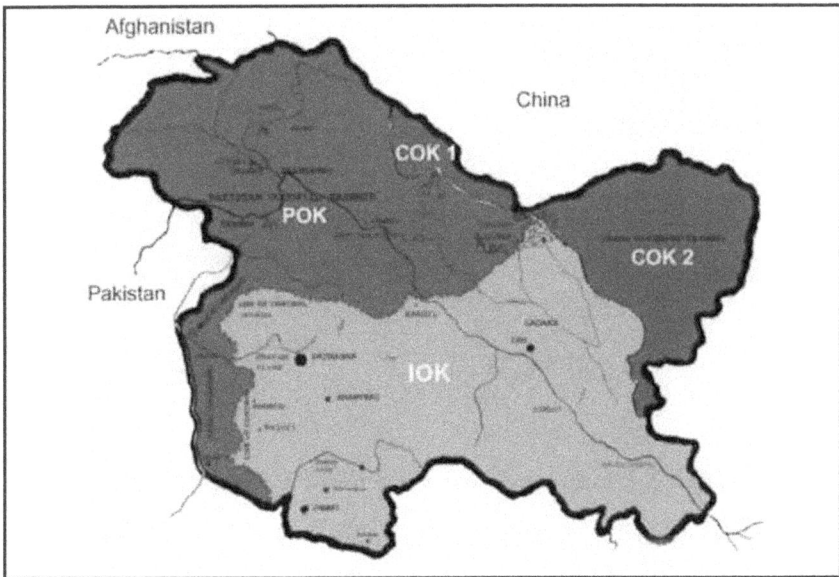

Map of Jammu and Kashmir Prior to 05 August 2019

The abrogation of the Articles 370 and 35 A of Indian Constitution of exclusive status to the State of Jammu and Kashmir is an internal matter and integration of the State under one constitution is the exclusive right of the Government of India, and there is no doubt that Jammu and Kashmir is the integral part of India. The State was bifurcated into two Union Territories of Jammu and Kashmir and Ladakh respectively. The world did not have any objection and have accepted, that it is internal matter of India and have all the rights to carry out amendments of its constitution or abrogate certain clauses. The present map of Jammu and Kashmir is inclusive of occupied territories which have been amalgamated with the two Union Territories of India i.e. UT Jammu and Kashmir and UT Ladakh :-

Map UT Jammu and Kashmir and UT Ladakh of India

On the other hand, India also blundered and lost opportunities, to bring to an end the issue of Jammu & Kashmir. Many Indians believe it was a blunder on the part of India, as it lost the initiatives gained in 1947-48 by going in for ceasefire and blaming the then Prime Minister J L Nehru and Congress Government. Followed by, in 1965 Indo-Pak War, returning the captured areas of the disputed territories in Pakistan Occupied Jammu and Kashmir thus recognising the status of Line of Control (LOC) by the Congress Government in power, giving away recaptured occupied areas was not warranted as LOC would have been realigned with captured territories becoming part of reclamation of occupied territories from Pakistan. After 1971 war with faulty vanquisher's conditions and lack of geo-strategic vision, Congress leadership was unable to pressurise Pakistan or gain a position of advantage by making Pakistan return the occupied territories of Jammu and Kashmir. In 1999 Kargil War, where the opportunity existed, to alter the status of Line of Control (LOC) in India's favour, by going in for pursuit of retreating Pakistan Army into the disputed territory, thus lack of political will and coming under USA pressure, made the BJP Government lose the initiative and the war was made localised one. Indian magnanimity has made India lose many opportunities to sort out the Kashmir issue.

In order 'to appease' the people of Jammu & Kashmir by then Prime Minister J L Nehru, the Congress Government went in for the introduction of Article 370 and 35A and granting State Autonomy under the Indian Constitution in 1954 with its own Separate Flag, Constitution, Assembly and Law & Judiciary, this made the issue of Kashmir more complex, as these articles gave opportunity to both the outside and the inside elements to create fissures, thus building the demand of freedom and providing scope of secession and merging with Islamic State of Pakistan. Restricted jurisdiction of the Indian Parliament in the State affairs further compounded the issue; this had actually created fault lines in acceptance by the people of Kashmir, the sovereignty of India. Polarisation on communal lines of the regions of Kashmir, Jammu and Ladakh due to parochial political developments, religious majority separation of the regions, sponsored terrorism, attempt of radicalisation of Muslim population and lack of socio-political integration with the mainland, became cause of instability in Jammu and Kashmir. This got exploited in creating perception changes in the Muslim population at politico–religious lines and demand of freedom by Kashmiri Muslims. The Articles were however termed as temporary inclusion and was not given any permanency, however, over last 70 years it made to exist due to socio-politico compulsion, as no political party was ready to 'bell the cat' or disturb the status-quo.

Political engineering since 1947 was another cause, which kept the Kashmir issue in continued existence, political blunders both at State and Central level kept recurring alongside political experimentations at all levels. The power politics became the norms and this lead to vote bank manipulations, especially in reference to creation of own turf and position of benefit. It was the political manipulation of elections, getting into position of power and resultant unethical practises in elections, led to discontentment among the people of Jammu and Kashmir. The outcome was insurgency and terrorism making in-road in Kashmir Region in particular and Muslim majority areas in the year 1989-90 and thereafter. Advantage was taken by Pakistan in sponsoring insurgency and terrorism, creating anti India terrorist organisations and operating these within Pakistan Occupied Kashmir, launching of Proxy War to create instability in Indian Jammu and Kashmir and sponsor separatists within the Indian State to bring about Islamic radicalism in the Kashmir Region and majority Muslim dominated areas adjoining Kashmir region. All this was due to Article 370 and 35A, which gave the scope of creating grounds for the people of Kashmir to demand freedom and breaking away from India, creating Muslim majority mandate on deciding breakaway and making Pakistan as the choice country. Own State and the power of self-rule created mindset towards total independence in Kashmiri Muslims, to top up, radicalisation of the Kashmiri Muslim religion was brought about, thus manifesting the desire of being part of Islamic State and distancing from secular and democratic India. The Hindus and Buddhists were never party to this since 1947 partition and never supported the Muslim majority, these communities were aware of religious cleansing in partitioned Pakistan, the Hindu population of 24 percent after partition in Pakistan stands less than 2 percent today. Hindus and minorities have equal rights as the majority Muslim to stay in their own State of Jammu and Kashmir, which the radical Muslims do not want.

The question which many Indians have been asking since long i.e. when comparison is made with Pakistan and its stance with regard to people of Pakistan Occupied Jammu & Kashmir. *Firstly,* why the voice of Azadi (freedom) has been suppressed by Pakistan and why the right to personal freedom which is part of Pakistan Constitution, not applicable to indigenous people of the Jammu and Kashmir of the occupied areas not been given constitutional recognition, then why India is giving so much to the Kashmiri? *Secondly,* to keep handful of Kashmiri appeased, through the constitutional safeguards of Article 370 and 35 A and also tolerate their call of Azadi (freedom) and support to radical Islamic insurgency, why? *Thirdly,* why India is continuing with the concessions of Article 370 and

35 A which gives the scope for demanding excision from India? *Fourthly*, when the articles were made temporary, why it continued to remain so and not absolved once the J&K Legislative Assembly was in place; however it remained in the Indian Constitution in spite of temporary inclusion for seventy years? *Lastly*, the Constitution of India's relevance, it is not there due to the Article 370 and 35A but Jammu and Kashmir has been getting favoured status in spite of its failed autonomy and poorly managed poor economy by its elected Governments under its own separate constitution? There are no answers, except for political gains, the Articles were made to exist.

Another question is why are the separatists who want separation from India to join Pakistan, are so concerned with Article 370 and 35 A to stay, as it is not going to be applicable in Pakistan or claiming independence under Islamic State. The simple reason is, spirit of freedom in the Kashmiri Muslim has been kept alive by Article 370 and 35A, articles have been used for fuelling the demand of freedom, as in its scope the provision exists and which can be interpreted to suit the convenience?

Actually, the State of Jammu and Kashmir is leaning heavily, on to the Government of India for its very survival, it does not have its own economic potential; it contributes only one percent of the total GDP of India, which is totally negligible and yet is the biggest spender of the exchequer as compared to other Indian States. The Indian Government is perpetually in the logjam of the special status to the State of Jammu and Kashmir. The Kashmir region is, far from amity and stability and in reality is considered as highly disturbed, the opinion of the masses are not yet congenial and is anti establishment, each player and stakeholders within the State have their own stake and no one is ready to lose an inch of its turf which includes the separatists, politics, so called indigenous freedom fighters and the people parse, the sentiments have the influence of Article 370 and 35A. Therefore the question remains, how long the temporariness of Article 370 and 35A is going to exist and when will the Government of India take the stand on its abrogation or abolition? There are only two options , *one* is to keep waiting and keep the issue open and *second* is go through a forced abrogation of the Article 370 and 35 A, various connotations and varied opinions are existing on the subject each of which are as vague as the question itself.

With the above backdrop and the situations as was prevailing prior to August 2019, let us discuss the relevance of 370 and 35A and why the abrogation was warranted by the BJP Government before going into the reason analysis; let us see what is Article 370 and 35A.

Article 370

- ❖ **History.** In October 1947, the then Maharaja Hari Singh of Kashmir signed the 'Instrument of Accession', which specified three subjects on which Jammu and Kashmir would transfer its powers to the Government of India, *firstly* Foreign Affairs, *secondly* Defence and *thirdly* Communications. In March 1948, the Maharaja appointed an Interim Government in the State, with Sheikh Abdullah as the Prime Minister. In July 1949, Sheikh Abdullah and three other colleagues joined the Indian Constituent Assembly and negotiated the special status of Jammu and Kashmir, leading to the adoption of Article 370. The controversial provision was drafted by Sheikh Abdullah. Inserted in 1954, Four years after the Constitution of India came into being in 1950, the Article 370 got incorporated in the Indian Constitution through a special order issued by the President of India. There were many objections and in the Instrument of Accession there was never any mention of special status when signed on 27 Oct 1947, it was the India Prime Minister JL Nehru who went with the amendment without going through the Indian Parliament both Houses and got it incorporated under the Presidential Order. Within the Congress Party, which was having single majority there were differences, opposition strength was negligible at that time thus it could not influence any government decision.

- ❖ **Provisions of Article 370.** Article 370 embodied six special provisions for Jammu and Kashmir. *Firstly,* it exempted the State from the complete applicability of the Constitution of India; the State was conferred with the power to have its own constitution. *Secondly,* Central Legislative powers over the State were limited and restricted, at the time of framing the article only three subjects of defence, foreign affairs and communications was bestowed to the Central Government. *Thirdly,* other constitutional powers of the Central Government could be extended to the State only with the concurrence of the State Government. *Fourthly,* the 'concurrence' was only provisional; it had to be ratified by the State's Constituent Assembly. *Fifthly,* the State Government's authority to give 'concurrence' lasted only until the State Constituent Assembly was convened, once the State Constituent Assembly finalised the scheme of powers and dispersed, no further extension of powers was possible. *Sixthly*, Article 370 could be abrogated or amended only upon the recommendation of the State's Constituent Assembly. These provisions surmounted to:-

➤ Indian Parliament needs the Jammu & Kashmir Government's nod for applying laws in the State — except defence, foreign affairs and communications. Article 370 granted special and separate status to the State of Jammu & Kashmir and had allowed it to have a separate constitution, dual citizenship, a State flag and autonomy over the internal administration of the State.

➤ Despite being a State of Union of India, the Article 370 defined that the Jammu and Kashmir State's residents would live under a separate set of laws, including those related to citizenship, ownership of property, and fundamental rights as compared to residents of other Indian States. The Article prohibited Indian citizens from other States from buying any land or property in Jammu and Kashmir. The law of citizenship, ownership of property, and fundamental rights of the residents of Jammu & Kashmir is different from the residents living in rest of India

➤ Under Article 370, the Centre has no power to declare financial emergency.

➤ It is important to note Article 370(1) (c) explicitly mentions that Article 1 of the Indian Constitution applies to Jammu and Kashmir through Article 370. Article 1 lists the States of the Union. This means that it is Article 370 that binds the State of Jammu and Kashmir to the Indian Union. The interpretation was taken as the State can any time move out of the agreement and this got exploited by various stakeholders.

➤ Under Article 370 the Indian Parliament cannot increase or reduce the borders of the State. This gave an impression to the people of Kashmir that they had all the rights to the freedom from India, if the terms of agreement with India on accession are not fulfilled.

➤ **Temporary Provision of Article 370.** The article was drafted in Part XXI of the Constitution as Temporary, Transitional and had Special Provisions. The Constituent Assembly of Jammu and Kashmir was only empowered to change status either with regard to continuance of the temporary provision of Article 370 or to abrogate it altogether. Indian Government need not be consulted for any amendment or change, it can only recommend for consideration. Article 370 was a temporary provision as its applicability was intended to last till the formulation and adoption of the State's Constitution. Since the State's Constituent Assembly dissolved itself on 25 January 1957 without recommending either abrogation or amendment of the Article 370, the Article stayed within the Constitution of India. Neither the word 'Constituent Assembly' was replaced with 'Legislative Assembly of Jammu and Kashmir' when it came into being, in the provisions by either the State Government nor did the Central Government care to take any action on the same, thus the temporariness remained in the following years, lasting seven decades. As such Union of India was empowered to abrogate, amend the provisions in Article 370 as there was no Constituent Assembly to which any reference could be made. However the Articles continued to remain in existence over last 70 years without any opposition, objection or amendments, thus the state subjects made it their right and people of India termed it as special status exclusive to Jammu and Kashmir. Since it remained operative and the Jammu and Kashmir Legislative Assembly which replaced the Constitution Assembly, had not made any effort as it was suiting the political powers. Thus status quo was made to remain, nor any change or additional provisions incorporated, as it would have racked up unwarranted objections. Many lacunas and gaps which existed got exploited especially by the Muslim population and political parties of Kashmir Valley parse. The Hindus and other minority communities never supported or became party to either continuation of Article 370 or its abrogation.

What were the ramifications on ground? These must be analysed to know why the abrogation was necessary and how the Article 370 got exploited in Jammu and Kashmir, by Pakistan and the Separatists:-

❖ Parallel Constitution for Jammu and Kashmir and India, however there was no similarity in the contents and at places it was found contradictory where the interest of the majority population mattered, the constitution was without any safeguard to minorities. The irony was *firstly* having a constitution within constitution, *secondly* the Indian Constitution which was making the provision had no power what so ever over the State Constitution, *thirdly* unlike in the Constitution of India, the rights of minority communities in Kashmir and many other fundamental rights like education, job, inheritance and property were not protected. As the status of Jammu and Kashmir was separate from rest of India, it was presumed that State is a separate entity and Indian Central Government had very restricted jurisdiction, thus the State subject were made to understand and create an mindset by interested parties, that option to chose freedom from India always exists, if people are not satisfied and the terms of The Article 370 are not agreed especially which impinge the right to self determination or liberty. It was for this reason and option the Kashmiri Muslims considered the State as not part of India.

❖ Separate constitution provided the scope to incitement of the Azadi (freedom) movement, radicalisation of Kashmiri Muslims and support to the proclaimed 'Jihad'. This was one of the major reasons in cleansing of the Hindus and other minority population in the Kashmir Region in 1989 - 1990. Kashmiri never wanted that any State subject other than Muslim , to settle in the Valley or the Kashmir Region, literally the Hindus and minorities in spite of being State subject could not purchase land or house in Kashmir and those who are still there are paying 'Jizya' (Tax on non Muslims) to militants in order to survive.

❖ The constitution had shades of 'Shariyat' laws. Thus education was not taken as a right. The female population was most affected as their rights were impinged with regard to marriage, right to property and citizenship of their children. The scheduled castes were deprived of basic human rights, as their job is looked down upon and below pure Muslim dignity. All the Indian States on the other hand are governed with the doctrines of Directive Principles of State Policy granting rights of education, inheritance, employment to each and every citizen and concessions to minorities and Scheduled Caste/Tribe. But in Kashmir it did not apply. The State Constitution in real terms had given leeway to the terrorist and militant organisation to force 'Shariyat' in Kashmir Region

❖ The constitution was exclusive for the people of only Jammu and Kashmir not as a State but as a country where the Indians do not have any rights of any nature including purchase of land or make use of the land of any Kashmiri for any business or industry, lease was also not permitted. This was a major drawback as no infrastructure developmental work could take place, State survived only on cottage and small industries which could not generate employment, economy suffered as there was no investment from the business houses of India and the provisions of the Article kept India from developing the State potentials by FDI or invite business fraternity to establish industries.

❖ Deprived Women of their Rights. J&K women who married Non-Permanent Residents of Kashmir would lose their Permanent Resident status and inheritance rights in Kashmir. So if a girl marries any Indian who is not a permanent resident of Kashmir she would lose all her rights and Kashmiri citizenship. Even if the person who marries the girl and wants to settle down in Kashmir, the family loses their rights. On the other hand if she marries a Pakistani (person of occupied Kashmir), all her rights are intact.

❖ Reservation of Government jobs except for sweeper which was for lower and backward caste that was brought to carry out the dirty job from Punjab in 1957. They could not get a Scheduled Caste certificate from the State Government and therefore were not eligible for any benefits under Central Government schemes. In Muslim society sweeper and scavenging job is considered as below dignity and this is left to non Muslims, it was this reason that low caste sweepers were brought from Punjab, and these people have been living in Jammu and Kashmir for last sixty odd years without citizenship of the State. How can this be possible in today's environment where the sanitization infrastructure have been modernised and the sanitization work has become more mechanised.

❖ Breeding racial discrimination. Muslims coming from Pakistan have been given the right of citizenship, while Hindus and Sikh refugees from West Pakistan have been denied citizenship. This communal discrimination has been an issue of contention. People who had crossed over in 1947 to Pakistan and have become permanent citizen are permitted to return and claim dual citizenship and right to property, the wards of such persons who were born in Pakistan have also been given the same privilege by the State Constitution. The person who had crossed over in 1947 and was just born will be seventy plus today and most with higher age would have expired by now, giving such concession today is not understood and totally illogical, as such people are no more State subject of Indian Jammu and Kashmir. Kashmiri Muslims want to stick on with the provision. Thus the abrogation checkmated ulterior motives of separatists and Pakistan in getting public support and have a major role to play in the issue of separation from India?

❖ Mr. Jagmohan, Governor of Jammu and Kashmir, wrote to the Indian Prime Minister Rajiv Gandhi *"Article 370 is nothing but a breeding ground for the parasites at the heart of the paradise. It skins the poor. It deceives them with its mirage. It lines the pockets of the "power elites." It fans the ego of the new sultans. In essence, it creates a land without justice, a land full of crudities and contradictions. It props up politics of deception, duplicity and demagogy",* he further added *"The fundamental aspect which has been lost sight of, in the controversy for deletion or retention of Article 370 is its misuse. Over the years, it has become an instrument of exploitation in the hands of the ruling political elites and other vested interests in bureaucracy, business, judiciary and bar. Apart from the politicians, the richer classes have found it convenient to amass wealth and not allow healthy financial legislation to come to the State."* There is no doubt that the Article 370 had many lopsided provisions, it gave opportunity to Muslim political parties to take advantage of majority in assembly and have helped them in parochial power politics.

❖ The provisions of the Wealth Tax, the Urban Land Ceiling Act, the Gift Tax etc, and other beneficial laws of the Union have not been allowed to be operated in the State under the cover of Article 370. Tax evasion using the Article 370 provision has been a known practise as no financial regulations of the Centre was applicable to the State. The article over the years became detrimental in development when the State was getting maximum grants from the Government of India; the largest Indian State Uttar Pradesh was getting less than Jammu and Kashmir. State law was found to be lenient and not detrimental to money laundering, amassing of wealth and property. Every stakeholder took advantage of the provisions of the Article 370 and the law of the State to make money. No political party till date has replied to Auditor General's central audit enquiries and there is large scale misappropriation of central funds. This is more so, because there is no jurisdiction of audit by central agencies in the State.

❖ Keeping the spirit of Two Nation Theory alive. Article 370 lacked the very spirit of secularism, as the majority population prevailed over the minorities and their rights. It facilitated the growth and continuation of corrupt oligarchies and puts false notions in the minds of the youth, which got exploited by Pakistan and Indian Separatists. It has given rise to regional tensions and conflicts. In practise the autonomy was impracticable due to Article 370 dichotomy in its provisions. Sheikh Abdulla had his own political interest which was evident in the Article 370, in which the option of accession to Pakistan and Independence was very much prevalent in the wordings of the Article 370.

❖ The very purpose of Article 370 got diluted over the years as changes kept creeping in the presidential order, it started with removal of Sadar-e-Riyasat (President) and Wazir-e-Azam (Prime Minister) and introduction of Chief Minister in place of Prime Minister and Governor in place of President. The Constituent Assembly became State Legislative Assembly. Acts passed by Indian Parliament have been extended to Jammu and Kashmir over a period of time under the clause of concurrence.

❖ The dilution in the provision of Article 370 has been going on since 1958. Still certain provisions continued which created fissures between people of India. Political parties of Kashmir Valley have been most vehement in abrogation but the people of Jammu and Ladakh have welcomed the abrogation, this population is approximately 34 percent of the total population of Jammu and Kashmir.

Article 35 A

Article 35A was introduced through a Presidential Order in 1954, to continue the old provisions of the territory regulations under Article 370 of the Indian constitution.

❖ The Article 35A permits the local legislature in Indian-administered Jammu and Kashmir to define permanent residents of the region.

- ❖ It forbids outsiders from permanently settling, buying land, holding local government jobs or winning education scholarships.

- ❖ The article, referred to as the Permanent Residents Law, also bars female residents of Jammu and Kashmir from property rights in the event that they marry a person from outside the State. The provision also extends to such women's children.

- ❖ While Article 35A has remained unchanged, some aspects of Article 370 have been diluted over the decades but 35 A was never touched.

There are school of thought, which do not support the abrogation of the Article 370 and 35 A, reason advocated by them is that when due to the appeasement under Article 370 the people of Jammu and Kashmir joined India and given independent constitutional rights, how can it be abrogated without the consensus of the Constituent Assembly of Jammu and Kashmir as per the provisions. The matter is now with Supreme Court of India. Pakistan on the other hand claim Pakistan Occupied Jammu and Kashmir as liberated, thus the issue of appeasement did not arise and neither it made any provision which were exclusive to Jammu and Kashmir. In the divided Jammu and Kashmir, Indian part is demanding liberation based on Islamic agenda and amalgamating with Islamic Pakistan, where as other part is raising voice of separation from Pakistan, what counts here is the Muslim majority; the minority communities do not have any say or inclinations.

There are many debates in the media and internet, and lots of materials are floating around, each giving out its opinion and view points, thus I am not discussing the Articles 370 and 35A any further. I have given just an overview and what are the sentiments. There are certain facts about Article 370 which must be known to the people of Jammu and Kashmir and India, these are actual historical facts which cannot be denied either by the right or the left liberals:-

- ❖ Sheikh Abdullah called the 'Sher-i-Kashmir' (The Lion of Kashmiri) is considered as instrumental in getting the Article 370 in the Indian Constitution. Maharaja Hari Singh who was still having the hope of ruling independent Jammu and Kashmir, had role to play in the incorporation of the Article 370 to suit his interest after normalisation of the situation and intervention of United Nations. The Article 370 in a way gave the connotation that Jammu and

Kashmir is separate and any abrogation will give it the option to move out of the Indian Union. Sheikh Abdulla taking advantage of the article was contemplating separating Kashmir from India and agreeing on accession with Pakistan. Kashmir Conspiracy Case of 1958, wherein Sheikh Abdullah was secretly planning merger of Kashmir with Pakistan, this backfired and he was arrested for anti national activities by Indian Prime Minister Jawaharlal Nehru and removed from Prime Ministership of Jammu and Kashmir. Bakshi Mohammad was placed in his place. For 10 years Sheikh Abdulla was kept away from politics. It was Article 370 which provided the scope of separation and in the later years the Kashmiri Muslims contemplated Azadi (Freedom) from India and resorted to insurgency after the debacle of 1987 rigged elections. Question thus remains, why have such an Article in the Indian Constitution, which gives scope to contemplation of separation and why was it not abrogated earlier?

❖ The Article 370 separated the State into three parts Kashmir, Jammu and Ladakh Divisions under the State Constitution, however the Muslim majority rule prevailed, first with single party NC (National Conference) ruling the roost and then Central Party of Indian Congress and its stooge party PDP (Peoples Democratic Party) joined to create a front to challenge the NC. All these parties were basically Muslim dominant with Muslim leadership. Article 370 was exploited by restricting Indian entry in development and business, this made selected few and political bigwigs own and hijack the complete tourist, cottage industries, handicraft industries and business establishments. As the State Financial statutes, had so many loop holes and power of the Indian Parliament being nonexistent, corruption was rampant and wealth went into the parochial fraternity of political families, their relatives and selected few who were close to the political parties. Question is when Article 370 gets exploited in such a manner, why should this not be abrogated?

❖ The State, for last 70 odd years is fighting for separate self-rule with no interference by the Indian Constitution and the Parliament, the Quit Kashmir Movement of 1942 by Sheikh Abdullah and declaration of Jihad and Azadi (freedom) by Kashmiri in 1980's, remained a prevalent factor all these years till abrogation of Article

370 and 35 A, it was evident during 1950's when Kashmiri Muslims were herded by their leader for separation from India and then in 1990's when the Kashmiri Muslims welcomed the terrorist and militant organisation in the Kashmir Valley to fight their Jihad and get them Azadi. From 1990 onwards the Muslim population, separatists and the Kashmiri political parties have been talking of Azadi (freedom), accepted the radicalisation of Islam and showed support to pan Islamic association and allegiance to Pakistan. It was Article 370 which encouraged the forming of perception of Azadi (freedom) and separation, the Muslims of Kashmir Division of the State considered itself to be separate from India and claimed number of times abrogation of the Instrument of Accession. This perception was taken as granted and used as instrument of blackmail to have their say with Indian Government. The separatists tagged on with the two nation theory and believed in separation of Kashmiri Muslims from the Hindu Nation. The statement of Muslim Political Leaders, Religious Heads, Liberals and Internet and Social Media savvy intellectuals, have similar sentiments and there are no inhibition what so ever, to speak openly on separation and allegiance with Pakistan and Islam. The Kashmiri Muslims have been radicalised to the extent that it considered India as enemy and its defence forces as occupational force. The Article 370 was made an instrument of dissension. Therefore the question is why a separate State Constitution should be there and why Articles providing scope of separation must prevail and not abrogated?

❖ The fact on ground and reality is, Kashmiri Muslim is only concerned of the Kashmir Region and the Kashmir Valley, they could not influence others who are beyond the boundaries of Kashmir Region, and it was a case of 'frog in the well' which has kept itself within the walls of Kashmir Valley. Hindus never supported the Muslims of Kashmir. Neither any Muslim leader could garner support; Kashmiri Muslims had no answer to the Hindus safety and security in case of separation and joining Pakistan. Pakistan's human rights violations on Hindu community and gradual cleansing, have left hardly any Hindus in Pakistan, it is barely less than 2 percent of the Muslim population. How does Kashmiri Muslim expect any supports from Hindus, it was this very reason Maharaja Hari Singh, went in for accession with India.

❖ Muslim are in majority in the Kashmir Region, thus based on the population density and numbers, the number of constituencies in Kashmir Region were more than combined Jammu and Ladakh Region. The situation is typical in Jammu & Kashmir; the Legislative Assembly was initially composed of 100 members, later increased to 111 by the Constitution of Jammu & Kashmir (Twentieth Amendment) Act of 1988. Out of these 111 seats, 24 seats are designated for the territorial constituencies of the State that remains occupied by Pakistan since 1947-48. These 24 seats of Pakistan occupied Jammu & Kashmir as per section 48 of the State Constitution remain officially vacant, and are not taken into account for reckoning in the case of deciding majority percentage of the party to form the government. Thus the total contested seats of the Assembly presently are 87, out of which the Kashmir Region has 46 seats, Jammu Region has 34 seats and Ladakh Region has 4 seats. Adding the Jammu and Ladakh seats it does not equal the Kashmir constituencies' seats. In Jammu Region the population of Muslim is approximately 30 percent and it is in the fringe districts neighbouring Kashmir Division which have Muslim majority, thus certain constituency seats of Jammu adds on to the Muslim Political parties' kitty. Thus it has always been the political parties of the Kashmir Region who had been in power in the political front; it was for this reason that parochial politics have been the centre of gravity of the Muslim Political party's ideology. It is the Kashmiri Muslims, who are more allied to Article 370, as it gave them the option of separation and choice of accession at their own terms. The Hindu Dogra's of Jammu and Buddhist and Shia Muslims of Kargil–Leh–Ladakh, are not at all interested of getting associated with Azadi (freedom) and Jihad of Kashmiri Muslims. This population does not have any desire of being part of Islamic State of Pakistan or having allegiance with Pakistan. Question is, was the appeasement by Indian Government since accession, applicable only for Kashmiri Muslims and for which the provisions of Article 370 was manifested and kept in vogue for seven decades. How long India will keep facing the threat of separation from Instrument of Accession by the Kashmiri Muslims?

❖ The development of the State entrepreneurship, industry and infrastructure was in the hands of the State, under the Article 370 and 35 A. Problem was, neither the Kashmiri nor Dogras or the

Ladakhi were professional, effective and smart entrepreneurs or industrialists. Frankly speaking they are like petty shop keepers or traders who neither had resources, skills, vision and initiative, thus the development suffered. I have seen huge loans were provided both at Srinagar for tourism industry and at Industrial town of BD Bari in Jammu, projects started but died its own death, very few survived, reasons are many but most important one was lethargy, lack of quality manpower due to Article 35 A and lack of initiative to grow. Whatever iota of development was there, it was through Central grants and resources. State never could come out of horticulture, handicraft, tourism and small scale industry, syndrome. Indian entrepreneurs and Industrialists were not permitted to establish industry, service infrastructure firms were denied lease and business institutions not provided land to develop. Question is why have an Article which is detrimental to Indian participation in the development?

❖ The question is why Pakistan is vehemently protesting the abrogation of Article 370 and 35 A. These Articles in no way is applicable in the Pakistan Occupied Kashmir (Azad Jammu and Kashmir and Northern Area of Gilgit –Baltistan), therefore the concern is having different connotation. The possibility of separation of Jammu and Kashmir from India is conditional as application of the clauses of accession, was the main apparatus which gave birth to Article 370, and which provided the linkage with India but ensuring separate political and societal entity. This in fact made Pakistan to launch Proxy War against India, when it found that it is beyond its capability to have military solution and liberate Jammu and Kashmir. Pakistan was of the opinion that it is only the people of Kashmir who can revolt and break away from India. Article 370 provides the scope of self determination due to the factor of self rule/ autonomy; it is at this angle Pakistan has been working way out through the Proxy War. The proxy war has military and sponsored Islamic state actors as the main stay, objective is balkanisation of Jammu and Kashmir on communal lines, radicalization of the Kashmiri Muslim population, talibanization through the imposition of ideology based on fundamentalist interpretation of Islam, sponsoring state terrorism, providing unequivocal support to separatists within Kashmir and ensuring instability through military actions along the Line of Control. Article 370 provides the scope of indulgence to Proxy

War; aim is people's revolt and accession of Kashmir to Pakistan. Question is where there is scope of separation in the provisions and interpretations in the Article 370 then why not scrap it and make Jammu and Kashmir as the State of Union of India. Moreover the issue of plebiscite or discretion with regard to choice of country for accession is not relevant anymore, thus why not have the State within the purview of one National Constitution?

❖ Everyone is only talking of Kashmir and is more concerned about it, all hypothesis, premise and opinion is about Kashmir and Kashmiri Muslims. No one has talked of 30 percent Non Muslims and who are also the State's subject, their numbers are small but they inhabit more land areas than Kashmir, and what do they want, or what are their aspirations, none is bothered. Left liberal, Lutyens, Kashmiri intellects and separatist or break away gangs (in Hindi called Tukre-Tukre Gang) have never accepted their relevance. This minority with their inhabited land mass wants to remain part of India, then what relevance the Article 370 will have and where does Azadi (freedom) by Kashmiri stands?

❖ The article 370 was temporary, as the plebiscite was yet to take place. This also warranted that no demographic change must take place as the very purpose of the plebiscite will be defeated. This clause in UN Resolution 1948 was also applicable to Pakistan. Thus certain assumption became part of Article 370 giving exclusivity to Jammu and Kashmir. The political compulsion at that time made India to accept certain aspects like separate flag, Prime Minister's (Wazir-e-Azam) and President's post (Riyasat-e–Sadar) for the State, inclusion of Article 35 A to ensure no demographic change or population inversion takes place and concurrence and consultancy of all matters in relation to Jammu and Kashmir by the Indian Parliament with the State Assembly. However the plebiscite has lost its relevance as Pakistan did not adhered to the stipulated conditions and over the years it lost its feasibility. The Article 370 and 35A stood their ground for last 70 years till August 2019. The political will was lacking, no one wanted to disturb the hornets' nest. Question is how the Articles can exist, in its temporary State for want of outcome of the plebiscite, when the relevance is no more in existence?

The above are the facts as on ground, people are and will be arguing on the legality, Left liberals will be supporting the Azadi and till date none of them are clear - what freedom and from whom. Separatists have been giving sweeping statements on rights and freedom of Kashmiri Muslim from India, whereas on the other hand they have promised their allegiance to Pakistan. The political parties National Conference and People's Democratic Party was keeping their options open if things took a 'U' Turn, thus keeping both India and Pakistan on to their side. No one talks of the terrorism and Jihad to liberate Kashmir from India by people's movement, the fact that Islamic radicalisation was accepted by the Kashmiri Muslims and making it the communal movement of 'Jihad for Azadi' is just brushed aside.. There are so many arguments and counter arguments, allegations of repression and fixed mindsets on counter insurgency and terrorism operations against the so called freedom fighters and Jihadis. The picture projected is of mayhem happening in Indian Jammu and Kashmir. Those who vehemently oppose the Indian Government give an impression that in Pakistan Occupied Kashmir there is ever lasting peace and tranquillity. So much has been hyped and fabricated making it a palpable story, which makes one believe as if everything is true, this was more with Kashmiri Muslims and sympathisers who were not at the scene, at any point of time and writing sitting in a foreign land especially Pakistan. Actions were not as rampant as described by many, yes aberrations were there and which were controlled and actions taken to remove the deficiencies, what India has done no other country would have ever done to ensure human rights were not violated by its security forces. No one talks about destruction, massacres, burning, looting and dishonour of Muslim women by the terrorists and jihadist mercenaries, they are from the same radical stock and for Kashmiri they are the 'Heroes'. I am not against the Kashmiri or the religion or the Article 370 and 35A or the autonomy. What I am against is the when the State is part of India one must readily accept it, for it cannot survive at its own and is lacking the very potential, it is exploiting the opportunities and benefit from dual citizenship but when it comes to the State Citizenship then become totally parochial and literally blackmailing the Indian political setup with 'Jihad for Azadi' (Freedom)?

Now the Article 370 and 35A have been abrogated, State divided in two Union Territories and these are federal territories governed directly by the Central Government of India for the time being, the dynamics have changed. The map of India now has claimed the status of Jammu and Kashmir as it was before the partition:-

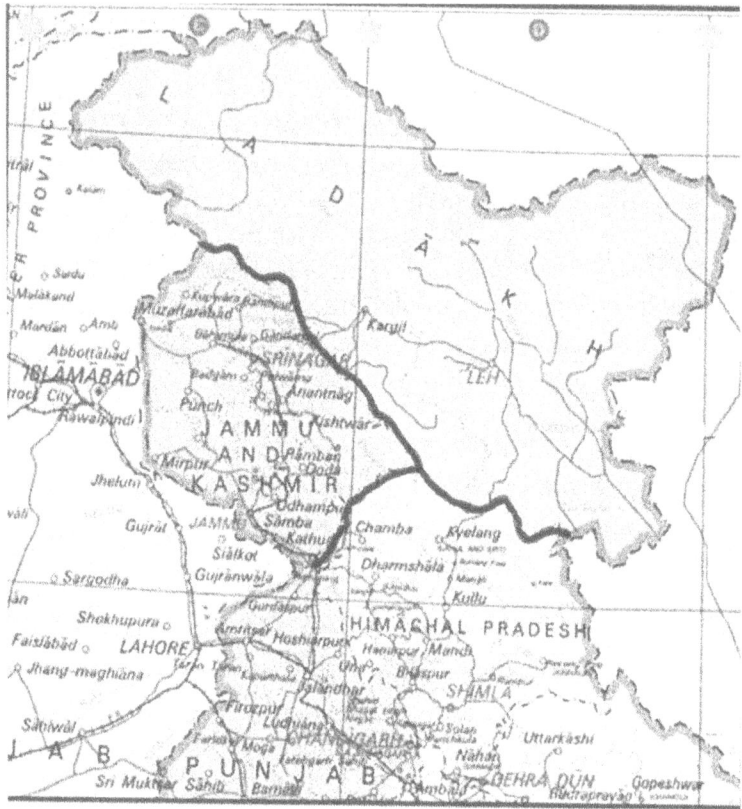

Map of Union Territory of Jammu & Kashmir and Ladakh

The above map is having objections of Pakistan and China, whatever is the case, the true fact was that the map is same as it was prior to 1947 partition, thus Indian claim is legitimate. In case of China and Pakistan, the areas held by them have been internationally claimed as disputed. Thus the map stands its ground.

Now the scenario has changed and there will be changes in the dynamics. There are parties, who would be going to Supreme Court especially the liberals and anti Bharatiya Janata Party (BJP) political elements, case will go on for ages and generations will keep changing. Pakistan will be instigating people of Kashmir and will be claiming their rights to Kashmir's dispute, which in their perspective includes whole of Indian Jammu and Kashmir, Pakistan believes as being Muslim majority State and as per two nation's theory Jammu and Kashmir rightfully belongs to Islamic State of Pakistan. The two nation theory which was applicable in

1947 and after seven decades is not relevant anymore; moreover the British are no more moderator of partition, past is history now. International lobbying have been attempted by Pakistan and China, but most of the countries have stayed away from abrogation of Article 370 and 35 A, stating it as internal affairs of India. People of Kashmir have accepted the abrogation as fait-accompli and are getting reconciled, people of Jammu and Ladakh as such had no objection to the abrogation. Lastly getting back the Article 370 and 35A will be a difficult proposition, party which tries doing so will lose its footings in Indian politics. It has been a great jolt to Left liberal, Lutyens, Leftists Kashmiri intellects and separatist or break away gangs. But whatever be the arguments, any provisions or law which are retrograde or creates discrimination or hampers national integration or gives scope of exploitation must be removed or abrogated, it should be taken in this spirit.

With this background it would be appropriate to analyse what is the future of India and Jammu and Kashmir, with the changed scenarios. After abrogation of the Article 370 and 35 A in August 2019 and followed by the pandemic of COVID 19 Corona Virus out break world over from December 2019 onwards starting with China, the issue of Kashmir has taken a setback and is not in focus presently, moreover Kashmir dynamics are going to see more changes as the time passes and depending when India will be coming out of the pandemic. I will be discussing the scenarios which can crop up and how India is going to or must be handling these scenarios to its advantage. It is high time that India comes out of the 'Panchsheel' (mutual respect, mutual non-aggression, mutual non-interference, equality and mutual benefit, and peaceful co-existence) and the 'Bhai-Bhai' syndromes, in respect of its neighbour especially Pakistan and China; India cannot get itself stabbed at the back time and again. India must make its power and vitality, matter.

"The clever combatant imposes his will on the enemy but does not allow the enemy's will to be imposed on him. Remaining one step ahead than your enemies which will cause the enemy to make plans in contrast to yours and there would be no scope where he can out manoeuvre you".

– Sun Tzu

Chapter - II

Kashmir's Significance

"Leaving out the question at issue, either of the parties takes resort to another; his previous statement is not consistent with his subsequent one; he insists on the necessity of considering the opinion of a third person, though it is not worthy of any such consideration; having commenced answering the question at issue, he breaks off at once, even though he is ordered to continue; he introduces questions other than those specified by himself; he withdraws his own statement; he does not accept what his own witnesses have deposed to; and he holds secret conversation with his witnesses where he ought not to do so. These acts constitute offence against the King."

- Chanakya

The question is why Kashmir is significant to both India and Pakistan, what is the present status and relevance, and what are the changed dynamics? The issue is not how the dispute is to be resolved and what is going to be the outcome. The issue is of the legality of the accession of Jammu and Kashmir and the dispute between Pakistan and India over Jammu and Kashmir. Remaining with the status quo is not going to resolve the dispute, and the question is how long India is going to tolerate the proxy war, Kashmiri Jihad and the call of Azadi (freedom) sponsored by Pakistan. Similarly, how the communal population of Jammu and Kashmir where 60 percent are Muslim and 40 percent are the others, and why Hindus and Buddhists who are approximately 36 percent are going to accept things as it stands today. The polarisation is very acute, the aspect of secularism does not hold its ground. Communal polarisation had been the existing phenomenon between the Regions of Kashmir, Jammu and Ladakh in the State (including the disputed areas claimed by India) before the partition of India and Pakistan in 1947 and after partition, this continued.

Thus, it would be better to understand the significance of Jammu and Kashmir to India and Pakistan, why Pakistan does not want to give away the occupied areas and why India is reclaiming the disputed areas, need to be clear to everyone. The people and sentiment of Jammu and Kashmir here is of no significance, as there is no choice for the people to decide now to which country it wants to go, as a composite State or partially in breakaway parts. The independent self-rule claim of the Muslims especially of the Kashmir Region, is not supported by other two Regions. Thus, question of independence does not arise even if Kashmiri Muslims of occupied Jammu and Kashmir are willing to participate. Seventy odd years has changed nothing much, the polarisation has been exploited year after year. The reason is that both India and Pakistan had to hold on the areas which are under their control at all cost, thus all actions are related to this prospective, which in turn has given rise to respective political ideologies of both the Nations. Librados, Left wing Liberals, Lutyens, cloying intellectuals and analysts, will be having their views, grudges, vehement objections, raising sentiments etc, nothing is going to matter, till such time the issue of Jammu and Kashmir is in suspension and there is face off, both countries consider the issue as internal affairs and each have been handling it since 1948 in their respective sensitivity and its related approach.

Pakistan & Jammu and Kashmir

Pakistan had always played the communal card in Jammu and Kashmir, under the pretext of two nation theory of partition. It always felt that India by deceit was trying to take Jammu and Kashmir into its folds, thus went in for strategy of forcibly taking Jammu and Kashmir. Pakistan was successful of getting close to Srinagar, it was at this stage that Maharaja signed the Instrument of Accession with India and India launched its Army to evict the invaders. Cease fire came when the Indian Army was in the process of pushing the invaders and it achieved success to a certain extent, and till today the status remains the same since 1948 after the cease-fire. Where the battle stopped, areas recaptured became part of India and balance held by Pakistan became occupied and disputed. Line of Control became the geographical demarcation line, between Pakistan and India. The significance of the area which Pakistan is holding and occupying need to be analysed, as this will answer to the question, why India cannot part with and give away the areas which are legally Indian Territory as per the Instrument of Accession and the UN Resolution of 1948. The occupied territories being declared as disputed, does not mean it is no more Indian Territory. This must be made clear?

❖ **Strategic Significance of Areas Held.** Pakistan always felt, handicapped with the land demarcated during partition. Pakistan was interested in having the whole of Punjab, Rajputana States of Jodhpur, Bikaner and Junagarh and Jammu and Kashmir in the West and in the East whole of Bengal. Mr Jinnah, the Pakistan Prime Minister, was keen to attract some of the larger Princely States of Rajasthan and Gujarat, hoping thereby to make other smaller Rajput Princely States to opt for Pakistan, this presumption was in order to compensate for the loss of half of Bengal and Punjab, this, however, did not materialise. Princely States bordering Pakistan in Rajasthan and Gujarat having Hindu Rulers and Junagarh having Muslim Ruler but Hindu majority had acceded to India thus Pakistan was not in a position to influence any merger, moreover partition of Punjab and Bengal had its toll on the then political set up of Pakistan. Attempts were made to have the Hindu Rulers of Rajputana States to come with Pakistan through luring, appeasements and promises of meeting all demands. Pakistan's Prime Minister actually wanted to have the areas as indicated by drawn lines in the Map below to acquire more land thus increase the strategic depth. If comparison of what Pakistan got in partition in 1947 and what Pakistan desired, the sensitivity of Pakistan's military thinkers to strategic depth can be understood. The depth between Pakistan's East to West border is considered the minimum which is approximately 15-20 KMs in the North, average depth in Central Pakistan is between 140 -160 odd KMs and largest being at Baluchistan above 200 KMs. The Map as under makes the point rather clear. The occupied territories act as buffers, thus it is reluctant to lose it, and Pakistan will fight to retain the occupied territories.

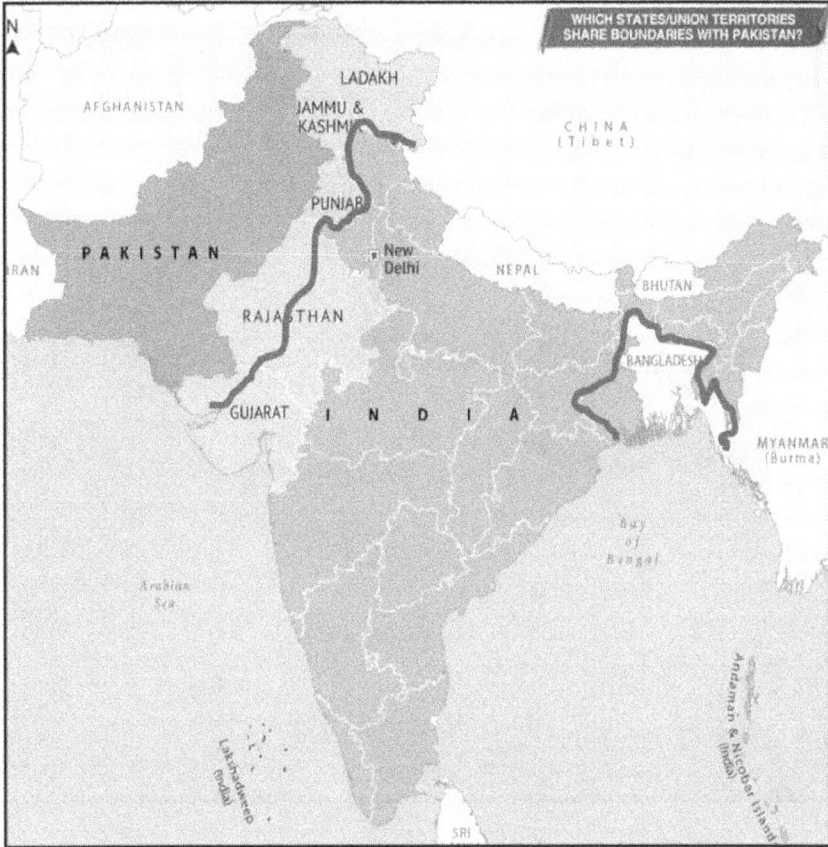

Map: Pakistan's Demand of Areas on Partition 1947

Pakistan military became apprehensive of the Strategic depth of West Pakistan on the culmination of first Indo–Pak War 1947-48. India, on the other hand, had amalgamated Princely States and Colonies irrespective of their inclinations. Thus, present Pakistan came into being in 1947, the East Pakistan was liberated and Bangladesh came into being in 1971 this loss also weighed very heavily on the Pakistan's strategic thinkers. The strategic depth has affected Pakistan psychology, which compelled it to include Afghanistan as part of its strategic depth; this has given it a substantial confidence. In case of loss of territories in any forthcoming wars with India, Pakistan can use the Afghan depth to fight back. For this reason, it is actively involved in Afghanistan especially the tribal belts of its Western borders to denying any Indian proximity in Afghanistan.

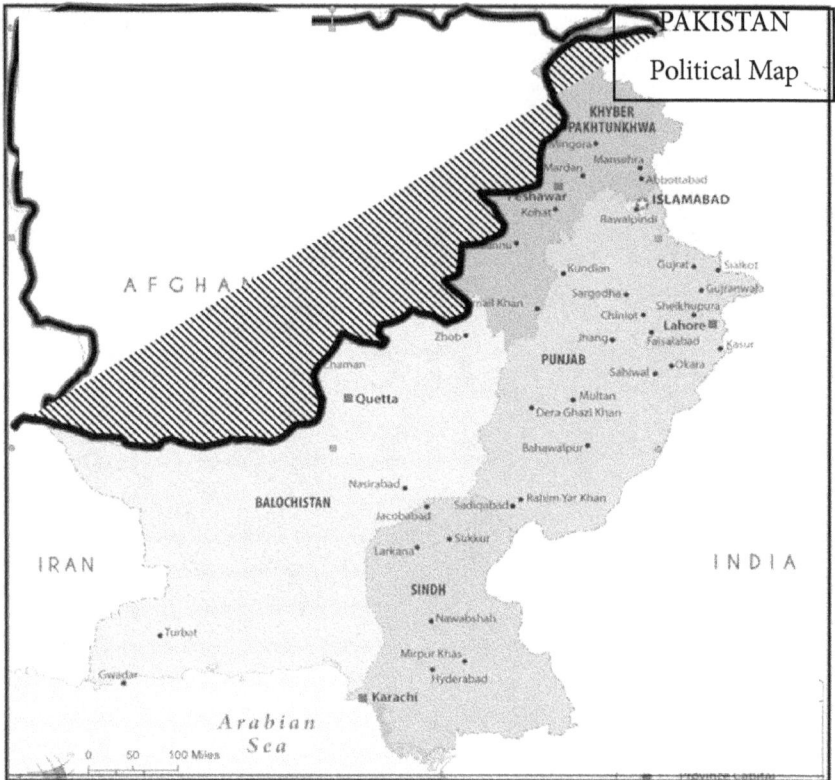

Map Showing Use of Afghanistan to Increase Strategic Depth

The realisation of inadequate strategic depth either from India or from Afghanistan/Iran was considered as the vulnerability by Pakistan and it became the mindset. Pakistan was more concerned with India, as it considered India as the first and only enemy and till date it remains so. As compared to the South and Central Pakistan, North Pakistan had the least strategic depth. The strategic imperatives thus made Pakistan:-

➢ November 1947 through mutiny in Gilgit Agency by Gilgit Scouts and handing over of the Maharaja's Governor of Northern Area, Brigadier Ghansara Singh by British to Pakistan Administrator, compelled withdrawal of Maharaja's State Forces from Gilgit -Baltistan, Pakistan consolidated its occupation of Northern Area by capturing Sakardu and Hunza. Simultaneously, with invasion of Jammu and Kashmir within one week of independence in Aug 1947, the intention of Pakistan was made very clear. Holding on to the disputed territories and occupied areas provided depth to its sensitive communication centre of Islamabad, Peshawar and Rawalpindi by having an effective buffer of Azad Jammu and Kashmir. The Khyber Pakhtunkhwa Province got the strategic depth due to buffer of the Northern Area.

➤ The Himalayan Ranges, Karakoram Ranges and Hindukush Ranges in the occupied Northern Jammu and Kashmir (Northern Area) provide depth to North-West Frontier Province (NWFP), obstacle value of mountains causes delay in any offensive and demand of enhanced troop ratio by the attacker, on the other hand as defender it provides better holding capability against any offensive in case of any war of reclamation by India. Improving and supplementing the strategic depth in North is essential to deny India land link with Afghanistan and safe guard NWFP.

➤ The Shaksgam Valley and the Trans Karakoram Tract is part of Hunza-Gilgit region of Pakistan Occupied Kashmir and is disputed territory and claimed as its own by India. It borders Xinjiang Province of the People's Republic of China (PRC) to the North, and is the under belly of the Northern Area of Pakistan Occupied Kashmir to the South, it guards the Siachen Glacier region to the East and provides launch pad for any assault on Saltoro Ridge and the glacier. This tract was ceded by Pakistan as confidence building effort with China in 1963. This gave China access to Karakoram pass, made it dominate the Siachen Glacier and provide direct connectivity to captured area of Aksai Chin, from Tibet it is the shortest route to China Pakistan Economic Corridor (CPEC). The sensitivity of the area will make China get involved in support of any Indo–Pak War by making India commit it forces to contain Chinese offensive or offensive posturing, as also activate Line of Actual Control to commit Indian Forces all along from Ladakh to Arunachal Pradesh. The ceded part of Ladakh to China added to the strategic significance of Aksai Chin which was captured by China in 1962 and not returned to India after the Indo-China war, as per the

Geneva Convention to which China is a signatory. The threat by China or opening a second front in case of China decides to support Pakistan will always exist. Pakistan's perception that Indian dilemma of opening two fronts, will cost in terms of force equation and with divided war efforts. Divided force application for containment/holding Chinese threat and attack on Pakistan would enhance the strategic concentration of forces at the point of decision thus enhancing the strategic depth. This way Pakistan has ensured its strategic depth by making the occupied territories as the buffer in the North. Over the years it has fortified the occupied territories and has large military presence, it is said that mountains eats away forces where the equation of minimum effort is 1:8, thus it would cost India very heavy as it was witnessed in the Kargil war 1999.

➤ On the other hand the occupied Northern Area provides option to Pakistan of grab actions into the Ladakh as it tried in Kargil War 1999, in order to alter the Line of Control and to outflank India and address Kashmir from North. Holding on to the Northern Area, provides Pakistan launch pad to any offensive either to Kargil – Ladakh from Skardu or to Kashmir from Chilas/Neelam.

➤ The occupied Northern Area also provides avenues across Great Himalayan Ranges to address the Kashmir Valley from North and West in combination with the Azad Kashmir approach. This would isolate Kashmir Valley and trap Indian Forces.

➤ The strategic location of Kashmir has made Pakistan to wage proxy war and low-intensity conflicts with India. The occupied Azad Jammu and Kashmir is serving the purpose of strategic depth and denying India direct approach / interference with sensitive nerve centres. The proxy war is in itself giving the strategic depth to Pakistan, just imagines if the buffer of occupied areas was not there, low intensity conflict and proxy war through sponsored terrorism against India, would have been difficult proposition. The hinterland of Pakistan in that case had to be used for bases and launch pads. In any Indian venture against the terrorist camps, bases and launch pads the hinterland of Pakistan is not affected as the occupied territories of Jammu and Kashmir is getting used extensively against India.

➤ From the North Afghanistan, the occupied Jammu and Kashmir especially Northern Area give strategic depth to FATA (Federally Administered Tribal Areas) and Khyber Pakhtunkhwa. This aspect has been of concern for the military and strategic thinkers of Pakistan. For Pakistan, the occupied Jammu and Kashmir especially Northern Area, can be used in stabilising any situations in FATA and Khyber Pakhtunkhwa arising in near future. In military term one can say occupied Jammu and Kashmir will then provide the firm base in case of any contemplated military action, in its own territory of FATA or against Afghanistan.

➤ To understand the Strategic implications as explained above, it would be pertinent to refer to the Map below. The sensitivities of India due to the occupied territories can only be negated by reclamation and merger. The Indian sensitivities from both Pakistan and China are:

- Siachen Glacier and approach to Leh.

- Strategic centres of Ladakh, Leh, Shyok Valley, Pangong Tso Lake and Chusul.

- Kargil District.

- Kashmir Valley and adjoining areas of Muslim majority population of Jammu Division.

- Kargil, Drass and Baltik if captured, Ladakh gets threatened.

- Sub-sector North spanning Galwan, Depsang plateau and Daulat Beg Oldi (DBO) which provides domination on China.

- Strategically Ladakh gives depth to Kashmir from North and major part of Indus flows through the ares and is source of power and water.

Map of North India Showing Occupied Territories

❖ **Geopolitical Imperatives.** By holding on to the occupied territories of Jammu and Kashmir, Pakistan has gained in terms of geopolitical advantage, analysing the advantages, brings out:

➤ Pakistan's occupation of Northern Area of Kashmir gave it tremendous strategic advantages in South Asia as the region shares common boundaries with Xinjiang and Afghanistan, and the Central Asian countries.

➤ Without Kashmir, the access to Silk route to China gets denied. Thus, Pakistan will not be having direct link with China. The link route, therefore, has to be through Afghanistan and Central Asian Countries or the sea route of Indian Ocean. Land link with China on which China Pakistan Economic Corridor stands, was not possible if occupied Jammu and Kashmir was not with Pakistan. Karakorum Pass gives China direct access into Pakistan Occupied Kashmir and not Pakistan. Accessibility of land route from China through occupied territories on which the concept of China Pakistan Economic Corridor (CPEC) is based gives China access to warm water ports of Gwadar in Pakistan; it is very economical for China to conduct trade with Middle East, Africa and Europe. CPEC is beneficial to both China and Pakistan.

➤ Land link with Central Asian countries. Proximity to Tajikistan oil and gas rich regions.

➤ Pakistan considers Jammu and Kashmir as pan Islamic link with Muslim countries of Central Asia. It also gives China its most reliable and strong ally, direct access to Pakistan. China will be providing access to Pakistan through its Trans Asian Highways to Myanmar, Malaysia, Thailand and other South East Asian Countries. The strategic value of Jammu and Kashmir and geo-political importance cannot be ignored. Pakistan had been making attempts time and again since last seven decades to seize Jammu and Kashmir out of India by force. In this attempt Pakistan went in for four wars and has been persisting with low intensity conflict and proxy war to create a position of advantage in accession of Jammu and Kashmir.

➤ Over and above the strategic interest of Kashmir which is vital to the security as its Northern Area and direct gateway to the North West Province of Pakistan (FATA and Khyber Pakhtunkhwa) and Northern Punjab, is the issue of water of the rivers flowing through the occupied Jammu and Kashmir and sourced from the Indian Jammu and Kashmir, these rivers do matter strategically and geopolitically. These rivers are crucial for survivable of Pakistan and the most important one being the Indus River. Source control of other rivers Jhelum and Chenab may be in the hands of India but Indus is fed by large number of rivers of occupied Northern Area. If Northern Area is taken back then Pakistan will be at the mercy of India for its river water? The occupied Jammu and Kashmir thus keeps strategic-geopolitical course as open option of actions.

➤ India's State of Jammu and Kashmir provides a valuable window to the other regional powers, including Afghanistan and the nearby republic of Tajikistan. By holding the occupied Jammu and Kashmir, it denies India the link with Central Asian countries through Afghanistan and Tajikistan.

Pakistan in the initial years of occupation of Jammu and Kashmir had not given importance to the Northern Area due to its barrenness, remoteness and difficult terrain. However, war against Soviets, the strategic importance of Northern Area of occupied Kashmir and its North West Province was realised and exploited. The occupied Jammu and Kashmir has been the firm base for 1947, 1965, 1971 and 1999 wars. Soviet withdrawal in 1988 and political turmoil in Afghanistan, tribal terrorism in the backyard of FATA and Khyber Pakhtunkhwa, the proxy war against India in order to keep India under tenterhook and frustrated, withdrawal of USA troops its aftermath and likely change in the dynamics of Afghanistan politics especially the Northern Afghanistan, are some of the issues which the occupied Jammu and Kashmir provides excellent pivot to manage the affairs. Moreover, obtaining direct support from China being a possibility in which the occupied Jammu and Kashmir territory will definitely be used. Pakistan will keep holding the occupied Jammu and Kashmir at all cost, not only due to its strategic objectives but for its geopolitical aspirations. Neither China will want Pakistan to lose control over occupied Jammu and Kashmir, as lot is in stake and Chinese strategic and geopolitical interest is rather large in the region. Pakistan under the strategic alliance and under the burden of dependency, have given access to China for usage of areas for its security and military interests, in a way Pakistan is gradually coming under Chinese expansionism, day is not far Pakistan will literally be the stooge of China. The day this happens, the people of Pakistan may revolt against its Military and the political setup which is controlled by the Pakistan Army.

India & Jammu and Kashmir

India was not very sure that Jammu and Kashmir will be part of its union; it was taken for granted that this bordering State, having Muslim Majority population will be part of Pakistan on the partition. It was the politics of the Hindu Maharaja and his desire to remain independent brought about the dilemma, his indecisiveness which became the turning point of the fate of Jammu and Kashmir. Three things were playing in the mind of the Maharaja; *firstly,* loss of faith on Muslim population as it was in revolt in Northern Area, Kashmir and the adjoining areas, *secondly*, the concern of the non Muslim population which was about 34 percent of the total population and was loyal to the Maharaja and *thirdly*, the question of monarchy. Sardar Patel, the Home Minister, was equally interested that the Maharaja opts for India, as Jammu and Kashmir was having strategic significance for independent India. It was J L Nehru lineage of Kashmiri Pundit and the interest that made him get involved with accession of Jammu and Kashmir, his friend Sheikh Abdullah was instrument in negotiating the accession. It was Muhammad Ali Jinnah of Pakistan who believed that the majority population will support the Muslim Tribesmen incursion supported by Pakistan Army, and Jammu and Kashmir will be forcefully made part of Pakistan, things which went against Jinnah's plan was the plunder and atrocities of the tribesmen, which made the Kashmiri Muslims resist and forced the Maharaja to sign the Instrument of Accession with India. At that point of time, what prevailed was the communal separation between Pakistan's Punjabi Muslims and moderate Kashmiri Muslims. The Kashmiri Pundits, Hindu Dogras and the Buddhist minority as such was not in favour of accepting the Muslim hegemony or having allegiance with Pakistan. The strategic and geopolitical matters at that point of time had no much relevance; it was more of land grabbing and acquisition of land holding actions.

The Indian held Jammu and Kashmir, is a separator between China and Pakistan, one can imagine if Jammu and Kashmir was with Pakistan and it would have given Ladakh to China, then India would have been on perpetual threat and sandwiched, on one side by the fundamentalist Islamic country and on the other expansionist China, only difference would have been 1962 would have been at NEFA and Pakistan demand of Punjab would have replaced Kashmir, the lost Punjab obsession still exists, even today Pakistan is all out supporting the Khalistan Movement in Indian Punjab, the desire of Jinnah 1947 of having whole of Punjab still is the reason of annexing Indian Punjab through anti India Khalistan Movement. Therefore, the importance of Jammu and Kashmir the integral part of India cannot be denied and India will not tolerate any deviation and get back the occupied territories. With this as the background, the significance of Indian held Jammu and Kashmir and Pakistan occupied parts must be discussed to understand the relevance and concern of India:

❖ **Strategic Significance of Jammu and Kashmir.** The strategic interest is similar to that of Pakistan; the only difference is that the Indian advantages become disadvantage to Pakistan, if reclamation takes place. One thing which made a difference to Pakistani advantage and the China ploy is, Indian part of Jammu and Kashmir like a fist jetting between Pakistan and China with Siachen Glacier being the thumb. Taking control of the 70 kilometre long Siachen Glacier was the most successful strategic move which changed the tactical equations. All the main passes and heights of the Saltoro Ridge immediately West of the Glacier including Sia La, Bilafond La, and Gyong La, became ground of domination and thus putting an wedge between the ceded Karakorum Tract and Shaksgam Valley by Pakistan to China in 1963 and Aksai Chin captured in 1962 but not returned by China. The strategic value of Indian held Jammu and Kashmir thus are:-

➢ The Ladakh region is a buffer to the Kashmir Valley, between the Pakistan occupied Kashmir of Northern Area and China from North. The Indian held Jammu and Kashmir in other words secures and denies the Northern approach, to both China and Pakistan to the mainland India and the plains.

➢ Safeguards the control of rivers of Kashmir flowing into Pakistan i.e. Indus, Jhelum, Chenab and Ravi. From economic point of view, Jammu and Kashmir is the lifeline of Pakistan, as it depends on the river water of India. Hafiz Saeed, the chief of Jamat-ud-Dawa (Lasker-e-Taiba), had said I quote *"All the deposits of water are in Indian Kashmir. The only way by which the economic prosperity of Pakistan can be granted and its farms can be prevented from getting barren is to increase its efforts in wresting control of Indian occupied Kashmir. Only if Kashmir is freed from Indian control, can Pakistan's interest be safeguarded"*. India can any time throttle Pakistan by denying water and abrogating Indus Water treaty with Pakistan. This is a big strategic advantage to India.

➢ The Indian held Jammu and Kashmir provides the launch pad for any operation into Pakistan occupied Kashmir and areas ceded and occupied by China of the Ladakh Region of Jammu and Kashmir, in other words the rightful claim of whole of Jammu and Kashmir can be made possibility in the contingency of going for military action for reclamation. Threat to China's sensitivity of under belly of Xinjiang Province, Tibet, Karakorum Highway and China Pakistan Economic Corridor (CPEC) in Pakistan occupied Kashmir from India cannot be denied both by China and Pakistan. This it puts considerable pressure on both China and Pakistan.

➤ Any build up of forces, in the Ladakh Region of the occupied territories, is difficult due to the inhospitable terrain and accessibility factors. The Chinese occupied areas are on the higher reaches; however, the areas under Pakistan towards Gilgit, Skardu, Hunza are on the lower reaches. Developing operations on Pakistan will be along the lay of the valleys from the heights of Kargil, Drass and Batalik i.e. along the grain of the terrain, to lower heights. From Pakistan side the approach is against the grain and it was for this reason, it could not replenish the logistic nor build up reserves in Kargil War 1999. In case India in 1999 would have under taken hot pursuit operations against the withdrawing and fleeing Pakistan forces, India would have reclaimed large part of the disputed territory in Northern Area, thus before agreeing to unilateral ceasefire the hot pursuit would have made substantial change in the alignment of line of control by going into the disputed area. I am of the opinion India really missed the opportunity of going into Northern Area in 1999. Whatever may be the political reasons or compulsions; a strategic opening was missed, which would have changed the dynamics of the disputed territories.

➤ The Siachen Glacier control gives strategic advantage and capability to monitor the sensitive Pakistan-China nexus. But the problem is that Pakistan has practically ceded to China the whole of Gilgit-Baltistan (Northern Area) for the CPEC project, the Shaksgam Valley and the Karakorum pass is being used for the link up by China with the economic corridor. However due to India's occupation of Siachen. China is not in a position to bridge the Aksai Chin – Shaksgam – Gilgit-Baltistan gap and dominate the Karakoram Pass. Control of the Glacier for India became even more critical, considering that just East – South East of the Glacier, lays the vast high altitude desert plains, that the Indian Army calls Sub-Command North (SSN). This is the area that saw much action in the 1962 India-China War. This includes the Indian Advance Landing Ground (ALG) of Daulat Beg Oldie, and contested areas of the Depsang plateau, that have seen numerous face-offs in the recent past between Indian and Chinese border patrols. Strategically, should Pakistan have taken control of the Siachen Glacier, SSN would have been sandwiched between Pakistani and Chinese forces, a fact that the Indian Army leadership well appreciated. The entire Siachen Glacier, with all major passes, is currently under the administration of India since 1984. Pakistan controls the region west of Saltoro Ridge, with posts located almost 3,000 ft below the Indian posts. Thus, Siachen Glacier strategic advantages are:

- The Saltoro Ridge of the Siachen Glacier serves as a divide that prevents direct linking of Pakistan occupied Kashmir with China, denying direct military support, geographically linking of military forces and manoeuvres to upset any Indian operations in Pakistan occupied Kashmir. Siachen also serves as an observation post for India to keep a watch on Gilgit-Baltistan region of Pakistan.

- Loss of Siachen, would become a big threat to India, from the West by Pakistan in Ladakh region, in addition Chinese threats from Aksai Chin will make Ladakh more vulnerable thus forcing India to commit forces at two fronts.

- Due to its control over Saltoro Ridge, India is better placed to strike a bargain while settling bilateral territorial disputes with Pakistan in the future.

- Siachen also helps India keep a close watch on the activities of China which has vastly improved its infrastructure in this region. China has developed all weather road links in the Shaksgam region, which was ceded to China by Pakistan in 1963.

➤ China is very apprehensive of Pakistan losing the occupied areas of Jammu and Kashmir and India reclaiming the same. China in this case will be in great disadvantage and have to negotiate with India, for the part of the China Pakistan Economic Corridor (CEPC) passing through occupied territory of Jammu and

Kashmir of India. In case India blocks the portion of the corridor passing through Jammu and Kashmir, the whole project collapses as China has already made huge investment. The Gwadar Port which is virtually under the control of China and is a threat to India in the Arabian Sea will be denied, if CPEC is denied. On the other hand, India can bargain the use the corridor for trade with China at its own terms, this will help in linking the Central Asian landlocked countries, if this happens then India will be at the position of advantage in all negotiations with China. By going in for an economic corridor using the disputed areas, China has committed two mistakes; *firstly*, it has increased its sensitivity level of threat from India and *secondly*, with forced incursion on the land of indigenous population the chances of disruption will exist if people revolt against Pakistan and Chinese nexus. This has already started due to Chinese atrocities and strong hand handling in the region of Northern Area.

➢ Indian use of the Chabahar port of Iran and road communication to Afghanistan is a concern for Pakistan. Relation with Iran is not that cordial and there is also difference of religious ideologies, as Iran is a Shia country and Pakistan being Sunni, chances of clash are always there. However, of late the relationship is on the high as China has joined hand with Iran against USA. On the other hand Afghanistan political viability is presently not stable, moreover, now the new Taliban government is going to run the country after US withdrawal, big question is, what will the quotient of Pakistan's involvement and interference, this will be a cause of concern for India. Pakistan on the other hand is apprehensive that the new government will go in for global support for survival and development and if India's diplomatic relationship becomes strong with Afghanistan then its role will diminish. Afghanistan's economic and infrastructure development supports are through two routes i.e. the routes of Iran for South and Central, and Gilgit–Baltistan land route for North Afghanistan. If Indo-Afghan relations become stronger, the strategic equation is going to change. Pakistan in this case will be strategically trapped and encased. Therefore, losing occupied Jammu and Kashmir is going to cost Pakistan and it will fight to retain it, as the strategic depth gets compromised both from West and East.

❖ **Indian Geopolitical Imperatives.** The imperatives which are applicable to Pakistan by occupying Kashmir are equally pertinent to India. However, in case of India, the Jammu and Kashmir parse has more relevance as compared to Pakistan in terms of geopolitical, socio-economic and strategic foreign relationships:

➢ Even though the border with Afghanistan is rather very restrictive in terms of land area, yet it gives access to North of Afghanistan and through it, the countries of Central Asia. Occupied territory of Northern Area will provide strategic, foreign and socio-economic relationship with Afghanistan. In the present context Indian relationship with Afghanistan is through Iran, this affects the direct trade and economic assistance. Pakistan is very apprehensive of Indian involvement in Afghanistan. Pakistan feels trapped between India, Afghanistan and Iran, thus any linkage with Afghanistan, Pakistan is very sensitive. In the sphere of international recognition and relationship, building of Afghanistan economically and development of the national infrastructure, Taliban is not going to and cannot rely wholly on Pakistan, it will look beyond Pakistan. India is going to play an important role in Afghanistan and Taliban very well understands this, the direct land link is going to make a difference in the sub continent. Presently India is isolated due to Pakistan occupied Jammu and Kashmir and the reach to the Central Asian countries and Afghanistan; the route is rather circuitous.

➤ Having link with Badakhshan Province, through Jammu and Kashmir (Ladakh Union Territory), will open up Central Asian Republics through the land route, this has been a concern for last so many years, thus reclamations is going to make difference. This will also put pressure on China, as its Xinjiang Autonomous Region is neighbouring Central Asian Republics and Indian geopolitical proximity is going to be a concern. Through the Badakhshan Province the project of having gas and oil pipe line from the Central Asian belt will be a possibility, however, due to Tarek-e-Taliban domination of the area the risk does exists. Thus the relationship equation with the Afghanistan Government will matter.

➤ Resource rich Central Asia countries of Tajikistan, Kyrgyzstan, Uzbekistan, Kazakhstan and Turkmenistan, geopolitical linkage from the Northern part of the boarders of Jammu and Kashmir will be an added advantage, thus the circuitous route via Iran or through Pakistan can be avoided. Route link through Pakistan, which is not going to materialise and is unlikely, even if it gains economically by having trade with India, thus gas and oil pipeline trade is handicapped and lying defunct, due to Pakistan's anti India attitude, any endeavours through its land or the occupied territories will continue to be a difficult proposition.

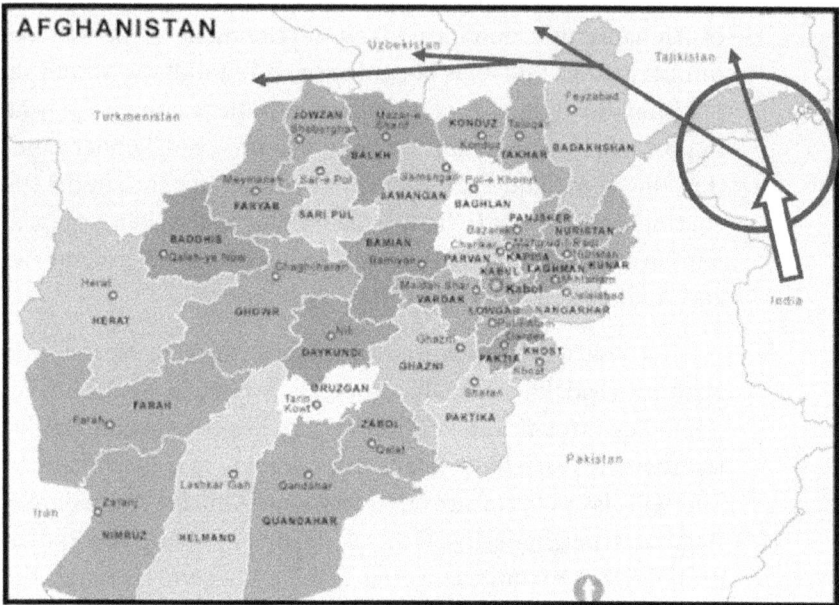

Map Afghanistan and Link Routes from India

> With Jammu and Kashmir the small window over the narrow stretch of Badakhshan Province located in the farthest North Eastern part of Afghanistan between Tajikistan and Northern Area of Pakistan occupied Gilgit – Baltistan Region, can be developed as trade high way, this would largely depend on the dynamics of provincial and Taliban's political synchronisation and the international relationship quotients. Taliban in their statement have clarified independent status of foreign relation and has side lined Pakistan, even though Pakistan is not going to rest with this and will be at its game in Afghanistan?

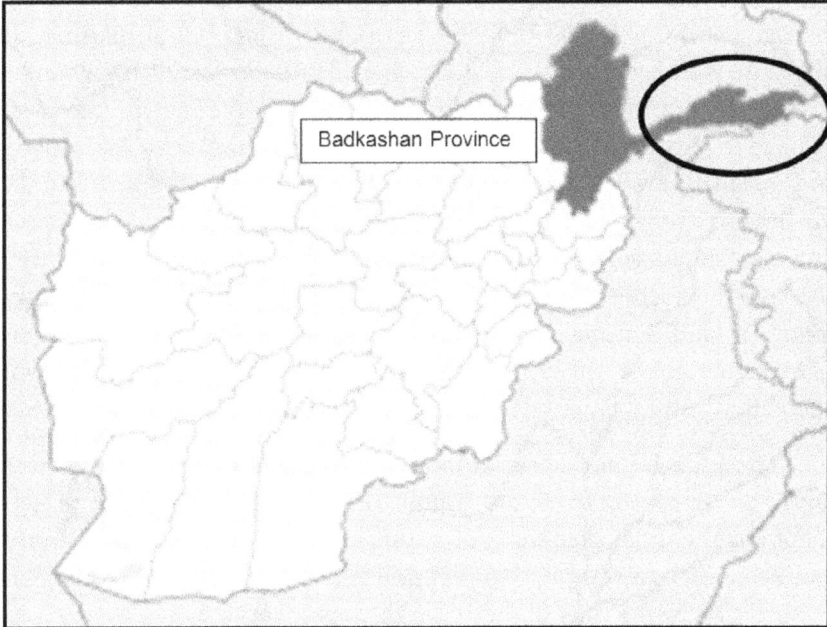

Map Showing Badakhshan Province of Afghanistan

➢ The likely balkanisation of China in near future or breakup like Soviet Union will definitely bring into reference the Xinjiang Province and Tibet. One cannot predict, at this juncture but possibilities cannot be totally ruled out. In that case Jammu and Kashmir will play an important pivotal role both strategically and geopolitically, especially the Union Territory of composite Ladakh. Importance and relevance of Jammu and Kashmir as a whole is there for both Pakistan and China. For India the composite Jammu and Kashmir including the Union Territories of Ladakh and Jammu and Kashmir, play pivotal role for India in the geopolitics of the Central Asia region.

The significance of Jammu and Kashmir, both strategically and geopolitically is very crucial and important. It is for this reason that both Pakistan and China do not want to give away advantage to India. Pakistan through proxy and low intensity war tries to create instability in the region. China also does not want India to have full control over the region, thus is supporting Pakistan. China's interests are too many and it has strategically and economically invested in the occupied areas and does not want any interference from India. Thus, Pakistan and China will be partners in the game plan against India and it is for this reason that, it has gone for irrevocable relationship. China also has interest in the region other than India centric, which is the USA dynamic with withdrawal from Afghanistan and installation of new government, Pakistan's total succumbing under the debt of China and the economic corridor and Iran's anti USA stance, provides China the opportunity of having dominance in the area and direct access to the warm water ports of Pakistan and Iran and reducing the trade routes to Gulf, Europe and Africa. China will never want India to gain significance and accept loss of Pakistan occupied Kashmir (POK), it will be totally against its interest.

There are certain school of thoughts that are very apprehensive with regard to India's stance on the Jammu and Kashmir, both in the present status and the anticipated status of getting or obtaining the whole of Jammu and Kashmir, as it was prior to partition and according to the Instrument of Accession by the ruler of the State. The arguments are:-

❖ India has not been able to manage Jammu and Kashmir in its present status and the communal card is very dominant. Even though the Article 370 and 35A have been abrogated, India is yet to be see the majority Muslim's reactions and demand of Azadi (freedom). The Pakistan factor is still very active and there has not been any respite, even though the control of the two Union Territories is with the Centre. The irony is that very few people know that out of 61.44 percent of Muslim population of Jammu and Kashmir, the sect wise distribution percentage is, Gujjar Muslim 9.8 percent, Bakarwal Muslim 4.4 percent, Phari Muslim 5.8 percent, Shia Muslim 8.2 percent Sufi Muslim 1 percent and Sunni Muslim 32.2 percent, out of this only the Sunni Muslims of Kashmir Valley want Azadi (Freedom). Appeasement of just 32.2 percent Sunni Muslim does not stand any arguments and those who are involved most of them are not aware of ground realities or have never been to Jammu and Kashmir except as tourists.

❖ The Maharaja did not have any control over the Northern Area due the remoteness and isolation, which was attributable to mountainous and difficult terrain. The coup by Gilgit Scouts conniving with the

British and people revolting against the Maharaja, thus making the situation untenable and the Maharaja's State Forces was compelled to withdraw, no reinforcement could reach in time. Maharaja's Rule was defunct, when people of Northern Area accepted the administration of the region by Pakistan and did not surrendered its independence. It will be difficult proposition to get the region into the folds of the Ladakh Union Territory, as India after partition never had any control over the occupied areas of Gilgit–Baltistan. As claimed by certain school of thought, the difficult terrain exhausted the Indian Army during 1947-48 war with Pakistan, thus the Army did not have the steam to venture into the Northern Area. Another school of thought attributed the calling of ceasefire on the advice of the Indian Army, when it found increased level of resistance as Pakistan by then had deployed the Regular Pakistan Army. This reduced the viability of reclaiming the balance captured areas. Pakistan Army was taking over the defences by faster build-up of forces, thus increasing ratio of combat forces. The stiff resistance and heavy consumption of troops placed Indian Army in 'no go situation', therefore, balance areas remained with Pakistan which it claims as captured territories, it was on advise of Indian Army that J L Nehru went for ceasefire and United Nations intervention. For creating Line of Control (LOC) and Pakistan occupied Kashmir (POK), many blame Nehru for going in for ceasefire and taking the case to UN. Indian Army never accepted that it was exhausted and to quote General Thimayya Chief of Indian Army said *"Prime Minister gives me three more weeks, I will recapture whole of Jammu and Kashmir"?*

❖ There are people who think that the Muslim population of Pakistan Occupied Kashmir (POK) will increase the total population in terms of comparative quotient with the minority population of Hindus, Kashmiri Pundits and Buddhists, this will add to the problem, as pro Pakistan elements among the Muslim population will be larger and controlling it, will be difficult. Moreover, the proximity to Pakistan and Afghanistan will bring fundamental Islamic terror influence in a larger way.

❖ The border with Pakistan and China will be larger, thus stretching the border management and challenges of defending such a large area, will add on the problems to guard the border, more acute.

❖ India has been trying to integrate Kashmir for last 70 years and integrating the Pakistan occupied Kashmir will add on to the issue and will have to commit more forces to contain and consolidate. The areas of FATA (*Federally Administered Tribal Areas*) and Khyber Pakhtunkhwa Provinces are trouble spots for Pakistan and is under dominance of various Afghan terrorist groups, this would make the Jammu and Kashmir susceptible to the influence of pan Islamic fundamentalism and terrorism.

❖ What benefits will India have by taking whole of Jammu and Kashmir, as the economic potentials are very less except tourism? The mountainous terrain is barren and any development will be a 'high end' issue and heavy on the exchequer.

❖ India will be inheriting problems of Pakistan occupied Kashmir and this will add on to the problems of Indian Kashmir. Containment and consolidation will be a serious issue which will compel India to invest very heavily in all spheres of governance; economy, development and people's confidence-building measures. India must only be concerned with the Union Territories of Ladakh and Jammu and Kashmir?

The above arguments do not stand their ground, all problems which India is facing today, is from occupied areas and it is being used against India, no status quo will ever resolve the issues or bring stability. Once reclamation is done, India is capable to handle the occupied areas dynamics and integrate with Ladakh, Jammu and Kashmir and mainland India.

Seeing the significance and going through the arguments, opinion and views with regard to the perspectives of India, Pakistan and China, there is no doubt that Jammu and Kashmir has strategic and geopolitical importance. The degree of significance will depend on the values given to the prospective of each Nation, its political prospective and the dynamics of the future strategic and geopolitical significance of the changing world orders. Now keeping this in view it would appropriate to discuss the Indian interest, thus the options and scenarios that would be presenting to the Indian think tanks will be, *firstly*, contain and consolidate the present status, *secondly*, question of claim over whole of Jammu and Kashmir occupied by Pakistan and China, *thirdly*, the legality of the Instrument of Accession signed by the ruler of the State Maharaja Hari Singh and connotation of the word 'Whole of Priencly State of Jammu and Kashmir' and *lastly* not to compromise any territory held either by Pakistan and China or coming to any agreement in order to resolve the Kashmir issue thus sticking on to the claim of whole of Jammu and Kashmir. In each of the scenarios there will be many gameplay, understanding of variables, analysis of all the pros and cons and the methodology, in each of the scenarios strategic and geopolitical aspects will have pro quo implications and interpretations thereof. For India and its people , there has to be a concentrated effort of national self interest and national security, to take back which rightfully belongs to India. Is this that easy, where the other parties are equally affected, their self interest and national interest are equally relevant to them, over 70 years have passed in status quo without any infringement or any deviation of intention of purpose. Ultimate question to India will it like to live with perpetual threat and instability or to sort out permanently 'the wounds of thousand cuts'.

"Before you start some work, always ask yourself three questions - Why am I doing it, What the results might be and Will I be successful. Only when you think deeply and find satisfactory answers to these questions, go ahead."

-Chanakya

Chapter - III

STAGE - I
Containment & Consolidation

"A person who is aware of future troubles, and fight against them with his intelligence will be always happy. And a person you remain inactive waiting for good days to come will destroy his own life."

~Chanakya

The Stage-I after abrogation of Article 370 and 35 A is the prevalent state, *firstly* was the declaration of reclamation of all the occupied territories, *secondly* sub division of Jammu and Kashmir into two union territories and *thirdly*, unification of Jammu and Kashmir under single Constitution of India. Even though status quo of the occupation as prevailing stands, except for the formation of Union Territories of Jammu and Kashmir and Ladakh and change in the Indian Map where Line of Control (LOC) and Line of Actual Control (LAC) with Pakistan and China respectively no more exists, as the occupied territories belonging to India historically have been removed from the maps of the occupiers or for that matter from the altered atlases and added to the Indian Map. Now, what actually stands contentious is the issue of Indian reclamation of what rightfully belongs to India. Presently neither Pakistan nor China who are involved in the occupation are budging from their stance, and sticking to the respective perception with regard to the position and occupation of Jammu and Kashmir; thus the LOC and LAC stands. Only difference which this had made on Pakistan and China is increased apprehensiveness and anxiety of Indian reclamation intentions. In this scenario, the ways out for India is, *firstly*, the containment both within and outside and *secondly*, the consolidation of what presently is the status of Indian Jammu and

Kashmir, after abrogation of Articles 370 and 35 A and then follow it up with reclamation.

There was no way out for India to bring under one umbrella and under one Constitution State of the Jammu and Kashmir. This could have happened only, when the standoff provisions and articles of the Constitution, giving exclusivity of separation to the State of Jammu and Kashmir were abrogated. Article 370 and 35 A had made the State especially the Kashmir Region, to take advantage and create environment of independent rights, on which the parliament of India did not have any say. The outcome of the articles gave the perception to the Kashmiri Muslims the rights of taking the decision and expressing their choice of accession, on religious and communal lines (with Pakistan), this aspect had been made loud and clear many times by the Muslim majority through number of anti national activities, irony is no Kashmiri is clear about Azadi (freedom) but have accepted the concept of 'Jihad' for the 'Azadi' (freedom), thus making it an fundamentalist movement and invited pan Islamic fundamentalist intervention in the State. The Kashmiri Muslims perception did not have any support from Jammu (Hindus), Ladakh (Buddhists) and Shia Muslims of Kargil. Start of the terrorism and jihad was only by the Kashmiri Muslims and this was exploited by the Pakistan and China. The entry of Islamic fundamentalism and overthrow of Kashmiri Sufism, brought about the perception of Jihad linked with freedom through the sponsored Islamic fundamentalist mercenaries and the anti-India terrorist groups. Kashmiri Separatists also supported the concept and gave voice to Kashmiri demand to freedom and Jihad. Kashmiri political parties' inviolable covert support gave Kashmiri Muslims the morale support. The perceived mindset of the Kashmiri Muslim population of separate state and Pakistan's existing proxy war are all reality and cannot be denied. There may be many arguments, but it is an actuality and a reality.

The irony is, that the 80 percent of Muslim population out of the total Muslim population of Jammu and Kashmir is concentrated in the Kashmir Region and balance 20 percent in the fringe areas of Rajouri, Poonch, Ramban, Doda and Kishtwar and Kargil. Kargil has Muslim population of Shia sect, mostly nomads and are not interested in the Kashmiri endeavours of Jihad for Azadi (freedom). The Muslim population of Jammu and Kashmir is concentrated in 1/4th of the total land area of Indian Jammu and Kashmir. To be very clear and being candid of the fact, that all the problems in Jammu and Kashmir are related to and is by the majority population of Muslims in the Kashmir Region, there is no denying of the fact that Kashmiri Muslims are the only ones, who have started the problems, lived with the problems and in future will continue to be the problem if not contained. Communal and religious overtones, emotions, reasons, reactions and passion are playing a major role and it is the fundamentalist brain washing, which has created mindsets and parochialisms. Politics, police, bureaucracy and civil administration have also been a big part, in getting the situation to this stage and cannot be totally be absolved. Mistakes, commission and omissions have taken place over the last seven decades, without coming out with concrete steps to address the issue, thus Centre also cannot be absolved. Therefore the first step to bring the people to the mainstream was removing duplicities, through abrogation of the Article 370 and 35A and dividing the State in two parts for having manageable administration and overall all-round developments. For people of India it was the right step by the Government of Bharatiya Janata Party (BJP).

Alongside with the abrogation of Article 370 and 35A, the areas of the Indian State of Jammu and Kashmir was divided into two union territories; this was a strategic decision of the Indian Government. It would be prudent to understand the reasons why such action was taken or why was it warranted:

❖ The State is having three geographical regions based on geographical separations and these had become politically bifurcated, each region was called Divisions i.e. Ladakh Division having two districts with land area of approx 59 hundred square kilometres, Kashmir Valley Division having 10 districts and land area of approx 16 hundred square kilometres and Jammu Division having 10 districts with land area of approx 28 hundred square kilometres. The choice was between dividing the State in three union territories exclusively based on geographical demarcations as shown in the Map:

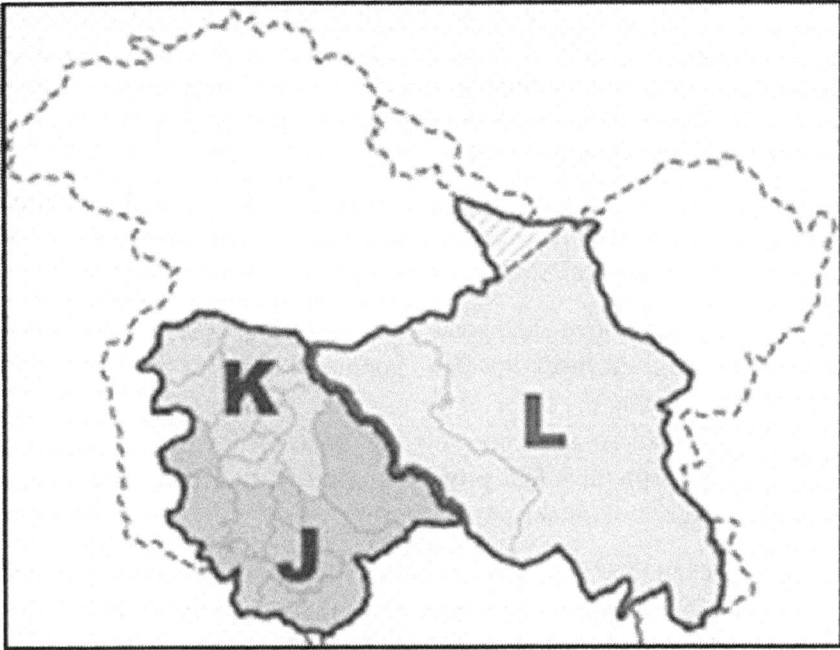

Map of J&K with Three Divisions

There were many advocate of dividing the State into three parts as indicated above, now the question is why two union territories? The reasons as per my inference and which I feel justified are:

➢ Separating Ladakh, with almost 65 percent of the area was a brilliant strategic move, as it has separate prospect of geopolitical importance and military strategic imperatives. The Union Territory shares its border with Tibet Autonomous Region of China, Xinjiang Uyghur Autonomous Region of China and Afghanistan. Separating Ladakh from Jammu and Kashmir will result in better administration and development. With better infrastructure development both at the interior and up to the border areas, strategically India will be at an advantage, deployment of defence forces will be faster and stall any ingress or expansionist endeavours by our neighbours. This will also increase the scope of settlement of people from the mainland and enhance economic development. Tourism will be good revenue earner. Ladakh is the gateway to Central Asian countries and places India in geopolitical advantage.

➢ For having a sustained and equal development of the union territories, the landmass was divided in nearly two equal halves keeping the contiguity and geographical separation in view. Moreover the communal separation was never warranted as this would create problems, and the actual concept of secularism which is part of the Indian Constitution will be lost. Communal parochialism has thus been avoided, which was the mainstay of the State politics.

➢ Densely populated areas of Jammu and Kashmir has been segregated with sparsely populated area of Ladakh, thus increasing the scope of planning the priorities of development, population shift to sparsely areas with development of infrastructures and providing strategic buffer between China and rest of India from the North.

➢ Separating Kashmir would have given more impetus to the Kashmiri Muslims to disassociate themselves and continue with the Jihad for Azadi (freedom). It would have given Pakistan an upper hand, in the attempt of annexing of the Kashmir Valley. This was a big setback for Pakistan and its proxy war, it was for this reason Pakistan reacted fervidly on abrogation of the Article 370 and 35 A.

➢ In case of Pakistan occupied Jammu and Kashmir integration is taken into account, integrating the mountainous regions of Gilgit –Baltistan with the Union Territory of Ladakh will be easy, and the link established with strategic townships of Skardu, Hunza, Gilgit and Baltistan. The infrastructure development in the areas of Drass and Kargil will facilitate connectivity with Northern Area; this will give India strategic advantage, in consolidation of the defensive posture and security of the new borders after reclamation of occupied territories. The Indus valley in itself provides alignment of connectivity and the lay of ground gives advantage to align roads and establish connectivity with Northern Area from Leh – Ladakh, similarly the connectivity from Leh to Aksai Chin and Tibet also exists; thus connectivity will not be an issue, only road infrastructure will require coming up after reclamation. Many military expeditions under the Dogra General Zorawar Singh during the reign of Raja Gulab Singh of Jammu and Kashmir, had used these routes for Xinjiang and Tibet. Thus, Ladakh Union Territory in fact, will be increasing the strategic reach and enhance scope of geopolitical links with the Central Asian Republics. The link with Union Territory Jammu and Kashmir from South is also enhanced as the present Kupwara salient jutting into Pakistan occupied Northern Area of Gilgit – Baltistan, provides the scope of connectivity from Kashmir with Chilas – Gilgit and further into Afghanistan from Srinagar and Muzaffarabad, refer the map below:-

Map: Communication within UT Ladakh

➢ Similarly the Azad Kashmir gets easily integrated with Union Territory of Jammu and Kashmir. Srinagar is better approachable from Lahore – Muzaffarabad through Pakistan occupied Azad Jammu and Kashmir; in earlier days every ruler used this approach to reach the Kashmir Valley. Reviving the old road alignments from Azad Jammu and Kashmir will not pose any difficulty. The Azad Jammu and Kashmir has better contiguity with the Rajouri–Poonch–Akhnoor (Mughal Road alignment)

➤ The two union territories have equal strategic value in respect of China and Pakistan respectively. Ladakh provides space and depth to India to take any Chinese threat, by effectively stalling and containing it, on the other hand it gives launch base to India into the Tibet Autonomous Region and Tibetan Plateau, and the Xinjiang Uygur Autonomous Region. China is sensitive to both the regions. India has disputed territory claim in the Xinjiang Region Southern borders, reclamation of the captured territory of Aksai Chin and the ceded Shaksgam Valley. Aksai Chin is strategically important for China as it connects Tibet and Xinjiang, it was actually encroached by China on the eve of partition of India and Pakistan and road construction commenced in 1950 and was the cause of 1962 Indo – China conflict, after the war it was claimed as captured territory. Pakistan as such feels highly threatened without the buffer of Azad Jammu and Kashmir, its strategic depth is compromised, this in turn threatens its economic corridor project of CPEC. In a way both Pakistan and China have been given a clear understanding of the Indian stance, this is the start point to stage one claim, of what actually belongs to India.

❖ Analysis of the population composition of the Divisions one must understand. The total population of Kashmir with land area of approx 16300 square kilometres is 6.8 million having 97.2 percent Muslims, 1.8 percent Hindus, 0.8 percent Sikhs and 0.1 percent others. Population of Jammu with land area of approx 28500 square kilometres is 5.3 millions, having 65.3 percent Hindus, 30.7 percent of Muslims, 3.5 percent of Sikhs and 0.5 percent others. Ladakh having the largest land area of approx 59000 square kilometres have approx 3, 00,000 population, having 47.5 percent Muslim, 46 percent Buddhists and 6.5 percent Hindus. Dividing Jammu and Kashmir into two union territories was the only solution:

➤ Abrogation of Article 370 and 35 A, thus breaking the hegemony of the majority population and concentration in specific areas.

➤ Improving the scope of distribution and settlement of population within the regions and the union territories.

➤ Keeping Jammu and Kashmir regions as composite thereby avoiding hegemony of any one community. The population of the Muslims in the valley and adjoining areas have its own peculiarities, Valley and its five districts have the fundamentalist Sunni Muslim which are the main party in fundamentalist jihad, the fringe areas in the Valley have population of Gujjars, Bakarwal and Pahari Muslims, this population have different beliefs, similar is the case of Jammu fringe areas of Pounch, Rajouri, Ramban, Doda and Kishtwar. Within valley, the Shia Muslim does exists, but maintain distance with the Sunni population. Separating Kashmir due to dominance of the majority of community would have been wrong, as this would have given impetus to one community sentiment and emotion, which would have further got exploited by Pakistan. The Pakistan calculation has got upset by having two union territories instead of three with Kashmir being exclusive Union Territory. If India would have done so, it would have amounted to giving special privilege to Kashmiri Muslims.

➤ Maintaining secularism, thus denying any dominance of any one community.

➤ Having areas with Hindu and Muslim majorities within the Union Territory dilutes the psychopathic dominance on religious and communal lines. It is a big counterbalance in the fields of politics, socio-economic issues and people's opinion and aspirations. Thus, having Jammu and Kashmir as one Union Territory is the right step to control the Kashmiri Muslims dominion. 20 districts, 10 each from Kashmir and Jammu bring equilibrium in the future politics when the Union Territory is upgraded to the status of a federal state.

➤ In case of integration of Azad Kashmir with Jammu and Kashmir Union Territory, it will keep at par the equation between Kashmiri Muslims and the non Kashmir Muslims therefore the factor of hegemony will not be there and the interposed Hindu population will create a counter balance, where the case of dominance of particular community does not become a factor. This one can say is the Stage-I of the process of integration of Pakistan occupied Kashmir.

➤ With 35 A being abrogated, people from other states will also be coming in, as the development progresses and infrastructure builds up, this to a large extent will create multi polarity in the equation of the population both within and from outside the communities.

➤ Ladakh as such provides large scope of people settlement from the other states.

➤ The Muslim population of Kargil District of the Ladakh Union Territory being from Shia sect and believe in Sufism, thus are not aligned or influenced by the fundamentalist Kashmiri Sunni Jihad prevalent at Kashmir Valley, they are mostly Bakarwal, Gujjar and Pahari Muslims. The separation is inherent due to the sect and geographical barrier, thus not being made part of Jammu and Kashmir, which has Muslim majority, doing so the majority equation of the Kashmir Valley got equally affected, which otherwise used the Shia Muslim in the overall majority factor of the erstwhile State of Jammu and Kashmir. Kargil Shias are not with Jihad and Azadi (freedom) of Kashmiri Muslims. The Gilgit – Baltistan are Shia-dominated regions and Sufism being prevalent in their religious life styles, thus its integration with Ladakh and Kargil is better facilitated. Even though Pakistan has gone in a big way after 1970 for population inversion by settling Sunni Punjabi Muslims in Gilgit – Baltistan, this will get automatically settled once integration takes place.

With abrogation of Article 370 and 35 A, the Stage - I has commenced, a concrete step has been taken towards the containment and consolidation of the State of Jammu and Kashmir, in its complete prospective. *"Dividing the State into two union territories has actually created the road map of future of Jammu and Kashmir as part of India. Government of Bharatiya Janata Party (BJP), which as a true nationalist has at last taken the initiative to do away with the ambiguity of accession of Jammu and Kashmir, position of the State in relation to mainland India and the Constitution. Commission and omission of over last 70 years by various political parties can only be salvaged, by containing and consolidation. My baptism in the Defence Forces was with the believe of the idiom 'Nation First, seen years of political process and game plans of 'gain and power', did not find any political party of having the guts to do, what BJP has done, when it comes to the 'Nation First' and India. I have doubts that any other political party can come up to this standard of nationalism and take bold decisions, the vote bank politics have to be done away and bold and able younger generation leaders who are languishing at the side lines have to be given opportunities. Left Parties and like minded people are nowhere near and do not have the ability to take risk and bold actions, they are better off with their ideologies and power play, nation has not been their priority and most are opportunists. What has been proclaimed is achievable, only when the political parties have the spirit of nationalism and 'will' to undertake consolidation of India, for this, aggressiveness is the only answer. In the land of 'Chanakya', we cannot forget his teaching on nation building, strategies and diplomacy"* this is what a retired Army Officer had to say, who had seen J&K very closely.

Pakistan Factor

It was Pakistan which vehemently objected to the abrogation of Article 370 and 35 A. In no way Pakistan can interfere with Indian internal issue and neither the similar articles were made applicable or existing in the occupied Jammu and Kashmir, under the constitution of Pakistan. The abrogation has affected Pakistan in many ways and upset its design of plugging out Jammu and Kashmir from India, through various planned operation and schemes.

Pakistan wanted to internationalise the issue, but no country supported, even China did not give support to Pakistan. Every country has treated the issue as an internal matter of India. Indian diplomacy really played its part of gaining favourable opinion and did make a difference inside tracking Pakistan out rightly.

Pakistan never expected that Articles 370 and 35 A will ever be abrogated, they always believed that Indian political 'will' is very weak and political parties lack courage, for last 70 years they have been testing and had firmed their opinion, the weaknesses were exploited to the hilt. As such the Pakistani public consider the Indians as weaklings. What are Pakistan's concerns?

❖ The issue of self determination on accession has got diluted on abrogation of the articles, exclusive constitution of the State became defunct and the legislative assembly stands automatically dissolved. Whatever hope Pakistan had about breaking away Jammu and Kashmir, have affected the momentum and conviction. Either Pakistan will renew its modus of Proxy War or for some time continue with the present status of the Proxy War to test the Indian tolerance.

❖ The Indian separatist's and the fundamentalist's cause of Jihad has now got totally diluted, as Kashmir did not remain exclusively to the Kashmiri Muslims. Moreover, the Ladakh region got detached from Jammu and Kashmir. This has made lot of difference to Pakistan but may not have affected the Indian separatists and fundamentalists of Kashmir, as they do not have any influence on the people of Jammu or Ladakh.

❖ The plebiscite which was as such defunct got further redundant as the State got divided into two union territories immediately after abrogation of Article 370 and 35 A.

❖ Sponsored terrorism from Pakistan occupied Kashmir and the proxy war got setback as Kashmir did not remain an exclusive issue and the communal angle got watered down. During the consolidation phase by the Indian Government there is going to be further division of the Muslim community due to shift to equal socioeconomic status, thus removing distinctions and bringing at par Gujjars, Bakarwals, Pahari Muslims and the Kashmiri Muslims in the development phase of human resources, the social distancing was very evident earlier. The very purpose of the Islamic fundamentalism gets diluted as the equilibrium between the sect gains predominance.

❖ Pakistan fears, with abrogation of 35 A, people from outside Kashmir will settle down, resulting in population inversion, this would upset the Muslim fundamentalists calculations of having people's movement and breakaway of Kashmir from India.

❖ Dominance of Muslim majority in the politics and legislative assembly will see a change, as Jammu will have equal representation. The communal factor will be less effective in the vote bank politics, due to differentials in the community of Muslims of Kashmiri, Pahari, Gujjar and Bakarwal.

❖ The claim over Azad Jammu and Kashmir and the Northern Area occupied by Pakistan and phrase 'disputed area', becomes totally untenable as the relevancy of the UN Resolution 1948 is no more relevant. The area of Jammu and Kashmir with India is legally justified and Pakistan's occupation is illegal, thus it is illegally occupied territories and not disputed territories. Pakistan and China is well aware of this. After the abrogation of Article 370 and 35 A, the special appeasement status given to Indian Jammu and Kashmir is no more applicable, moreover, the provisions were temporary. In fact, Pakistan purposefully kept the environment unstable and flared it up at will, to keep the articles in force with the view of annexing the State through people's movement and revolt is the actual intention. What has hit Pakistan is the word 'disputed' as claimed by Pakistan, has also totally lost the meaning, on which it was internationalising the issue as bilateral. Jammu and Kashmir is the integral part of India and under one constitution, and it is the whole of Jammu and Kashmir as per the Instrument of Accession which now matters. The map of Princely State of Jammu and Kashmir prior to August 1947 is relevant as it covers the State boundary and is mentioned in the Instrument of Accession. Not only Pakistan but China also is now apprehensive of the Indian claim, and Indian stance has been declared as internal matter of India, thus bilateral part is now unrecognised.

❖ The people of Azad Kashmir and the Northern Area of Gilgit – Baltistan are the state subject of India, in spite of the claimed disputed status or for that matter the forced population inversion in the said areas. Pakistan has till date, not given the constitutional privilege of Pakistan Province, to the occupied areas of the Jammu and Kashmir, these two areas of Azad Kashmir and Gilgit-Baltistan are only centrally administered, thus not having any legislative powers, in the hindsight Pakistan is aware that areas of Jammu and Kashmir is occupied and is disputed, whereas it is not the case in respect of India. This keeps frustrating Pakistan and with abrogation it has taken a serious twist which is bound to bring apprehension in the Pakistani psyche. Pakistan is now thinking of giving province status to Gilgit-Baltistan and merge Azad Kashmir with Punjab to legalise the occupation.

❖ Lastly the map of India after abrogation and division of the State into two union territories include the whole of Jammu and Kashmir including the occupied areas of Pakistan and China. After 70 odd years it is for the first time that line of control (LOC) is not existing or mapped. This surmounts to authenticating the claim and legality of the accession by India. Any unilateral decision by Pakistan will get contested by India in case of Azad Kashmir and Gilgit-Baltistan.

Pakistan is not going to lie down and bear with these new developments, Kashmir will be kept boiling and in the coming times modus will change, but the strategy against India and Kashmir will stay. For Pakistan, it is matter of survival of its political fraternity and the Army, Indian Kashmir and India is the bogey on which their very existence depends. They may not be bothered about the occupied Kashmir, but concern is more about the Indian State of Jammu and Kashmir, reasons are many but primary ones are dismemberment of East Pakistan (Bangladesh), loss of Siachen and professing the theological belief of 'Ghazwa-e-Hind in exploiting the terrorist organisation as part of revenge against India and to create instability in Jammu and Kashmir resulting into Kashmiri people's revolt. Operation Topac of General Zia-ul-Haq (thousand cuts), proxy war, low intensity conflict and India bashing will continue for some more time or until India gets back whole of Jammu and Kashmir. To achieve its objective, Pakistan will continue to:

❖ Violation of ceasefire and cross border firing.

❖ Sponsoring terrorism and infiltrating militants.

❖ Supporting the separatists and boosting the indigenous militancy.

❖ Firming- in of fundamentalist Islamic organisation and total radicalisation of the Muslim population.

❖ Disruptions in developments.

❖ Firm in Muslim brotherhood to bring all Muslims under one umbrella.

❖ Use social media to create mindset and radically change the youth's perception.

❖ Keep the drug business thriving and use it as force multiplier of favoured people's movement.

❖ Play the Khalistan card, by resuscitating the Khalistan movement to keep India in tenterhooks and make it the counter balance for India's involvement in Baluchistan.

Pakistan has a well laid out plan; its intelligence agency ISI and Army is fully involved. Even though the facade of democracy is there, in reality it is the dictatorship, which is prevalent in Pakistan, which makes the decision. Kashmir is money churner, it brings in Jihad donations, Islamic countries aid and financial support, illegal arms factories are surviving on the jihadists and unconditional Chinese support. Lot of planning and effort has gone into Kashmir by Pakistan since 1979-80 onwards; Indian mainland has also not been spared. The plans included creation of sleeper cells, psychological and pecuniary scheming of liberals and sections of Indian Muslim population, fanatic and monomaniac supporting from within India through sponsorship and using social media to build up frenzy by targeting Indians against India.

Pakistan has become sensitive to Indian strategic strikes and it would not be that easy, to have such adventurism time and again. Moreover, the recuperation after strategic strikes is very fast and activities recommence nearly immediately. The nuclear threat is omnipresent against any endeavour of war on Kashmir; this to an extent brings in audaciousness in Pakistan's endeavour in Kashmir. There are certain guarantees on which Pakistan keeps acting; *firstly,* the nuclear equilibrium, *secondly,* its relation with China and Chinese support as it also occupies the territory of Jammu and Kashmir, *thirdly,* pan Islamic support and *lastly,* anti India rhetoric has always paid Pakistan. In my book 'Kashmir: An Affair of Continued Existence' the game plan of Pakistan, its state actors, the use of Indian weakness has been covered in detail, book gives insight to the continued existence of the problem of Kashmir before abrogation of Article 370 and 35 A. Nothing much has changed, there had been certain lull when Indian Government had taken strict precautionary action. But as opening up of people to people contact has taken place and India being busy tackling with Corona COVID 19 pandemic, Pakistan and its non-state actors have now indulged in reviving the game plan. Under International and FATF (Financial Action Task Force) pressure, Pakistan is claiming about disbanding and abolition of terrorist organisations operating from its soil and the occupied Jammu and Kashmir. Certain arrests were made, accounts have been frozen, to show to the world that it is making efforts.

But the terrorist organisations as usual at their game, now have changed names but have the same masters and cadres, it's repackaging of terrorist organisations to hoodwink the World. In Jammu and Kashmir, it is giving an indigenous touch to the terrorist and fundamentalist movement of Jihad for Azadi (Freedom).

There is not much change, as Pakistan carries on with its Operation Topac (Proxy War) and Low Intensity Conflict, thus trying to raise the tempo. Now with Jammu and Kashmir being a separate Union Territory therefore for the time being, the focus will be on Kashmir and Muslim majority areas of Jammu, will target Jammu region and Ladakh Union Territory selectively at a later stage. To divert the Indian pressure from Kashmir it will try to reinstate the Khalistan Movement in Indian Punjab. It is going to make itself strategically stronger in the Occupied Azad Kashmir and Gilgit- Baltistan with the help of China and improve its offensive and defensive postures, certain defensive and offensive military infrastructure will now be created with help of China thus grounding its claim over occupied territory and rest of Jammu and Kashmir. Pakistan is going to induct more forces and militants into its occupied Jammu and Kashmir creating the psychological superiority ratio issue for India, in case of any planned attempt to recapture occupied Azad Kashmir and Gilgit-Baltistan. Nuclear threat will be played up to create pressure and fear on the world, the nuclear flashpoints will be created in Jammu and Kashmir. Pakistan is well aware that the Article 370 and 35 A in respect of Jammu and Kashmir is not going to be revoked and any party coming to power after BJP will not have the courage of revoking the articles in spite of pressure, it is now an permanent resolution, thus Pakistan will be redesigning its modus operandi, some of the anticipated modus in its proxy war against India will be:

❖ Bring about Muslim fundamentalism all over Jammu and Kashmir and not confine it to Kashmir Valley. The Bakarwal, Gujjar and Pahari Muslim communities will be brought in the ambit of radicalisation. Jammu and Kashmir Shia Muslim will be put under pressure; however, the Muslim leverage will be kept alive to make the majority count, matter!

❖ Populate the Hindu areas with Muslims both from within and from Other States of India. Take the example of demographic change which Pakistan was bringing in Hindu dominant areas of Jammu for quite some time under Jihad. With abrogation, Muslim land

Jihad and involvement of land mafia in purchasing land for Muslim settlement will be accelerated and activated. Pakistan will be making use of the abrogation of article 370 and 35 A in increasing Muslim settlements from other Indian States, thus meeting its agenda of population inversion by increasing Muslim population ratio and using the communal angle to keep fermenting problems for India, so that it gets entangle in handling the Islamic fundamentalist issues.

❖ Claim of occupied Jammu and Kashmir by India will get contested, by total population inversion of the Northern Area of Gilgit-Baltistan. It will further give access and build-up Chinese presence in the area and create total Chinese polarisation, thus involving China equally in safeguarding the territorial integrity of the area in case of any Indian attempt.

❖ Distance India from Afghanistan. With the Taliban taking over the governance of Afghanistan, Pakistan will create mistrust against India. The militant part of Taliban will be used in the Kashmir front to give boost to pan Islamic Jihad for liberation of Jammu and Kashmir.

❖ Likely to bring the issue of Jammu and Kashmir in the International Court and bring status quo to stand. Will get the issue in the UN Security Council. Even though the abrogation of articles and division of Jammu and Kashmir is an internal matter of India and this has been proclaimed by the world. Pakistan will try to make the abrogation as human rights and give a communal angle to it. Movement of self-determination of the Muslims will be made to gain grounds, by creating a situation of revolt and rebellion in Kashmir and the Muslim majority populated areas, thus forcing international intervention. The aim will be to have the Muslim areas with Pakistan, then go in for converting the line of control to fixed International Border and having chunk of Kashmir and Muslim areas in its ambit of border with India. Pakistan knows, that it cannot take whole of Jammu and Kashmir but if the Muslim card payout fructifies, then foregoing Jammu and Ladakh, will not matter. With abrogation of the Articles 370 and 35 A, the aim will be to impregnate maximum areas with Muslim population, so that radicalisation and fundamentalism will bring people's movement, which will aid in annexing Indian Jammu and Kashmir territories.

❖ Threat from India and claiming of whole of Jammu and Kashmir will see change in defence posturing. Both state and non state actors will be actively participating in this posturing, aim will be to put caution into India. China will also be equally participating in this posturing. Nuclear threat will be omnipresent.

❖ As China's interest is very much there, as large investment has been made on the China Pakistan Economic Corridor. Chinese involvement will be coexisting and this gives extra confidence to Pakistan. China being member of the Security Council, the veto will be creating hindrance to any solution which goes against Pakistan.

❖ Exploitation of the social media and artificial intelligence will be the order of the day. This will not only be applicable to Kashmir but will include Muslim population of India. Psychological warfare is and will be the main weapon to keep the Kashmir issue alive and stall any attempt by India to annex the occupied territories. Its intelligence agency ISI and Chinese Intelligence will be actively involved and easy targets of liberals, left parties, sympathisers, Muslim separatists, vocalizers and students, will be made the extended arm and who will be speaking in favour of Pakistan

India is going to see many changes in the strategy, defensive build-ups, and extensive pan Islamic terrorists' organisation involvement in a big way. All claims of India will be contested vehemently and violently by Pakistan. It will also change the political and socio-economic quotient to make the occupied part of Jammu and Kashmir as its integral part and remove the clause of disputed territory; it is going to bring changes in its constitution and legal apparatus. It will keep trying, in internationalising the Kashmir issue and will be lobbying with the Muslim countries and its friendly associates.

India has tough task ahead and has to systematically and logically plan approaches, thus in the Stage-I, India has to first contain and then consolidate before getting into the Stage-II , which will be, to take back the occupied part of Jammu and Kashmir firstly from Pakistan and then China. Stage-II will be the real testing of the Indian grit and will involve all round efforts to first create opportunities, following up with making the opportunities into possibility and then going in for the claim, this would be a difficult proposition but not impossible. The second option is to run Stage-I and Stage-II concurrently, this would require great political will, determination, enhancement of capabilities and resources. This process will be time consuming and require political continuity with similar zest and determination, in spite of differences. There will be many opportunities coming in the process, which has to be exploited to create position of advantage, India cannot let go such opportunities due to political indecisiveness and buckling down under pressure, all window of opportunities have to be exploited to the hilt and ensured it is not lost due to irresolution or for want of action. Pakistan has to be handled by strong hand; India has experienced many agreements, reconciliations, ceasefire decelerations and diplomatic initiatives for peace, many chances have been given to Pakistan, it is high time Pakistan must be dealt in the same way as it behaves, just see the venom which each Pakistani spits on India. Till such time Pakistan is not paid back in the same coin, it is not going to mend its ways.

India's Containment & Consolidation

After creating two Union Territories from Jammu and Kashmir, and after the abrogation of Article 370 and 35 A, there is a requirement now to get Pakistan on its knees. The first stage is of containment of Pakistan and the terrorism in Kashmir and followed by consolidation of the position, which can be concurrently or tackled individually separately, both the Union Territories have to be addressed concurrently in the sphere of development and functional environmental changes. Stage I, will require formulating strategies in all the fronts of diplomacy, economy, intelligence, governance, politic, developments, education, infrastructure, institutions, control mechanism and enforcements. The abrogation has to be used in building the Union Territories, here one has to be prudent with the actions and not get politically involved or being sentimental. I would be discussing containment and consolidation in Stage-I strategies and give out the imperatives, which are going to matter and provide insight to the Indian think tanks in implementation of the Stage-I.

Containment

The very first step of the Stage-I will be the acts of containment. India is faced with many problems internally and externally in respect of Jammu and Kashmir. Dividing and making Jammu and Kashmir as Union

Territory of Jammu and Kashmir and Ladakh, was a prudent strategic step and will facilitate in containment and consolidation. Division of the State and abrogation of Article 370 and 35 A had brought in built-in containment with Governor's Rule and dissolution of the Legislative Assembly, enforcement of control measures did not allow political parties and the separatists either to vent their anger, views or call for protests. This had also silenced Pakistan, as it did not get any support from the International fraternity or from the Muslim lobby, most had viewed it as India's internal matter. Immediately after abrogation of the Article 370 and 35 A, the country from March 2020 got into the fight against COVID 19 pandemic, in spite of being under lockdowns and managing control of spread of the virus, the cross border activities resumed with violation of ceasefire by Pakistan and infiltration of terrorist cadres from the occupied Kashmir, violence has seen an increase, encounters continued and number of terrorist cadres where neutralised. Terrorist activities were seen more in the districts of Srinagar, Shopian, Phulwama, Kulgam and Budgam, these are Sunni Muslim dominated areas. In reality the situation is similar, as it was before and will see increased tempo, once political and separatist leaders are released from detention. Thus, containment is the first step through which the normalcy has to be brought and this will facilitate in consolidation. The areas which will require addressing by the Indian think tanks thus will include:

❖ **Pakistan**. This is the most critical issue and is the root cause to the problem of Kashmir. The outlook of dominance and temperament of revenge has been burning in the Pakistani's hearts, never wanted to accept the fact that India is a power in reckoning and is better placed in the world order in comparison to Pakistan. History of Pakistan has been manipulated to convince the public that, as a clan Pakistani's are superior to Indians. This attitude gives them the courage to take offensive posturing against India. Earlier it was blatant, as the Indian politics and political parties in power never retaliated but kept offering the olive branch to Pakistan. It was the present BJP government under Prime Minister Narendra Modi, which has retaliated offensively and pro actively, this to an extent, has shaken Pakistan's government. Still Pakistan, under its Army and Intelligence Agency ISI contemplating strategies to rejuvenate the ongoing efforts to destabilise Jammu and Kashmir and India. It is at its old game, but now will be putting new ideas. Thus, containment will involve multidimensional approach and multitude of actions, which India must plan, these are:

➤ **Isolating Pakistan.** All out efforts have to be made at the international, regional and sub continental level to isolate Pakistan. The diplomatic front has to be proactive in bringing Pakistan into the open. Whatever be the gestures of reconciliations, compromise or offer of bilateral meetings, must not be believed and treated as bluff. India must give the cold shoulder to Pakistan and get the International fraternity on board. This will bring frustration and make Pakistan to commit mistakes, and these windows of opportunities must be exploited to further deepen the wound. Indian intelligence agency RAW (Research and Analysis Wing) has to penetrate into the political and military system of Pakistan in a big way, to gauge the moves and motives, so that pre-emptive actions can be planned and executed to upset all calculations. Irony is that RAW operations was made totally defunct in Pakistan, during the Prime Minister Manmohan Singh's tenure and during Congress Government being in power; renewed efforts have to be put in to reactivate the cells and sources. Diplomatic isolation can only create the grounds to weaken Pakistan and create fissure between the state and non-state actors. This will facilitate reclamation of the occupied areas.

➤ **Projecting Real Face of Pakistan.** So far India has not taken this seriously and is lacking in perception management at international and regional levels. All intelligence, cyber and media apparatus has to be brought under one umbrella and properly organised. The real face of Pakistan, its polity, Army, bureaucracy, administration and law & order has to be exposed to its population and the World. Social media need to be exploited to create people's movements; pro-active application of media to change the public perception and give true picture to the Nation by exposing the Pakistani Government. The indigenous population of the occupied Jammu and Kashmir has to be supported in their agitations and the World has to be made aware of their plight and grievances, atrocities committed by the Pakistan Army and Police, have to be constantly highlighted in the International media. The political and socio-economic discrimination of the occupied areas have to be done very imaginatively and with authenticity. Mainland Pakistan and occupied areas comparison, need to make it an issue of injustice and parochialism of the indigenous population of occupied areas, thus raise the voice of secession from Pakistan. Showing real face of Pakistan must not be confused with propaganda; it must be fact and factual reporting with full authenticity and must be supported by evidence. Reality over a period of time will affect the perception of the people of occupied areas.

> **Cradle of Terrorism**. Aim must be to show Pakistan as a rogue nation and supporter of fundamentalist Muslim terrorism. Indian intelligences need to keep updating the latest happenings and activities about each organisation, leaders and cadres. This has to be made public, it is only then the target population will know the truth, this will definitely impact the fixed mindset perception of the people both in Pakistan and India. The cradle has to be shaken very frequently, so that there is a continuous 'relay racing' among the organisation to keep shifting its activity centres, this must be without any respite, thus exhausting all the alternatives or making the outfit unable to resuscitate. Breakup has to be initiated within the anti India militant organisations and selective neutralisation of the leaders and cadres to be made both covertly and overtly. To create fear and instability concept of sneak, search and destroy operations both shallow and in depth, must be a regular feature. Line of Control (LOC) must be kept constantly volatile on the Pakistan side, the philosophy of retaliatory cross border firing must be done away with, and all cease fire agreements abrogated as none has been honoured by Pakistan. Retaliation should be at India's will, place of choice and time, instead of keen jerk reactionary action, it must be planned to target real targets. Active LOC and International Border(IB) will instil fear in the infiltrating terrorists, couriers, guides and the Pakistan Army's BAT (Border Action Teams). Randomly all identified launch pads must be targeted both across the LOC and the IB, this will require planning and prudent resource utility management, it is a costly proposition, but will have impact in shaking the cradle. Fear of retaliation must always be prevailing. Thousand cuts have to be now inflicted on Pakistan to bleed the

cradle. Leadership neutralisation both inside Pakistan, occupied territory and within India has to be constant and continuous. In fact cradle must be made to rock hard.

> **Turning the Proxy War.** The proxy war of Pakistan needs to be turned around, overt support to disgruntled people of regions where majority population are having differences with the Pakistan Government must be made to raise their voice under support from India. Internationalise the human rights violations of the Pakistan Military and Administration on people of Baluchistan and FATA, who are anti Pakistan and indigenous communities of occupied Jammu and Kashmir. Supports to separatists' organisations who want freedom from Pakistan. In other words giving back to Pakistan, the same coin. This would require going to the drawing board, taking on board all the agencies and state actors. This would need a proper planned operation centrally controlled. The inter sect and religious heads will need addressing to create instability within Pakistan, an environment of panic and alarm in civil society needs to be created. Till such time it does not pain Pakistan, it is not going to mend its habits and ways, it is time that thousand cuts have to be applied to keep bleeding Pakistan. Chanakya on dealing with enemy neighbour had said "*An enemy destruction shall be brought about even at the cost of great losses in men, material and wealth; otherwise he will not allow you to rest in peace*". Therefore, India has to think on making Pakistan bleed; the Gandhian philosophy cannot work here.

> **Neutralisation of Militants and Terrorists.** The perennial flow has to be stopped; it is only possible when neutralisation is far higher than the flow. Indian forces are at it and have been very successful; however, the frequency of resuscitation is equally fast. Neutralisation has to be on both sides of the LOC (Line of Control), sneak operations have to be more frequent both shallow and in depth. Idea is to create fear of 'Indians are coming' and to incapacitate the operative apparatus. There will be difficulties, which have to be surmounted, use of Standoff Disruptive Warfare Technology i.e. use of artificial intelligence, drone swarms, standoff long distance precision weapons, directed energy weapons, algorithmic warfare, internet among

others have to be used to make survival difficult. This has to be a consistent effort till it breaks the back of the anti India terrorist organisations. The gap between the population and the militants has to be created to isolate and throttle their survivability arteries. Stringent laws, making people go against the militants, stoppage of fund flow and changing the people's perceptions have to be applied to detest people supporting militants and terrorists. Militant Leadership both within and on the other side of LOC have to be targeted MOSSAD style.

➤ **Claim over Occupied Jammu and Kashmir.** India has to project to the world that Pakistan is illegally occupying part of Jammu and Kashmir; the word disputed has to be removed, as there is no question of dispute at all. India has started with weather reporting of the areas under occupation, it has happened for the first time in 70 years, otherwise people on both sides of LOC had taken it for granted and reconciled to the status quo of disputed territories. The geography has to be brought back to what it was in 1947 prior to partition, not only maps require change but also the perception of people of the World, Pakistan and India. At every given opportunity Indians have to claim it as 'Our Land'. National resources from scientific satellite exploration to mass media apparatus have to be co-opted in the reclamation process and gaining favoured International recognition of aggrieved country, to claim the occupied territories. Diplomatic support has to be garnered to make the rightful claim viable in the times to come. Pakistan will be going in for infrastructure and defence development projects or recreate old defence infrastructure, this has to be contested and made ineffective by taking the legal course at International level, use of indigenous unrests and other such means. India must keep planning projects, infrastructures, resource explorations, canalising water resources and having water reservoirs with power grids and all such activities within its areas, giving no concession or considerations to Pakistan whatsoever. What presently exists as an international river water sharing agreement must be made conditional without any favoured nation treatment, the blunder which Congress did. Take the case of China in North East, no concession has been given to India on rivers flowing into Assam.

➢ **Flow of Funds**. The proxy war funds which are filling the pockets of the separatists, agitators, terrorist operating inside Jammu and Kashmir and political funding, need to be stopped totally or rather throttled, 'Eagle Eye' watch need to be constantly maintained and Indian Enforcement Directorate to be pro actively engaged to weed out the source and the culprits, swift action have to be taken to eliminate the source and the operator. Income Tax must have watch and regular raids on sympathisers, separatists, agitation syndicate leaders and the Over Ground Workers; this is warranted to create fear. Bank loans have to be monitored and ground execution checked. Financial control has to be strictly enforced. The 'Hawala' transactions (money laundering) need to be made difficult. In other words, all funds have to be brought under stringent control, special cell has to be made to plan, monitor and control, take penal and legal actions. Fund flow will throttle the Proxy War and make difficult survivability of the terrorist groups and supporters. Mosques and Madrasas need to be kept under surveillance and Maulvis' tracked, the religious source of funds need to be nipped at the bud, these institutions are the biggest source of routing funds to various functionaries. Pakistan involvement in funding need to be exposed and made universal, dossiers to be prepared and in diplomatic meetings shared. Pakistan's counterfeit syndicate and printing units have to be destroyed; all the routes sealed, Indian intelligence agencies have to be involved in breaking the chains and the printing.

➢ **United Nations Organisation**. It is time that the issue of Kashmir should not be allowed to be raised by any party, it is internal matter of India. Pakistan to be barred from raising the point, as it has defaulted on the UN Resolution of 1948, in a way it had not given cognisance to UNO. The aspect of bilateral issue need to be removed and international pressure to be directed on Pakistan to give back the occupied territories to India, there cannot be any bilateral arrangement between India and Pakistan, as the right over Jammu and Kashmir is exclusively of India, this has to be made the diplomatic imperative and opinion of the world to be synchronised with rights of India. India must never allow comparison of Kashmir with Palestine or allow communal interpretation as the cause of the problem.

➢ **Domicile Certificate Act**. This was a big blow to Pakistan after abrogation of Article 370 and 35 A. The Muslim brotherhood support by Pakistan has got a big setback; this act is now effective and under implementation, the Muslim factor was the root of the State politics. The abrogation is going to change the dimensions and dynamics of the political gambit, earlier single community 'Kashmiri' based power politics was in vogue in which Jammu was the bench sitter. Legislative Assembly seat distribution and alignment will also see changes and is going to give opportunity to other indigenous Muslim and Minority Communities to come forward and challenge the Kashmiri hegemony, which has been the case for last 70 odd years. Implementation of this act will contain Pakistan to an extent of making the issue exclusively Kashmiri. The Census and the Domicile Certificate Act is going to change the dynamics in the political and electoral equations. India has to guard against the Muslim Land Mafia who are all out to increase the Muslim settlements in Hindu dominated areas. This game plan must be checked.

➢ **Pakistan's People Perception**. There has to be constant attempt to change the Pakistani people's perception, shift is required to compel the politics of Pakistan to come out of the obsession of 'Kashmir and Kashmiri'. There were views in Pakistan that *"Pakistan is unable to manage its own Provinces and financially crippled, why add to problems by having Kashmir"*. Such sentiments need to be reinforced. Indian Media has to play a big role in this and have to be pro-active, comparative analysis of both countries with regard to their Jammu and Kashmir have to be brought about to fuel the sentiments of the public of occupied Jammu and Kashmir of what they are missing and what will they gain when it becomes part of India, visualisation has to be holistically made to create an perception setup. This would put pressure on Pakistan politics. The level of frustrations is to be hyped among the Pakistani people by using the unrests in occupied territories and raised economic cost in pleasing the agitated public. The effect must be felt by the people of Pakistan and aspect of futility in holding occupied territories at the cost of people of Pakistan to be part of perception management to change the mindset. Issue of giving up of occupied territories of Jammu and Kashmir must come to the forefront to make people realise that it is not necessary to hold on to the occupied territories. Pakistan people will play an important role in future, thus initiative need to be taken to garner their support, all types of media, media apparatuses, artificial intelligence, perception management and diplomatic skills have to be synchronised to achieve this. In the present status Pakistani people's perception is very much against India, Pakistani News reporter had asked "*if Kashmir comes to Pakistan, what will be the capital?*" the comment was "*Islamabad 2, Hindu name 'Srinagar' must be removed*". There is two facts of the perception, *first* is communalism of the freedom and *second* is confining too exclusively to Kashmir only.

➢ **Indian Counter Terrorist Operation**. The containment is best achieved when the superiority of operations are proved, time and again. This has effect on the morale of terrorist organisation, operating terrorists and the country sponsoring terrorism from its land. Indian counter terrorism operation is based on multi faceted engagement of all units of national institutions which is directly and indirectly connected. Indian forces fighting terrorism over last 40 years have made these Indian forces operationally effective units, with good success rate. If the equation of induction and source is made lower and slower and neutralisation rate continues to be consistent, it creates psychological impact of invincibility of breaking through the Indian forces and inability to establish dominance in an area or make it free, this frustration among the cadres will create inadequacy and make realise the public the futility of the Jihad for Azadi (freedom). This helplessness will make the terror organisation accepting the futility and shift focus to other lucrative targets elsewhere, this is going make a difference in the mindset and fixed perception of the Kashmiri Muslims, the movement will die its own death. Let there be any organisation, ISIS, Al-Qaida, anti India terrorist organisations or Pan Islamic anti India States, it is a fact that these individually or in coalition cannot on their own achieve anything against Indian Forces. Pakistan also knows that any war with India is going to disintegrate it. Thus, the pin pricks will remain and to contain, India has to maintain its pro-active and offensive posture in combating proxy war of Pakistan. The fear of Indian retaliation must be consistent from LOC to the depth of occupied areas and into Pakistan's hinterland and beyond, where these militant organisations have sanctuaries, pressure has to continue unabated keeping the surprise factor in view. Another issue is not to allow resuscitation of the destroyed targets or permit relocation. Threat of war must be looming on Pakistan and realisation of futility of Jihad for Azadi by both Kashmiri Muslims and Pakistanis' must be prevailing in their dreams at all times. Thus, morale ascendency over Pakistan and Kashmiri Muslims will matter in containment. As Azadi (freedom)of occupied Jammu and Kashmir from Pakistan is the issue which has to be more focused and deliberately worked on.

➢ **Kashmiri's Perception of Futility of Effort.** It is to make Kashmir Muslims realise the futility of Jihad for Azadi, earlier is this realisation honed-in better will be the consolidation. Neither Pakistan, terrorism and terrorist organisations, separatists nor the radicalisation could give Kashmiri Muslims their Azadi (freedom). Pakistan had the opportunity during the Kashmir people's movement in 1989-90, when there was rebellion all over the Kashmir valley and the administrative control was defunct, the Kashmiri Muslims had sent in their request to Pakistan to liberate Kashmir Valley through military operations. Pakistan lacked the courage and 'will' to go for an all out war with India and face a repeat of 1971 Bangladesh liberation War. The Kashmiri Muslims were specified by Pakistan with the plans of Proxy War. The Proxy War as was expected and anticipated, did not have the desired impact, it is being continued as face saving measure to show the people of Pakistan, concern for Kashmiri Muslims. In fact Pakistan could not create the 'Bear Trap' of Afghanistan in Kashmir, in other words Proxy War has been a total failure. Now the threat is looming on Pakistan of losing the occupied part of Jammu and Kashmir, this threat has to be persistent and serious. The pseudo nuclear flash point of Kashmir by Pakistan and the international fear has kept India at bay, otherwise the issue would have been sealed long back, moreover the Indian political 'will' was lacking since last 70 years. With BJP coming to power in 2014 under Prime Minister Narendra Modi, start has been made to mend the political approach and pro-activeness is evident in resolving the pending National controversial issues, which were becoming threat to issues of national integrity and sovereignty, if this Government stays little longer things will change. Containing Pakistan will, then not be an issue as by then the dynamics within Pakistan would have seen many changes and it would be that which will then become the cause of concern, windows of opportunities will be coming forth which must not be wasted. Kashmiri Muslims have to realise that they were and are part of India since ages.

Pakistan has to be contained, using all the resources at hand and from all fronts and directions. Pakistan must be made to get so engaged, with its own survival and containment of the internal problems, so that sponsoring Proxy War becomes a costly affair and that it will be unable to economically support, as its own economic survivability is a matter of big concern. Pakistan should get tired with the load of Proxy War and low intensity conflict, under frustration either Pakistan is made to go in for war with India thus calling its own destruction or move away from anti India bashing and get its own house in order.

> **ISI.** Pakistan's Inter Services Intelligence is the agency which is handling all terrorist and militancy activities in its neighbourhood countries. In case of India, it is under the operation called as 'Operation Topac', the Proxy War is being stage managed since 1990's by this organisation and Pakistan Army. Actually, this organisation is under control of Pakistan Army. There is a need to checkmate this agency; the only answer is in having a proactive and pre-emptive approach. The Indian intelligence agencies and counter terrorism organisations have to gear up, what is required is the real time intelligence and countermanding the anticipated moves. RAW (Research and Analysis Wing Indian Intelligence) has to penetrate the ISI and the anti India Terrorist Organisations. Think tanks must be thinking on the same lines, what is required is create unrest among the local population of occupied Jammu and Kashmir against the Pakistani establishment and at the same time fermenting trouble in the Pakistan hinterland to create chaos and instability, thus getting the Army committed, to some extent this is already on, but intensity has to be increased. Proxy War both from inside Pakistan and in the Jammu and Kashmir has

to be checkmated, for this ISI has to be first penetrated and cells and agents infiltrated to create network which can be used for countering the ISI moves. ISI network inside India has to be exposed and neutralised. Neutralising ISI is tough task but has to be undertaken at all cost. It is containment of ISI which will make consolidation of Union Territory of Jammu and Kashmir and Ladakh, without any disturbances.

➢ **Chinese Factor.** Chinese interest in Pakistan occupied Jammu and Kashmir and Pakistan parse is very large, China has committed lot of money in China Pakistan Economic Corridor (CPEC) and the Gwadar Port. The corridor is literally in control of the Chinese, not only its manpower but its military is equally involved. China will never like that the corridor or the Pakistan occupied Jammu and Kashmir through which the corridor is passing goes to India, due to two basic reasons, *firstly,* the threat of India claiming Aksai Chin and the ceded areas by Pakistan the Shaksgam Valley and *secondly,* the apprehension that part of the corridor passing through Pakistan occupied Jammu and Kashmir, not being made available by India or the same can be used as bargain instrument to improve India's posture in relation to the border dispute. Therefore, China assisting Pakistan in its Proxy War cannot be discounted, not only this, it will assist the Pakistan's state and non state actors, in the ongoing Kashmir embroil covertly. This will give impetus in infiltrations and organised terrorism within Kashmir. This factor has to be considered seriously in the containment phase of Stage-I. The border issue in Jammu and Kashmir in particular will now be frequent Chinese endeavour, so that the areas under Chinese occupation and the claim by India creates diplomatic and military pressure points to keep the issue at bay, this will continue as was done in the yesteryears and go on into the future, it will a battle for 'who will blink first'. China will be a big hurdle in India's claim over Jammu and Kashmir. We have made a strategic start and the steam must continue at the political level. It is the Bharatiya Janata Party (BJP) government which has taken the initiative of putting the Chinese in back foot, by developing the communication and strategic infrastructure in the border areas with China, thus increasing the mobilisation pace for build up of forces, on the similar lines as it has been done by China in the Autonomous Region of Tibet, this initiative was lacking for last 70 odd years, the same must be maintained henceforth after, to reign on China. China can be made to make Pakistan detest from the Proxy War, by threatening the CEPC and its infrastructure, this angle must be considered by the Indian think tanks, if executed to perfection the dividends will be there, Chinese sensitivities must be mercilessly exploited.

➢ **Making Pakistan Economically Weak.** As such Pakistan is in doldrums in the economic front with heavy debt and near zero reserves, from which it cannot recoup that easily. The economy is barely running and Pakistan is dependent on relief and loans. The 'Modi' Government has to a large extent globally sidelined Pakistan economically by bringing perception change with regard to virtually calling Pakistan a terrorist state; this impacted the economy and investment including FDI. In containment, making Pakistan economically further defunct should be the aim of India. In foreign countries especially Europe and USA word 'Pakistani' makes people uneasy, thus as a way out Pakistanis have adopted calling themselves as 'Indian' to hide their identity, this is the state of affairs. India has to throttle Pakistan economically in the containment phase of Stage I and the continuity must be maintained. This will bring frustration and when the Pakistan polity takes certain counterproductive steps, as was the case of threatening OIC (Organisation of Islamic Cooperation) of withdrawal of membership, blaming it for not giving any importance to Kashmir issue and insulting by doubting the organisation integrity by Pakistan's Foreign Minister, the repercussion of the same was UAE demanding immediate return of loans from Pakistan. Actually, funding by Pakistan in sponsoring of terrorism against India must become costlier and it can happen only when it gets financially and economically weak. Black listing of Pakistan by FATF (Financial Action Task Force) and the World Bank must be the aim of the Indian Government, Pakistan will play games and try to hoodwink the World by showing its concern and reigning in militant organisations and terrorists, would be agreeing on compliance by ordering seizures, freezing of assets and arrests, in order to gain favours of loans from World Financial bodies. Pakistan is to be constantly exposed, one thing is sure Pakistan without supporting the Islamic Terror outfits, organisations and syndicates cannot survive, day it does so the same day it will break, which the Pakistan Polity, Army and Intelligence Agency ISI knows very well.

➢ **Baluchistan Factor.** Presently the movement of freedom by Baluchi's is not full grown, Pashtun population is not involved which consists of nearly 40 percent of the total population, moreover the Pastun Taliban of this belt is with Pakistan. Another issue is all Baluchi's do not want to break up with Pakistan; it is the tribes which face the wrath of Pakistan Army which want to break away. To contain Pakistan, the Baluchistan Freedom struggle needs not only be sustained but made to grow out of proportion and made a people's movement. The RAW (Indian intelligence agency) need to be reactivated, to support the movement. What is important is the political 'will' on the lines of 'Bangladesh and Mukti Bahini'. India can do it and is capable of bearing the cost involved. This threat must be looming on the head of Pakistan and will be the best way to contain Pakistan's Proxy War against India. Baluchistan is the sensitivity of Pakistan due to its size and the natural resources of oil and gas and it does not want repeat of East Pakistan, it is for this reason Pakistan wants that liberty movement to be controlled and kept suppressed, but the mistakes which gave birth to Bangladesh loom large in the Pakistan Army's psyche. North and North – West Baluchistan is the insurgency areas and fighting Pakistan's Army atrocities and human rights violations. Human Rights violation in Baluchistan need to be made point of issue and internationalised, India has to play a big role, what is being presently done is insufficient, coagulated media projections is the need on which India has to work upon to make the World aware of Human Rights violations and the cause of distrust against Pakistan.

❖ **Separatists.** The separatists have been one of the elements within the Jammu and Kashmir, especially the Kashmir Valley, who have overtly and covertly abetted the Proxy War of Pakistan and supported the radicalisation of the Kashmiri Muslim community. In the Kashmir

Valley, they had absolute control over the people, mosque, madrasa, educational institutions, over ground workers, sleeper cells, stone pelting syndicates and the operating militant groups especially the indigenous ones. These separatists are from a congregation of anti India Muslim religious and political parties of All Party Hurriyat Conference (APHC). These separatists are confined to the Kashmir Valley and do have any influence on Muslims who are outside the Kashmir Valley i.e. Gujjars, Bakarwals and Pahari Muslims. After abrogation of Article 370 and 35 A most of them were isolated by detention, thus they could not ferment problems and agitations in the Kashmir Valley. These separatists cannot be indefinitely held under detention, thus measures to contain them need to be worked out. Measures which are already applied, need to be further reinforced, aim must be to neutralise their effectiveness, break the link with the people and distance them from Pakistan. Before understanding the modus of containment of the separatists, one must know how these separatists function:-

➢ The Indian Kashmir separatist leaders and organisations are the political front which is pro Pakistan and is aiding Pakistan's the Proxy War and cross border terrorism. The political leaders who could not come to power after elections or were not part of any party had created their own organisations or parties even with limited supporters; the list of these parties is very large. During the elections of 1987 in the Jammu & Kashmir State, all these petty political parties formed one single party called Muslim United Front (MUF) and contested the elections; National Conference wins the elections in coalition with the Congress Party and Mr Farooq Abdullah is made the Chief Minister. The Muslim United Front (MUF) alleged that the elections have been rigged by the Centre, at that time Indian National Congress Party of India was in power at New Delhi. The insurgency came into the Kashmir Valley during this time and in the following year it gained momentum; Kashmir 'Azadi' (freedom) was turned into people's movement. The Indian Governments mostly the Congress during last seven decades committed many commission and omissions and is also to be blamed for consistent failure of democratic process, not taking cognisance of grievances seriously. Fermenting of pent up anger among the people and political parties not exploiting the offered political opportunities adequately when situation was under control, made the situation grave and gave boost to the insurgency. The Muslim United Front (MUF) candidate Mohammad Yousuf Shah claimed that he was not only cheated in the rigged elections but was also imprisoned and he later crossed over to Pakistan to become Syed Salahuddin, Chief of Hizb-ul-Mujahideen militant outfit, similarly other party leaders had created breakaway groups to continue fighting the political battle of liberation of Kashmir within Indian Kashmir under Tarek-e-Hurriyat merger.

➢ On 9th March 1993, an alliance of 26 political, social and religious organisations were formed; the party was named as All Parties Hurriyat Conference (APHC), with the agenda of united political front to raise the cause of Kashmiri freedom. The party challenged the claim of the Indian Government over the State of Jammu & Kashmir. This was a boon to Pakistan, and it exploited the sentiments by supporting the call of freedom. APHC was nurtured with lot of care by Pakistan's Inter Services Intelligence (ISI) and was made the extended arm of Pakistan's Proxy War within the Indian Kashmir. The paradox is that the Indian Government mistook the organisation as a political front, and hoped through APHC the Kashmir issue could be controlled and resolved; the organisation took full advantage of this and enjoyed the Indian pampering. For the members of the All Parties Hurriyat Conference (APHC), it was win-win situation i.e. having the bread buttered from both sides. It became a business for the All Parties Hurriyat Conference (APHC) to appease Pakistan, to sustain the embroil and get paid to finance the same, on the other hand it enjoyed the appeasement of the Indian Government and taking favours for personal gains, thus it kept throwing tantrums to show their importance to Indian Government, not a iota of nationalism existed among any of the Separatist leader.

➢ In its present form, All Parties Hurriyat Conference (APHC) is a political organisation and majority of the members are pro Pakistan and are having separatist agenda. The protests, student movements, stone pelting on Police and Security Forces, arson and sabotage, activities of burning of schools and education institutions and raising radical issues to influence the perception of the masses, were all organised and regulated by these separatists. Of late it has become a business for these All Parties Hurriyat Conference (APHC) members, it is involved in money laundering from Pakistan, illegal financial transactions through 'Hawala' deals from Pakistan and Dubai, organising religious contributions and donations to facilitate financial support to anti Indian militant organisations in Pakistan and within the State and diverting Indian Government development funds towards anti India movement through coercion of contractors and State Political Party in power. The modus of functioning of the members and the affiliated organisations are:-

- Political agenda is a facade and is used in creating own turf on which the issue of Kashmir and the special status under Article 370 and 35 A of Indian Constitution are weighed, by keeping the sentiments of the local population in the forefront and making it an instrument of blackmail when taking the political front. Any dilution or abrogation of the special status, can tantamount to creating the conditions of civil war and breaking of the Indian State of Jammu & Kashmir, thus facilitating Kashmir's annexation with Pakistan. The issue has already been given a communal angle, moreover, privileges of all the three provinces of Kashmir, Jammu and Ladakh having Muslim population are equally affected, and in such an environment raising ante against India sentiments is not a difficult proposition.

- The question of the special status, in case of joining the Islamic Pakistan and sacrifice of appeasement provisions which is being enjoyed being part of India, have been kept camouflaged under the Islamic card, the local Muslim population is brainwashed by fundamentalist and radicalised ideology of Shariyat (Islamic way of governance). Inter Services Intelligence (ISI) of Pakistan is providing support to All Parties Hurriyat Conference (APHC) to keep the pot boiling. For doing this, All Parties Hurriyat Conference (APHC) is being well paid for sustaining the status of continued existence of the Kashmir issue, in terms of Pakistan's political support, finances and favours.

- Making use of various religious institutions to breed radical Islamic ideology and making them breeding ground of fundamentalism. The 'Kashmiriyat' and 'Sufism' in the initial phase of the insurgency were literally forced out and the separatists compelled the people of the Kashmir into the Islamic way of life and follow 'Shariyat'. Muslim majority areas of the Jammu and Ladakh region was never under the influence of All Parties Hurriyat Conference (APHC) and neither it could establish its influence thus did not get affected. Hurriyat's failure outside Kashmir has been a cause of concern for Pakistan.

- So far the influence of Al-Qaida and Taliban is non existence, but ISIS is said to be trying to establish its foothold. All possibility is there, that the separatists and All Parties Hurriyat Conference (APHC) may be making preparation of creating a turf, to get these extremist organisations bedded in. Even though the basic fibre of 'Kashmiriyat', which still prevails in the personal life, marriages, food and habitat of the people of Kashmir in spite of forced Islamic social values and radicalisation, however the changing influences have created perception changes, which is exploited to create conditions where 'Jihad' becomes the sole solution to independence. Pakistan will be waiting for the opportunity to get fundamentalists and extremist outfits of Al-Qaida, Taliban and ISIS which are operating in its back yard, get into Kashmir thus creating situation like Afghanistan, Iraq and Syria. It is also a known fact that Indian Security Forces are not an easy game, but against mass people movement with pan Islamic support, the tenability factor of Indian security forces may break resulting in disintegration of Indian Jammu & Kashmir. Trans Islamic militant organisations are capable of involving in genocide and mass human rights violations against the non Islamic population leading to large scale exodus. Any strong arm tactics and strategy by the Indian Forces resulting in battle like situation, and in order to deny dominance and containing the terrorism unleashed by these trans Islamic outfits, will result in heavy casualties, thus allegations of human rights violation will then be orchestrated by the separatists to put pressure on India.

- All Parties Hurriyat Conference (APHC) at no point of time will like, that situation gets stabilised or try to create an environment for talks. In order to show allegiance to Pakistan distant themselves from Government initiatives, will invariably ask for inclusion of Pakistan as third party, knowing very well that this will not be acceptable to the Indian Government. This game plan has been going on for some time, getting into any solution to the grievances of the people of Kashmir is not part of their existence, the aim is to keep fermenting trouble to make belief that nothing is being done at the Government and political front and publicise the same in various National and International forums. Moreover, with active social media this task becomes much easier. Social media is being exploited by All Parties Hurriyat Conference (APHC) in instigating people and get them collected to ferment protests and mass movements, what Pakistan's intelligence agency was unable to do, the same is being achieved through All Parties Hurriyat Conference (APHC), in actual terms it is the extended arm of Pakistan's Intelligence Agency ISI and the Army.

- Another task which is being performed by All Parties Hurriyat Conference (APHC), is taking advantage of the weakness of the Indian Government, difference of opinion among the political parties of India, ambiguousness and uncertainty among the stakeholders in the State. To add to the problem it influences the militant organisationso to keep the people of Kashmir subjugated. To put pressure to destabilise or take favours, the activists of All Parties Hurriyat Conference have infiltrated the State political parties of National Conference (NC), People's Democratic Party (PDP), Indian Congress and some of the minor political parties all having majority Muslin dominance in their cadres, some of the members of these parties literally speak the All Parties Hurriyat Conference's language and most members are covert sympathisers of these separatists and easily play into their hands. Pakistan has made full use of All Parties Hurriyat Conference (APHC) as it helps in internationalising the issue of Kashmir and force India to react in order to make its position clear. Till the time the issue of Kashmir is kept alive in the International Front, it will be beneficial to both All Parties Hurriyat Conference (APHC) and Pakistan.

• The present ideology is no more 'freedom of Jammu & Kashmir' as a Nation. The sole motive has now become radically biased on communal lines starting with Islamisation of the Kashmiri, establishing the supremacy of Kashmiri Muslim and Shariyat, thus giving a pan Islamic dimension to Kashmir. Thus, opening the scope of Trans Islamic Fundamentalist Organisations involvement in the 'Kashmir Jihad'. Human and democratic rights are not permitted in Islam and Shariyat is the way of life, this has become part of perception management by the separatists, of the population of Kashmir. Gradually the syndrome of 'Freedom of Kashmir as a Nation' is losing the relevance, thus All Parties Hurriyat Conference (APHC) has totally endorsed pro Pakistan alignment, without letting any option exist. Pakistan is playing its cards very well; as the time passes any political reconciliation in Indian Jammu & Kashmir will become nonexistent. Pakistan believes that when Islam can divide the country in 1947, same can still be applied to Indian Jammu & Kashmir.

• Ensuring flow of funds by using innovative modus of money laundering, exploiting cross border trade in generating profits which get diverted to funding militancy, tour and hotel operators fudging, manipulation of admissions and donations in educational studies both within India and Pakistan, organising donations to religious institutions etc, the flow of the fund is kept well regulated and regular. One of the modus in tour and hotel fudging, is booking of hotels from a foreign country and cancellation just before or after scheduled check- in, thus the cancellation is not refundable as per the rules; such money is then withdrawn and sends to All Parties Hurriyat Conference (APHC) for funding. Similarly, many innovative modus orchestrated in laundering of money through various business and trade activities. Parallel taxation in form of donation is in vogue. Another way is siphoning the governmental funds from State Governments Departments and projects through the All Parties Hurriyat Conference cadres employed in various State Government institutions. There is no doubt money laundering is a big business to All Parties Hurriyat Conference, in order to sustain its agenda and assist Pakistan in its Proxy War.

- Develop the image of spokesperson of the Kashmiri cause, and the only agency which understands the sensitivity of the Kashmiri Muslim population. In any agitation, it takes the position of the leader of the cause and saviour of people. It has the capability to move masses and make people follow the dictates of Pakistan and the prominent leaders of Hurriyat Conference. The organisation has promised, people of Kashmir in meeting justice, fulfil Kashmiri's aspirations, freedom from the yoke of India and keeping alive the Islamic customs and traditions of 'Shariah'. They have gained sympathy and admiration, of fighting for the cause of Kashmiri Jihad. The popular support and trust of the people of Kashmir has made Hurriyat Conference powerful and it uses this as the fulcrum, for bargains and demands from the State political parties in power and the Indian Government. This helps Hurriyat in making itself party to any talks on Kashmir and demand for inclusion in any India and Pakistan initiatives, to resolve the Kashmir issue. Pakistan's unification of Kashmir and keeping the state of instability intact in order to pressurise the people of Kashmir in not succumbing to any Indian initiatives have become part of its propaganda.

- Provide base and intelligence for militant and their operations against the Indian Security Forces and threatening State Government officials, with the view to destabilise the State Government machinery and generate fear of terror. Provide covert support to the militant outfits and help meet the agenda of sponsored militancy, of Pakistan.

- Assist Pakistan's endeavours of Proxy War, by creating sleeper cells, establish intelligence and informer net work for gaining information in planning of terror actions by militants, identification and establishment of hideouts, providing safe haven to militants and permeate sympathisers in the police and bureaucracy ranks to gain favours and assist the militant cadres. They are in total sync with the Pakistan's intelligence agency ISI, in organising such despicable activities in support of the Proxy War of Pakistan.

- When any organisation is working on the agenda of separation and joining any Nation to fulfil the obligations of its support, such organisations are called separatists. All Parties Hurriyat Conference as such meets all the parameters of being a separatist organisation, its leaders like Peoples Conference's Abdul Ghani Lone, Jamat-e-Islami's Syed Ali Shah Geelani, Awami Action Committee's Mirwaiz Umar Farooq, People's League's Sheikh Yaqoob, Itehad-ul-Muslim's Mohammad Abbas Ansari, Muslim Conference's Abdul Ghani Bhat, Jammu & Kashmir Liberation Front's Yasin Malik, Jammu & Kashmir Democratic Freedom Party's Shabir Shah , all are hand in glove with Pakistan, they are the main players in the game of money laundering, organising protests, radicalisation of the Kashmiri religious beliefs and make belief promises of 'Jihad' for 'Azadi' (freedom). Any arrest or detention by the Government becomes a sensitive issue due to the popular support enjoyed by each one of them; moreover, a syndrome of immunity to arrest has been created by posing threat to the State Machinery and the Government Apparatus of strikes and protests. Their existence is a matter of compulsion, they keep changing their stand based on their convenience in dealing with the State or Indian Government, but when it comes to Pakistan it blatantly toes the line by keeping the spirit of Kashmir Jihad alive. Their opportunism have kept them engaged in politics of personal gains and purposefully kept themselves away from any positive solution or initiatives on the Kashmir issue, thus always ready to 'put a spoke in wheel' to derail any attempt.

- In other words, the union of self centred and narrow-minded parties and their leadership under one political front i.e. the All Party Hurriyat Conference (APHC) was what Pakistan had always wanted. This provided the scope of astute control, making the leadership puppets of Pakistan and brainwashing to meet its ends. All of them together are playing into the hands of Pakistan; the denial is the facade behind which the ulterior motive keeps procreating. The fence sitter in the Indian Kashmir are of concern to both Hurriyat and Pakistan, and if these fence sitters get acclaimed and made to step down to their side this would be meeting the agenda of Pakistan. From the Indian prospective, as long as the strength of the fence sitters increases, better will be the effects of the initiatives to win over the people of Kashmir. Till the time fence sitters are indecisive about which side to step down, it will provide the scope of time and space to India to plan and implement confidence building measures to get them into the main stream and build faith on the Government initiatives..

❖ Some of the containment measure which need to be applied to keep the separatists in control are:

➤ **Money Laundering.** The financing of the Proxy War was through the separatists for the militants, over ground workers, stone pelting syndicates, agitators, Mosques, Madrasas and the party functionaries. Separatists are directly involved in the 'Hawala' transactions and fund generations through donations. Their own coffers were getting filled with this money. These separatists were also involved in paying the family of killed militants and organising the martyr procession through money laundering cash. Even though the Enforcement Directorate is after these separatists, what is more important is to cut off the flow of the money from Dubai connection, Pakistan and Drug Money from the tribal belt of Afghanistan and Pakistan. Full scale operation need to be planned to kill the source. Second aspect is, not letting the money flow into India, the source are Nepal and Bangladesh, the laundering through these nations are mostly in counterfeit money and 'Hawala' transactions, the modules operating need to be neutralised within the country, intelligence based offensive actions and strategic strikes need to be carried out in Nepal and Bangladesh.

➢ **Road Route Trade with Pakistan.** This was one of the ways to control the business of the Kashmir Valley, trade was totally through the separatist's syndicates, which decided the rates and the transaction including the batter system as was prevalent. This trade was stopped immediately after abrogation of the Article 370 and 35 A. Money used to change hands and the share of profit was being paid for the cause of Jihad. Separatists were sitting and making money. In case India is serious to contain the cash flow, no trade with Pakistan must take place and road route trade to be totally stopped. Kashmiri horticulturist, fruit growers and dry fruit traders were hand in glove, Indian market provides better market price and this needs to be stopped. No consideration of any nature must be given to Pakistan.

➢ **Recruitment of Indigenous Youth.** Separatists have been intimately involved in motivating youths and helping in recruitment, Mosque and Madrasa are used exclusively for this purpose. The fundamentalism and indoctrination of the student community within the State and students studying in other Indian States, has been providing the fodder to the terrorist organisations through the separatists. Choking the separatists, will bring the numbers down of the recruitments, presently most of them are under detention yet few of them are free and some have gone underground, there is a need of having constant surveillance and all provisions of law must be applied to keep these recruits at bay and distance them from the public. The stone pelting syndicate is guided and controlled by them, social media and mobile communication is used to collect and direct them to the target areas, these modules and the chain needs to be intercepted, neutralised and eliminated, it is only then there will be control. If separatists are throttled, the cash going into the hands of stone pelters will get stopped. State intelligence, National intelligence agencies, Enforcement, Income Tax, Security Forces, Police, Legal prosecutions and other monitoring and surveillance agencies need to be employed in synchronised manner to bring the separatists to books.

> **Religious and Political Parties of Separatists.** These must be declared anti national parties and banned. Till this happens, the organisations must be made defunct or factionalised. As the laws have changed, as the State was divided into two union territories, validity of registration of the parties naturally changed, reapplying for new registration must have stringent clauses and religious parties must not be allowed in the political arena. All there separatists had been enjoying the appeasement of Indian Government since last 40 years, these personalities were considered as spokesperson of the people of Kashmir, given due cognisance to their security and were even regularly paid by the Indian Government. These deceitful people enjoyed the favours from India but were protégées of Pakistan. They supported Pakistan in its Proxy War, radicalisation of Kashmir and internationalised the Kashmir issue in support of Pakistan, thus back stabbing India. All of these separatists are the richest people of Kashmir, dominating business, tourism industry and real estate and property business. What is important is the isolation of these separatists. Some of them are old, these must be faded out, mid aged ones to be kept on the constant run and made to tire out and the younger ones kept confined and constricted, so that they are not able to establish link and lose the touch with the people. Separatists must never be allowed to come up and need to be treated as militants and terrorists. This is the only means to contain them and in turn contain Pakistan. Separatists are Pakistan's eyes and ears, these separatists have to be plugged out, to make Pakistan blind.

> The local Kashmiri are feeling that the Hurriyat has failed, new Hurriyat must come up with new agenda, some Hurriyat source had said "The *separatist youth are of the opinion that the entire Hurriyat leadership, especially the most influential Islamist leader Syed Ali Shah Geelani, failed to keep the state of Jammu and Kashmir together. They believe that the use of religion (Islam) by the Hurriyat in the separatist movement turned out to be counter-productive. They are now going to re-launch a new separatist movement under a new Hurriyat type of organisation which will*

be purely political in nature. The focus of the movement would be Kashmiri ethnicity rather than Kashmiri Muslim identity". This was bound to happen, in order to get the Hindus in the movement of Azadi (freedom), there is need to change the ideology and come out of Muslim majority syndrome. But the question still remains about the radical elements accepting it and the acceptance of hegemony of the Kashmiri Muslims by the Hindus. The continuation of the Jihad for Azadi by anti India Islamic fundamentalist terrorist organisation and Pakistan's involvement and demand of self determination will remain in continuation of the 'Jihad for Azadi'. However the issue of Kashmiri ethnicity will be in favour of India in the process of getting Pakistan occupied Jammu and Kashmir back, and will not be acceptable to Pakistan, for the obvious reason of large scale population inversion and settlements in the occupied territories, thus making the ethnic population a minority. The aspect of separatists must be deleted from the Kashmir chapter and not be allowed to crop up once dismemberment takes place. Separation psyche of any nature must not be acceptable to India.

➢ Separatists need to be isolated and kept out of the way; their dismemberment and disbandment must be the priority. What they have done and the evidence available, legal action initiated and law should be used to keep them on the run. The Intelligence and enforcement agencies must be used to track all illegal income, tax evasion, disproportionate properties, frauds or scams and anti national activities. Best is to confine them in legal tussle and make them ineffective. No new leaders must be allowed to emerge, the heredity pass-on have to be nipped at the bud especially their sons and daughters, who can exploit the turf and be a nuisance in future. With the exit of Syed Ali Shah Geelani from the Hurriyat Conference after leading it for 17 years, Pakistan has lost an important link through which the ISI was able to foment trouble in Jammu and Kashmir, this was more so due to Pakistan's loss of interest and faith in the older leadership and their inability to stop the abrogation of Article 370 and 35A or create people's revolt. Pakistan must not be allowed to put its candidates in the All Party Hurriyat Conference, in the leadership position. India's effort has to be consistent and must keep astute watch over all activities of Political Parties, Religious Institutes and the Likeminded Clubs.

❖ **Kashmir Valley Based Political Parties**. The recognisable parties are only two, National Conference (NC) and Peoples Democratic Party (PDP). Both are totally Muslim dominated party and with Kashmir affiliations, both are of Kashmiri parochial leaning and their vote bank was confined to 10 districts of Kashmir. Both are State and National party but have no influence in Jammu and Ladakh, at National level these two parties do not have any standing thus goes into an alliance to be part of power. Both play Muslim card and are fence-sitter, thus keeps Pakistan in the good books and speaks the same language. Dual faceted politics has been the main cause of continued existence of the Kashmir issues. No party seems to be in the mood to resolve the problems and are happy with the status quo especially when the political gains are obtainable in such an environment.

➢ **National Conference** Leadership has mastered the art of duplicity; it wants to keep all stakeholders at its side including Pakistan, that's why the leaders of the party frequently give such statements which keep the ball rolling in dual facet of its political ideology. Pakistan does not trust the party but the party feels that Pakistan is an important stakeholder in Kashmir and it cannot be made unhappy. Such intentions can be attributed to the political and personal interest of the leadership, *firstly,* in case any solution comes, it will be party to it, *secondly,* in case of any chance of Pakistan getting the advantage in any International mediation, it can prove its allegiance and *lastly,* by any chance International community press for resolutions under UN and both India and Pakistan agree, it can decide to change sides seeing where the advantage is more. National Conference is said to be an opportunist party, it advocates secularism but is very parochial and provincial. However its contribution in Jammu & Kashmir cannot be denied, it was the pioneer party which made the accession of Jammu & Kashmir a possibility, party has been active participant in the National politics and has been championing the Indian stand on Kashmir. The dynastic leadership has been erratic at times but has been supporting India. National Conference (NC) has the history of its founder leader Sheikh Abdullah planning to detach from India the Kashmir and Muslim majority areas of Rajouri and Poonch. He was arrested for anti national activities and put behind bars. NC's heredity party leadership and autocratic control over the years has made it stubborn, of late the party has seen drastic fall in the voter bank equation, which has made it very apprehensive and tentative in power equation thus willing to go for alliance with any party. The party is not liked by non Muslim population. Of late it got involved in appeasement and soft politics with the Kashmiri public, militants and separatists. Pakistan factor does play an important role, but NC is not open about it, leaning tendency does exist. With abrogation of Article 370 and 35 A, the party opposed vehemently and threatened India of losing Jammu and Kashmir. Leadership wants that Article 370 and 35A be reintroduced and will be waiting for Congress party, its old alliance, to come to power at centre.

➢ **People's Democratic Party (PDP)**, this party came into Jammu and Kashmir politics very late and was formed to challenge the single party domination of National Conference, the present leader Mehbooba Mufti openly sympathises with the terrorist, militants and speaks the language of Pakistan. Dual faceted politics has been the order and rather more bothered about the political and personal gains in the present environment. The party believes in appeasement of all participating stakeholders, including the anti India militant organisation to keep the vote bank equation in its favour especially in the Kashmir valley. The People's Democratic Party philosophy of politics is based on the concept of self-rule, which is distinctly different from the issues of autonomy, the leadership believes in policy of condonation and appeasement of the people, the anti-India groups/organisations of the agitators, militants and separatists. The party has been engaging in new political initiatives by keeping all doors open and non antagonist approach. The People's Democratic Party was founded in 1998 by the former Union Home Minister Mufti Mohammed Sayeed, when Congress was in power in the Centre. PDP came to power in Jammu & Kashmir in October 2002 Assembly elections. It was a member of the ruling United Progressive Alliance (UPA is a Congress lead political alliance of like minded parties). Mr Mufti Mohammed Sayeed headed the first coalition Government of People's Democratic Party (PDP) and Congress from October 2002 to November 2005 under rotational Chief Ministerial arrangement with Congress. The PDP withdrew support to the Congress in the wake of Amarnath agitation in Kashmir in 2008 thus breaking the coalition. The party came to power for the second term with support of Bhartiya Janata Party (BJP) in 2015. After Mufti Mohammed Sayeed demise in January 2016 the reins of People's Democratic Party went to his daughter Mehbooba Mufti. This coalition of Muslim and Hindu Party did not last long and the support was withdrawn, there were differences in the political philosophies and ideologies of both the coalition partners, the arrangements with BJP did not work out thus in 2018 the coalition broke as BJP withdrew its support. This party is also run on the lines of dynastic leadership as of date. The party actually had come to power when the situation in Kashmir was towards normalcy and the level of terrorism was seeing decline, it was during this period most of the militant outfits were marginalised, thus the numbers had decreased. Governor Rule was imposed by the Centre, as no other party was ready to support PDP or prove their strength to form the Government; none of the parties were interested in any coalition. There are certain contradictory aspects in the party's philosophies, which has been main cause of its failure, *firstly*, the policy of appeasement of people and the militants, *secondly*, the anti establishment protagonist attitude and *thirdly*, soft separatism outlook made the party communally inclined and capricious. No attempt to resolve the Kashmir issue was ever evident during its rule; on the contrary it kept wearing the cap of soft separatists by supporting the anti -establishment elements. Abrogation of Article 370 and 35 A, the party opposed it vehemently and threatened India of losing Jammu and Kashmir to Pakistan and bloodbath on the streets of Srinagar.

➢ The leadership of both the parties were detained under National Security Act and have been put under surveillance. The political setup will require certain rearrangement, especially after Kashmir Division and Jammu Division merged as Union Territory of Jammu and Kashmir, therefore the containment efforts will involve:

- **Rearranging the Politics.** First task will be to have multi party system in place and not allow single party dominations. Local political parties need to be created without any discrimination, which can keep the heavy weight parties in pressure thus maintaining the balance, it should not so happen as was the case of All Hurriyat Conference congregation of likeminded parties with agenda of separation. People's representative parties will be more appropriate and this would of help during the consolidation stage. The seat distributions have to be balanced so that total one sided leaning is avoided. Restructuring of the political system is the need, backward classes like Gujjars, Bakarwals, Pahari Muslims and other minorities have to be boosted up, so that their representation is there, this had been neglected for last 70 years, by dominance of Kashmiri Muslims. More than National Parties the importance need to be on Regional Parties. Break away from the present two dominant parties National Conference and People's Democratic Party and heredity syndrome prevailing in these parties, to be encouraged to deny any type of domination. The present political parties must be made to come out of manipulative politics to survive, with changed dynamics new political parties encouraged.

- **Bureaucracy and Administration**. The concept of only state subject cadres which was prevalent, now need to be changed. Also, the shifting of the State capital need to be considered. This historic legacy of dual Capital and Legislative Assembly at Srinagar and Jammu respectively for summer and winter cannot be carried on; it is costly affair and puts heavy load on the exchequer. Even though this is a sentimental legacy and with better communication and reduction of time and space in transit due to improved communication infrastructure, the logic of Winter and Summer Capitals or Assemblies does not stand. The administration and bureaucracy having parochial affiliations to the political parties will require a relook and cadres from centre and other states inducted to change the working culture, this will eliminate the infiltrated supporters of the separatists and Islamic fundamentalists. Only one capital either Srinagar or Jammu to be selected or alternately have a new capital at Udhampur. Moreover, the myth of 'Srinagar' being seat of power need to be broken. Other legacies must also be removed; clinging on to history of Raj must be negated and discontinued. In Jammu and Kashmir the discrimination is too large, everyone talks of secularism, but it does not exist in the politics, administration and bureaucracy.

- **Concentration of Vote Banks**.   Jammu and Kashmir vote banks are in fixed pockets based on majority factor, like in Kashmir it is all Muslims and in Jammu it is nearly all Hindus. This has been the main reason of divide from pre partition times, it is high time population movement is encouraged to have mixed population regions, moreover with abrogation of 35 A the citizenship has opened up. This will impact well, in containment of anti India forces. To build the confidence of the people, the internal security have to be made stable, law and order situation are brought under total control and Proxy War and militancy brought to an end. But this utopian situation to come, might take some years and will depend on allowing Pakistan to keep itself involved with Kashmir issue by Proxy War. In the containment stage, this population shifts have to take place irrespective of the Proxy War of Pakistan, initially security arrangements have to be catered and the shift must be in terms of colonisation concept to ensure safety and security, if need be one must follow Israeli technique of settlement. This way the political perception will change, as the vote banks will get equally distributed and spread.

- **Political Sensitivity**. The Indian political sensitivity both at internal and national level have to be more sensible and down-to-earth, ground realities has to be understood and people must not be taken for granted, politics has to be for development and must be people's welfare oriented, no more are the days existing when people can be herded and lead by their nose by charismatic leadership alone. Till results are not seen on ground, people do not believe and the anti incumbency factor then becomes the cause of frequent change of political parties in power, and this to an extent brings instability. Whichever party comes to power, there must not be any type of parochialism either between Muslims or Hindus. The parties must have cosmopolitan attitude and not be communal baised, this will make the Government more transparent. In Jammu and Kashmir the divide has been very predominant; including the National Political parties had the same tendency. In containment, the safe turfs to practise politics have to be created and established, thus terrorism and terrorist have to be neutralised in totality. People keep saying Jammu and Kashmir is going through militancy, this is not happening in Kashmir. What is happening in Kashmir is that militancy has got infused by Jihad for Azadi (freedom) and fundamentalism on religious lines has become the cardinal issue. This is called religious terrorism, and this is more dangerous than militancy. In Kashmir there is no clear defined agenda and aimless pursuit of communal alignments and purpose of allegiance with sponsoring country Pakistan, no more is the demand of independent Greater Kashmir existing among the Kashmiri Muslim. Here issue of ceasefire and negotiation does not exist, as was the case in North East India where political possibilities always existed. All political parties in Jammu and Kashmir have to keep this in mind and under no terms ever favour the sponsor and its state and non states actors. This was what happening under National Conference and People's Democratic Party in Jammu and Kashmir governance.

❖ **Ladakh Union Territory.** To contain the State of Jammu and Kashmir and the Proxy War of Pakistan, especially when it was eying for complete State, was something which required taking action to put to rest the claim. Pakistan desire for Ladakh was not communal alignment but having areas for strategic linking with China, but importance wise not in the priority. This dream was shattered by dividing the State into two Union Territories. Moreover, Pakistan strategic thinkers wanted to annex the State in phases, First take Kashmir and adjoining Muslim majority areas, Kashmir for Pakistan was the road to Ladakh or follow up with taking Ladakh with the support of China and lastly try to take Jammu Region by force, if Jammu is not obtainable then forego the demand and be contended with Kashmir and Ladakh.. Now dividing the State into two parts

Jammu and Kashmir and Ladakh has upset the Pakistani calculations and has given heavy heartbeat to China. In the containment stage, what is required by the Indian Government is to, build up the communication infrastructure and improve the accessibility of Ladakh. The tourism potential need to be exploited and make it world adventure tourism attraction, what is important is first having infrastructure. This area has very large tract of land but very low population, the population ratio to land need to be increased. One thing which must be known to the political masters of India that, accessibility to Skardu, Gilgil and Baltistan of Pakistan occupied areas, is through Ladakh Region, this areas provide the launching pads for all the occupied territories in the North. Therefore the area has to be firmed in from the strategic and tactical point of view and having a stable and sound governance system with viable political arrangements, this can be achieved in very short time. Ladakh is very important for containment of Pakistan for it keeps, both Pakistan and China on tenterhooks. Next issue is linking Ladakh with Gilgit and Baltistan, which must keep the tension and apprehensions hanging as 'swords of Damocles' over the head of Pakistan. This will either compel Pakistan to control the state and non-state actors of the Proxy War, in case they decide to change the policy of confrontation with India or plan to take the battle into India. It is Pakistan who has to decide, what do they really want?

Reintroduction of Abrogated Articles, the political parties of National Conference (NC), People's Democratic Party and State Congress Party have come together to demand rejoining of the state as one composite state, reintroduction of the Article 370 and 35 A and claim over the State Autonomy. As most of the political leaders have been released, a coterie of likeminded political thinkers has been formed. The national Leftist Parties and Congress have also given their support. This was going to happen and the arguments given by theses self interested personalities are nothing new than what was threadbare answered in the Parliament before passing of the Abrogation. Happiest is Pakistan, as its agenda is getting revived by the Indians only, there are so many Mir Jafers in India who are there to open the gates, for Pakistan. There are already opinions in circulation, that after the BJP Government, if Congress or its coalition comes to power, the status quo will be restored to Jammu and Kashmir? Pakistan will also be waiting for this to happen in order to rejuvenate the efforts with new dimension. It will be the greatest blunder ever committed by any political party, which reintroduces the abrogated articles. The BJP in the containment and consolidation phase has to ensure, that the changed established dynamics and dimensions are well founded, the hegemony of Kashmiri Muslims have to be dissolved and get the abrogation ratified legally. BJP under Modi has to really workout, just abrogation and no follow up with containment and consolidation, is going to work, containment and consolidation must be concurrent!

Consolidation

Consolidation is the second phase in Stage-I, which either has to run concurrently with the containment or planned independently. Only issue which must be kept in mind is that the delay cannot be to infinity. Basically, consolidation is people related activities and the confidence building measure. No one wants to be shaken from the comfort zone and the enjoying separate constitutional benefits as part of appeasement, abrogation of Article 370 and 35 A has brought some disgruntlement specifically in the Muslim population. The abrogation was welcomed by the Hindus and the minority communities; as they were hardly having any benefit out of the Articles 370 and 35 A.

Consolidation must not turn into appeasement to any one particular community. Consolidation thus will include and involve restructuring, revamping, development, promotion, drive and initiative for people's participation and prudent road map. This is a long drawn process and will require continuity. Both the Indian Government and the Union Territory administration have to be equally involved:

❖ **Restructuring.** There is difference between revamping and restructuring, in restructuring it is organising things differently and revamping is giving new and improved form. Actually, restructuring comes first followed by revamping. In this process, the existing systems and provisions are to be collated and analysed to find out what is to be retained and what is to be done away with. Here lot of sentiments will be involved which had been existing for last 70 years in Jammu and Kashmir. It is a tricky turf and has to be treaded carefully, thus gaining confidence of the people will be an important facet. Every aspect cannot be restructured in one go, schedules have to be worked out, starting first with employment which has been the grievance of the youth, followed by education and educational institutions, healthcare and medical, economics and financial management systems, the working of the Administration and Bureaucracy, focus on the ongoing projects and its completion, lastly the political atmosphere and prevalent legislative provisions and systems. What will be of importance is getting the people involved and making them accept the changes and challenges, here the issue of confidence building is very important. Restructuring must not be on papers, it should be visible and the impact felt. Indian Government has already started the process with the issue of citizenship. Other areas are equally important.

❖ **Revamping.** Restructuring will lend to revamping. The revamping needs to be in two parts, *firstly,* under the Governor of the Union Territory and later when the Legislative Assembly gets elected and *secondly,* under the Central Government through directives, amendments and provisions. Revamping is very critical part of the consolidation and will require expert handling, here Government initiative will matter, in working out the road map. With abrogation of Article 370 and 35A, revamping is a necessity and step to bridge the gap between Jammu and Kashmir and Indian mainland. Revamping field will be large as the complete spectrum of governance will be falling within its preview. The state has been neglected by its own political parties and the Centre, insurgency got added to make the problem large, terrorism and fundamentalism was responsible for destruction of the educational institutions and denial of basic human rights, rampant corruption in bureaucracy and civil administration, unemployment due to slow infrastructural and economic growth and large disparity in development among the three Divisions. Actually, revamping is required in every field to improve the efficiency and the output, hegemony of communities cannot be allowed or creation of interferences accepted. Really there is need to have complete overhauling, in the consolidation stage.

❖ **Development.** This is the key result area (KRA) for both the Union Territories and the Central Government. Communication infrastructure is the first requisite of development, for only then other developments can take place. Construction of communication infrastructure is a challenge in the mountainous terrain and is time consuming, this brings frustration, there is need to get people of the state involved by first training and then employing them, this will ease the pressure, however scheduled base project completion has to be ensured. India has gone a long way in planning and executing communication linkups with rail and road in Jammu and Kashmir and Ladakh, there is yet lot to be achieved; linking remote areas must be given priority. Connectivity will bring development; remote areas will be linked with the interior lines, thus increasing the reach up to the remotest corner. This will significantly enhance the strategic objectives and economic infrastructural development. Uniformity of development will be the need of the hour and to ensure this simultaneous enhancement of the infrastructure must take place, addressing all the industries and affairs of the state. The development must bring oblivious comparison with the Pakistan occupied Jammu and Kashmir, thus making the indigenous population of occupied areas realise the same and there is change in the perception of prospective, this will be helpful later in Stage 2, annexation of the occupied Jammu and Kashmir.

❖ **Promotion.** This is an important aspect for both Jammu and Kashmir and Ladakh, both are underdeveloped regions. Ladakh in that case is more underdeveloped than Jammu and Kashmir. Now the Article 370 and 35 A stands abrogated, industries and institutions have to be enticed through promotions and providing sustainability by both government and the people of the union territories. Just abrogation of the articles will not pull entrepreneurships and the industrial houses. The issue of radicalisation, fundamentalism and terrorism still stays in Jammu and Kashmir particularly in the Kashmir Valley, this is going to put hurdles as security is going to remain an issue, stability has be to brought about, otherwise 'what is built will be burnt' . The concept in Jammu and Kashmir has to be based upon 'Makes one side brighter so the darker sides feels the glare', here sensitivity of the areas will matter, first non sensitive areas, followed by low sensitive areas and ultimately highly sensitive areas after situations are brought under control, should be the priority need of addressing. Thus, first the controllable areas have to be taken in the gambit of promotion, seeing the development other areas due to public pressure will fall in line and people will keep the militant elements at bay by withdrawing support. Ladakh that way is free of the issues of instability or fear of terrorist activities, thus promoting here will be far easier. The Central and the UT Governments have to carry out potential mapping of the region and then prepare the road map of every development activities starting from settlements, infrastructure, tourism, industrialisation, employment generation to explorations etc, till such time the convincibility factor is not existing promotion will not be possible. Promotion is part of consolidation and has to be well planned, issues which need to be ensured are progressive, proactive thinking and perseverance in the approach and planning, continuity will count as projects will be time consuming. Another aspect will be to promote foreign investment, if government is willing and why not?

❖ **Drive and Initiative.** Consolidation is possible only when there is drive and initiative at all levels of participation. Consolidation is a process and it has to be having datelines along with the road map, otherwise the there will be tendencies creeping up of bureaucratic delays, red-tapism and sidelining of projects for want of funding. In case of both Jammu and Kashmir and Ladakh, there has to be more seriousness, as lot many factors are linked with consolidation i.e. the status of containment, strategic considerations, issue of geopolitical assertions, options with regard to dealing with Pakistan and China and confederacy with the mainland India and its people. The drive and initiative has to be consistent without any letup, if there is any gap the wheel of progression can turn back and come to zero, resuscitating at later stage will be difficult and by that time counterbalancing forces will become defunct, giving rise to the issues which had been effectively contained. The Central leadership has to be strong and capable to taking decision, what will matter is keeping the Nation's interest at the forefront with total selflessness, here political agendas, personal or party's political compulsion gaining predominance over the paradigm of containment and consolidation will not stand good.

The consolidation of the Union Territories, in isolation will not meet the purpose; the consolidation has to be simultaneously at Union Territory and National levels, this would make a difference and matter. The consolidation will depend largely on containment, core issues will involve isolating and making diplomatic gains against Pakistan's occupation of Indian Jammu and Kashmir, reconciliation of the Kashmiri Muslim and meeting their socioeconomic aspiration and grievances, making them detest from supporting the sponsored terrorism, make grow all the region simultaneously thus generating opportunities for development and employment and lastly changing the mindset perceptions which have been prevailing for decades. India must become more vocal about Baluchistan and it should be made looming threat for Pakistan, in its present status the Baluchistan insurgency is not full grown and is not supported by all tribes and only by percentage population. Another important aspect which India must address, is involvement in Afghanistan and establishing diplomatic and economic relations, this will make Pakistan very nervous as the threat of India having influence in its western borders, two of its sensitivity of Khyber Pakhtunkhwa Province and FATA (Federally Administered Tribal Area) and North West Frontier Province) which is in the vicinity of occupied Northern Area of Gilgit – Baltistan and Baluchistan which is disturbed. Something on the lines of Bangladesh has to be thought about to keep Pakistan in its right palce.

What will matter in consolidation is making perception change in the people of Jammu and Kashmir on both sides of the Line of Control, the primary aim must be to uplift the people's living standards and provide opportunities. The impact has to be universal, so that the present perception based on religious and fundamentalism get changed to 'quality of life and stability'. The realisation by the people 'this is possible only in India' need to be achieved in the consolidation stage. The people's realisation must percolate to occupied Jammu and Kashmir to create shift towards India. The other aspects which have been discussed must be running concurrently with the primary aim. The social media must be exploited in the perception change, to further weaken Pakistan.

In this chapter, two basic issues have been discussed, before getting proactive and offensive with regard to claiming forcefully occupied Jammu and Kashmir. In Stage I actions and preparations cannot be exclusive or sequential, the variables are non consistent and highly fluctuating, therefore India's actions and reactions has to be graduated accordingly. Till such time the Stage I is not taken into serious cognisance and due importance is given or if there is lack of shrewdness and pragmatism at political level in handling the issues discussed in stage I, then it will be difficult to launch claim back actions of occupied areas of Jammu and Kashmir which are under Pakistan and China. What is important is to resolve the in house pending issues and it putting the house in order and shaking the nerves of Pakistan and China, nobody is going to just vacate the occupied areas on diplomatic tact's exclusively or merely rhetorically demanding the vacation of occupied areas, these never work. Part of the Stage I has to run concurrently with the plans of reclaiming the occupied territories in Stage II, certain aspects of Stage I have to be continued to maintain the pressure, thus keeping both Pakistan and China in the state of uncertainty and on tenterhooks. The Stage I must put pressure on Pakistan, the impact will be equally felt in China. This can turn tables, earlier than what has been expected and provide grounds to launch Stage II. Containment and consolidation until or unless provides a formidable firm base as called in military terms or providing solid foundation of taking calls by the political party in power, it will be difficult to take the options for going in for military solution. In containment and consolidation stage, the Indian Military power has to be upgraded and capabilities enhanced to carry out the Stage II reclamation of occupied territories.

"Whenever there is a disagreement between history and sacred law or between evidence and sacred law, then the matter shall be settled in accordance with sacred law. But whenever sacred law is conflict with rational law, then reason shall be held authoritative"

- Chanakya

Chapter - IV

STAGE - II

Get Back Occupied Areas

"If you were to choose between an evil person and a snake to keep company with, opt for the snake, because the snake will bite you only in self defence. But the evil person will bite for any reason and any time and always."

~Chanakya

This is the stage where; the will and power of the Indian Government is going to matter and be tested. The seriousness with regard to decisions and the obtainable outcome will matter, as it will be affecting the geopolitical imperatives, change the strategic scenario and impact the political and diplomatic equations. This stage will definitely having issues, which will bring absolute and final outcome as well as change the dynamics in the political environment in the subcontinent and India in particular. The containment and consolidation phases to certain extent will continue to operate in Stage II also. Before coming to Stage-II India should have created and changed the world perception on the issue of Kashmir in its favour; here the issue of nuclear flash point and threshold will be the hold back factor, this need to be tackled getting onboard the powers which really matters. Stage II will not be an easy ballgame, lot of National and International fall outs will be occurring, each of which has to be dealt suitably and with firmness.

The options which will be available in the case of getting back the occupied areas will require prioritisation as both Pakistan and China are equally involved, this will depend on the capability to address two fronts or tackle sequentially first with Pakistan and then China. In my opinion it would be prudent to address both differently and in this Pakistan comes first followed by China, however while going in for Pakistan first option, its strategic partner China involving itself cannot be totally be overruled, then India will not have any other options but to take on both the fronts simultaneously. The options which are available with India in respect of Pakistan is; *firstly*, diplomatically compel Pakistan to hand over the occupied areas having bilateral talks followed by international intervention while carrying on with containment and consolidation, *secondly*, creating situation in Pakistan for its dismemberment or one can call it balkanisation of Pakistan and thus taking back the occupied areas, *thirdly*, get declared Pakistan as terrorist State and along with international intervention of 'fight against terrorism' get back the occupied areas or with international mediation get the occupied areas back and *lastly*, taking occupied territories militarily. All the options have their pros and cons, this is where the Indian think tanks have to balance out and assess the risk involved in each of the options. Therefore, lot of pragmatism and expediency has to be there, while advising the Indian Government.

The factors which will be playing predominant part in any of the option will be appreciation and study, understanding of the applicability of the appreciation, tasking and responsibilities to each participating force, ensuring availability of power and force multipliers and lastly the political will to go on with the selected option. Each of the factors has to be supported and contingencies worked out. The country has to be economically sound and must have adequate reserves; diplomacy will play an important role here. Compatibility of the participants and the State resources has to be synergised, capability has to be built up and effective command and monitoring mechanism made operative. The exercise will be something on military lines of appreciation of battle plan, aim and terms of reference identification, ground factors study, interpretation of inferences and deductions, assessment of the relative strength and calculations of the time and contingencies, all these will give out series of courses, these courses are required to be compared with pros and cons or advantages and disadvantages and lastly selection of most appropriate course of action which covers the complete gambit of operations including catering for contingencies in case cons i.e. disadvantages or negatives become hindrance so that the same can be addressed in the pre-planned manner. This is a simple process but has complexities and at national level it becomes more complicated as agencies involved are multifarious and in numbers. Whatever be the option thought of or adopted by the think tanks and at Prime Minister Office level, the ultimate decision will be political. Except for the military solution, all options are long drawn affair and will require continuity, it should not so happen with change of government the plans get changed or there is back-out, then all efforts will be in vain and the issue of Kashmir will continue to exist. India in that case will have to live with status quo as existing today for years to come and forget about occupied Jammu and Kashmir.

The initiative taken by 'Modi' Government is the first of its type in last 70 odd years; it is the first Government who has reclaimed all occupied territories. In the last 70 odd years 60 years were Congress rule in India since the partition in 1947, it was Congress doing due to which the areas were occupied, first by Pakistan in 1947-48 and China in 1962, never was any attempt made to get back these occupied territories. India's first Prime Minister Jawaharlal Nehru who commented when China did not return the captured Aksai Chin *"what we are going to do, where a single blade of grass does not grow"*, this attitude continued with Congress, it was only Narshima Rao who had taken some initiative but the same got sidelined during Manmohan Singh's premiership. The interposed Governments were busy with the party politics and alliances, thus did not have time to think about it, this was applicable to both Janata Dal and Bharatiya Janata Party under Atal Bihari Bajpai's premiership. Now the present Government under Modi have shown the willpower and determination to get back the occupied territories both from Pakistan and China.

The aspect of China, I will cover in the next Chapter, in this Chapter I am covering exclusively Pakistan and the occupied Jammu and Kashmir. The options which I will be discussing can be individualistic and sequential or can be concurrently linked with all the options to make it a viable plan of action.

Option –I Diplomatic Offensive

This is the option where the world has to be convinced about the legitimacy of the demand to reclaim the occupied territories, legally the accession of whole of Jammu and Kashmir (as per the mapped boundaries of British India) to India was signed by the ruler of the State Maharaja Hari Singh (historically and politically documented). The Instrument of Accession is a legal document executed by Maharaja Hari Singh, ruler of the Princely State of Jammu and Kashmir, on 26 October 1947. By executing this document under the provisions of the Indian Independence Act 1947, Maharaja Hari Singh agreed to accede to the Dominion of India. There is no doubt here as the law of majority was not applicable, however the will of the ruler was very much there and in his wisdom decided to join India which was very much part of the Indian Independence Act of 1947.

In the diplomatic front there are two basic factions, the United Nations (UN) and the power lobby. Falling back to the UN again will not be worth it, till China is part of the Security Council, earlier also UN could not resolve the Kashmir issue and it went into the backburner. However the assertion and denials as being done in UN and giving apt reply to Pakistan whenever the issue of Kashmir is raised in any UN forum, this must continue to keep the interest of India alive to declare Pakistan as aggressor State which occupied part of Jammu and Kashmir in 1947, and supporting fundamentalist Muslim terrorism against Indian Kashmir, Proxy War since 1989-90 and the Khalistan terror movement of Indian Punjab since 1984. UN must be reminded of terror attacks on India from Pakistan soil and overt support to terrorist organisation. Pakistan Army and ISI have been the master mind behind terrorist renegades who have taken shelter in Pakistan, and in instigation of Jihad for Azadi in Kashmir. Even though the chances of any initiative coming out of UNO, but keeping alive the reclamation demand of occupied territories, must continue. This will put pressure on Pakistan, as well as on China.

The next important aspect of diplomacy is the pan Islamic confederations and organisations. Pakistan being an Islamic country will always look to make use of the Islamic countries, confederations and organisations to put the issue of 'Kashmir' on religious and communal lines. The diplomacy here will be to isolate Pakistan in the Muslim world; this is going to be no easy task as the word 'Islam' makes the issue a matter of unison subsistence of Islamic countries against the others. India has been trying for some time especially under 'Modi' Government, but the results are not very satisfactory. Muslim countries are still contributing for 'Kashmir' in terms of donations and supporting the call of 'Jihad'. Most important will be to isolate Pakistan and take the agenda of 'Kashmir' out of not only Islamic States confederations but the world forums also.

The diplomatic offensive has to be astute and sustained with no let up. India has always been considered as tolerant and magnanimous country, this is taken as weakness and many exploit it, it all started from Nehru era and continued thereafter for 70 odd years. It was only during Indra Gandhi's premiership during 1971 that Indian diplomacy was proactive and aggressive. It is for the first time that under Modi's premiership that diplomatic initiative has been taken to create an impression and make position of India clear. In the present context of Jammu and Kashmir and the abrogation of Article 370 and 35 A of Indian Constitution, being termed as internal affair of India in the international arena, this is a great achievement of the government and was made possible by diplomacy initiatives of Premier Modi. India has to intensify the diplomatic offensive, some of the issues which can put pressure on Pakistan and make it recoil, are: -

❖ The economic and the financial support of the Islamic States to be made conditional with the term India, return of occupied territories and non interference in Kashmir. Throttling Islamic States economic and financial support to Pakistan is one of the ways out, especially by the powerful Islamic countries of Organisation of Islamic Corporation (OIC). The Organisation of Islamic Conference (OIC) according to its manifesto describes itself as "*the collective voice of the Muslim world*", and its stated objective is "*to safeguard and protect the interests of the Muslim world in the spirit of promoting international peace and harmony among various people of the world*". This is very fine, but if we see the organisation, it consists of Islamic countries and not countries having large percentage of Muslims population but are non-Islamic Countries. Thus OIC Contact Group on Jammu and Kashmir, in real terms cannot only be with part Kashmiri Muslims exclusively, when the State has more than 39 percent of non Muslim as part of the population and the Country to which the State belongs is a non Islamic Country, this sub organisation has no jurisdiction and must be made defunct. Issue of Kashmir must be taken out of agenda of OIC, where it has no role to play in the internal matter of a Country which is not part of OIC and recognised as non-Muslim Country. Diplomatically this aspect needs to be argued and make the Islamic countries sideline Pakistan. Chanakya the Indian philosopher 320 BC on diplomacy had said "*When neighbouring country is enemy and contemplating to create instability, it is wise to have relationship with its allies to isolate the enemy country. Make it succumbs to submission due to lack of support from the allies, weaken by keeping it under threat, till its capture*".

❖ The support and dependency, Pakistan in a way have kept two powers on its side USA and China. Both the powers are dependent on Pakistan, differently. USA for its strategic goals in the Middle East and Central Asia has used Pakistan and in turn had handsomely returned the favours. In case of China, it is using Pakistan to have a foothold in the Middle East and use its territory for economic benefits, on the other hand India factor made Pakistan to go in for strategic alliance as a save guard, declared China as it's 'Brothers at Arms'. This alliance is inclusive of military, economic and financial support. USA and China are the two nations which can put pressure on Pakistan. However, in case of China, as it is occupying Shaksgam Valley and Aksai Chin part of Jammu and Kashmir, therefore the dynamics of diplomacy will be having different connotation and arrangement. The only country which can have say is USA; therefore, there is requirement of having power lobbying shift and establishing diplomatic dialogue with consistency. India can take the call of being partner with USA in the 'Fight against Terrorism'; this will provide many avenues of applying pressure on Pakistan, this has its own pros and cons in the relation equations with supporting the 'cause' countries or the countries which are against USA. In the case where extremism and terrorism becoming the political power, developing situation like Afghanistan/Syria, then in global intervention under USA, India will be have no choice other than being part of participating forces. However in the likely case of Pakistan falling in the hands of terrorist groups and intervention by USA to free Pakistan, the Indian participation in that case will be beneficial to reclaim the occupied territories as these will be liberated and annexed with Jammu and Kashmir. The Governments in India have to take the call, survivability in the changed world order have to be pragmatically measured, there will be the need of choosing one of the power block and be part of its partnership, governments may be changing but consistency of diplomatic relationship has to be maintained by the party in power, here it is the matter of nationalism and not 'tit-for-tat' politics of government in power with the previous party in power, with a view to take political revenge and prove the party wrong.

❖ Now the question is what about Russia, who has been a strong ally of India over 70 years. During the Cold War and thereafter, India and Russia (Soviet Union - USSR) had a strong strategic, military, economic and diplomatic relationship. After the breakup of the Soviet Union, Russia inherited its close relationship with India which further strengthened the special relationship. In the time of need India has been depending on Russia, both the countries term their relationship as a *"special and privileged strategic partnership"*. The modernisation and self reliance of Indian Military, to a large extent was due to the technology transfer and support of Russia. However after the breakup of USSR there was a down slide in the relation due to the geo-political and geo-economic shifts both at the regional and global levels, the old romanticism of the Indo-Soviet ties saw ups and downs. However, the divergences in the objectives of the both the nations in recent times due to bilateral and international factors, and the shift in the respective outlooks, due to changed scenario is impacting the Indo-Russia relationship, in other words the issue of national interest has become more predominant in the case of Russia. Pakistan's relationship with Russia is tentative and Russians have not forgotten the Afghanistan episode and the hand of Pakistan in their ouster. Russia cannot be ignored and neither it can be sidelined in totality, diplomatic endeavour must be there to rebuild the relationship with the changed dynamics, this will be worth, when dealing with both Pakistan and China. The fact that Russia holds a permanent seat at the UN Security Council and has been a supporter of India on various issues including Kashmir at the international forum, and is of critical importance for New Delhi.

❖ South Asian Association for Regional Cooperation (SAARC), the neighbouring countries of India. India has to keep the diplomatic relation and pressure to an extent that Pakistan influence gets nullified and there is no teaming up against India. Whatever the political environment of the SAARC say about 'Big Brother attitude' and the 'bully syndrome', being the regional power, such comments and remarks must be taken lightly in the stride and realisation created among the countries about Indian support. Frankly speaking here India can emulate China and take some lessons. Issue of concern for India, is that most of the SAARC Nations due to its economic and development predicament, seek support and help from various nations and power centres, in the bargain they mortgage their sovereignty and national assets. The fear in these nations against India is similar to Pakistan, as number of disputed territorial and maritime issues exists; diplomacy here plays an important role, moreover like Pakistan large chunk of land under forceful occupation is not involved. The amicable settlement will pave ways for better diplomatic relationship; the support of SAARC will matter in making world opinion in favour of return of occupied territories of India by Pakistan. This diplomacy will be more on image building and demonstrating the fairness, thus exposing Pakistan who has been keeping the occupied territory of India's Union Territory Jammu and Kashmir and the Union Territory Ladakh illegally, issue of negotiation does not arise since India has the legitimate rights over the said forcefully occupied territories and it is not the case of border dispute.

❖ Where India is part of world groups or confederations or organisations, it has to diplomatically address individually each one of them to get the point across of the rights over the reclamation of occupied territories from Pakistan and China. Where Pakistan is part of such groups or confederations there also efforts must be there to isolate Pakistan or make such confederations to put pressure on Pakistan, the agenda of 'Kashmir' has to now take a 'U' turn and India has to vehemently project its case and obtain international opinion of return of its legitimate territories. In the case of Pakistan lobby; this is to be targeted with astute diplomacy and attempt made to make such lobby realise that they are wrongly supporting Pakistan. India has to think about having a dedicated team, as it is not diplomat alone who is responsible to handle, the other department of artificial intelligence, media, bureaucrats, articulators and interlocutor are equally important, who have to support the diplomacy. This team is to function under External Affair Ministry within the purview of the planned road map. Getting the world in favour is a long process but a definite one. Pakistan game plan is to be playing the game on at its own turf and own terms, with planned counter moves, decisions are taken at the level of Army and ISI, political head is not intimately involved, as there is no opposition the actions are at a faster pace. The ball has to be kept at Pakistan's court at all times and do not allow it to throw back. India is doing it, but pro-activeness and aggressive posturing is not there, time is unnecessarily wasted in reactive impulsive counter actions.

❖ Afghanistan, is going to play pivotal role in the diplomacy battle, Pakistan is of the view that Afghanistan is its back yard and will never allow India to have dominance in the strategic, diplomatic, economic and socio-cultural relationship. The Indian participation in Afghanistan and Strategic and political agreements, puts Pakistan in the syndrome of getting sandwiched from East and West by India. Afghanistan is in due course going to have Taliban at the helm of affairs, with withdrawal of the US Forces. Taliban has already given indications about their intension of having international relationship for development of Afghanistan. This has been a great setback for Pakistan, as it is against Indian participation of any nature. Moreover, Taliban is aware of the economic potential of Pakistan; it has reservation with regard to having partnership with Pakistan in development and strategic matters of Afghanistan. Therefore, Indian participation will matter, the best will be achieved when accessibility is there both from land through Northern Area and sea through Iran. Therefore, the return of Pakistan occupied territories assumes greater importance. Any threat to Pakistan's strategic interest, either by military action or the diplomatic offensive will put pressure, Pakistan will never like breakup of the country thus the diplomatic pressure can make it give-in to returning occupied Jammu and Kashmir.

❖ Pakistan has been surviving on grants and aids, economically it is not strong thus dependency is more on loans and aids. Economic asphyxiation prevails heavily in the psyche of the political masters, moreover, scams and corruption keep adding to the problem. Literally Pakistan has become economically dependent on Middle East, China, USA and World Bank. It is under heavy debt and is incapable to pay back, leave alone the principal amount but interest also. With no economic growth, the financial debts will become the noose which will strangle Pakistan. India need to create caution in the financial world bodies about the financial stability of Pakistan and the flow of funds in terror related activities. Economically weak Pakistan in the immediate neighbourhood of India is not desirable, it will make Pakistan to get involved and depend on drug money, money laundering, fake notes business, and donations for Jihad in Kashmir including extortion money of terrorist organisations, and this will get diverted into India. The diplomatic offensive thus need to focus on the three weak nerves of CPEC (China Pakistan Economic Corridor), debts and low economic growth, the diplomatic offensive must bring to fore in the world forums and financial organisations/ banks the risk and economic uncertainty prevailing in Pakistan. The issue of abetting, provisioning of safe haven and sponsoring terrorists and terrorist organisations need to be fixed with evidence and dossiers. The proof of loans, grants and aids of Pakistan funnelled to its military and the terror organisations or sponsoring terrorism, the idea is to black list Pakistan. Pakistan is very well aware of Indian endeavour especially under the premiership of Narendra Modi of the attempts to black list it. Pakistan will depend on its saviours, thus will play the communal card to survive, the Islamic confederation will be there to bail out. The target of India must also include Islamic Confederations, thus putting pressure on Pakistan on the similar lines e.g. UAE which has asked Pakistan to pay back the loan of $3b.

❖ CPEC is sensitive to Pakistan and China, which is passing through occupied Jammu and Kashmir. The case of ceding of Shaksgam from Northern Area of Gilgit- Baltistan by Pakistan to China in 1963 had the provision of transfer back, subject to the outcome of the final Kashmir settlement between Pakistan and India, in other words it is a temporary transfer and will be restored to Jammu & Kashmir once the differences are settled with India. Similarly, the word disputed in case of occupied Jammu and Kashmir puts a caution to Pakistan, as it is illegally occupied and Pakistan knows that this territory it cannot hold indefinitely. China is also very sensitive to the infrastructure of CPEC and its manpower deployed, threat is always looming large on the sustainability of operations due to the status of area coming under the term 'disputed' and the Indian stance of reclaiming whole of occupied Jammu and Kashmir. This is the best diplomatic bargaining and negotiating platform which need to be exploited and keep China in tenterhooks. This in turn will also make Pakistan more apprehensive and nervous as it has committed heavily in the CPEC project and if the start point itself gets cut off it will affect the rest of Pakistan and the corridor. India has already initiated the diplomatic initiative but it has to be progressed aggressively to corner Pakistan.

❖ Indus Water Treaty, so far India has been magnanimous with regard to sharing of water of Indus, Jhelum and Chenab. As most of us know that whole of Pakistan is dependent on the river water, which have source and flows through India. It is high time that India plays it diplomatic card to make Pakistan to realise the futility of the Proxy War and return of occupied Jammu and Kashmir. The water card will have a big pay back as Pakistan's agriculture is wholly dependent on the river water and is the main stay of its economy. The power generation dams which Pakistan has or are planning to have will be defunct if source is regulated. Pakistan might go to the World Court claiming its rights at this point the issue of return of occupied Jammu and Kashmir can be used in the same court to get to the point of correlated justice. Here the diplomacy is of making the world realise the validity of the rights of India over Jammu and Kashmir and there is no compromise whatsoever. Pakistan is to be made to realise the cost of water and mend its ways of interfering with India and its affairs. This is the pressure point, which will fail the Pakistan's nuclear black mailing and threat of nuclear flash point.

❖ Human Rights, it is high time these organisations are shown the right picture of violation by Pakistan. Human Rights are highly lobbied organisations which at times go in for partisan discrimination based on one side of the storytelling. Diplomacy here will involve highlighting the case and point of occupied Jammu and Kashmir, media is to be intensely integrated with the diplomacy. The human rights organisations and world opinion has to be changed which is presently against India, as Pakistan and its sponsors within India have been aggressive in projections. Diplomacy here will involve management of the global media and within India.

Diplomatic offensive is not only of being aggressive and involves only politician, it will encompass having various departments, bureaucracy, administration, media, intelligence agencies, selected government officials and think tanks of calibre. Diplomats are a coordinated group of emissaries of their field who diplomatically evolve tact and their field skills to mould the perception, opinions, views and the mindsets in favour of the Nation to meet the political objectives, and to achieve this having a planned road map is must, in other words it is a concentrated joint effort, to quote Chanakya who spoke of an all round efforts to make diplomacy effective said "*No deliberation made by a single person will be successful; the nature of the work which a sovereign has to do is to be inferred from the consideration of both the visible and invisible causes. The clearance of doubts as to whatever is susceptible of two opinions, and the inference of the whole when only a part is seen is possible of decision only by ministers. Hence the king shall sit at deliberation with persons of wide intellect".*

Pakistan is good in propaganda and use media pro-actively; it is not only the Muslims of Kashmir but also of Indian Muslims which is targeted. Pakistan intelligence agency ISI is actively involved in all the diplomatic endeavours and even the agenda points of diplomats are approved by them, it is also engaged in management of multimedia and the social media, the Pakistani posturing is aggressive in the field of diplomacy. India need to give a rethink on the aspect of diplomacy, it has to be offensive and aggressive diplomacy and not a mere approach. The diplomatic offensive can be addressed individually or concurrently run with the other options, but it is an important arm of the politics and the government. Pakistan has been and will be projecting their point and the claim to the world for justice against India, in such a scenario India has to take initiative and resort to aggressive lobbying. The options which are there with India are:-

❖ *Firstly,* convincing the world about the justifiability of demanding return of the Pakistan occupied territories of Jammu and Kashmir.

❖ *Secondly,* taking the case to the World Court or having outside intervention, this will be a long drawn affair and will depend on quotient of cognisance value given by Pakistan, in case of decision is in favour of India.

❖ *Thirdly,* by showing the muscle power and out rightly taking back the occupied territories, militarily. For this the World has to be made aware of the justification and support Indian cause.

❖ *Fourthly,* wait and engineer breakup of Pakistan and claim the occupied territories.

❖ *Fifthly,* make the population of the occupied territories to revolt and get annexed with India or liberate the area and get it merged with India.

❖ *Lastly,* maintain the status quo and coming to permanent solution of accepting the Line of Control (LOC) as the border thus there is no dispute , the question will still remain unanswered i.e. will Pakistan in this case, cease to instigate problems against India and Jammu and Kashmir, that is very doubtful. An ungrateful political party will choose this option and make the nation suffer for years ahead.

Thus, diplomacy to get opinion in favour of India, of the legitimacy of the rights over the occupied areas, will be a challenge and renewed dynamism need to be infused in diplomatic manoeuvres with dexterity and tactfulness. Diplomatic offensive is the prerequisite of getting the captured territories back from China and Pakistan, and this will require complete and competent handling. *"He who wishes to serve his country must have not only the power to think, but the will to act"* said Plato; this is what the political parties have to keep in their considerations.

Option-II

Dismembering of Pakistan

"A son of enemy, who wants to uproot his own father, should be treated as friend and should be protected. This may be called opportunism but is and should be necessary part of polity and statesmanship. Moreover, if a father is not an upright man to have friendship with his son, can be a meritorious person. A friend, even if he be the enemy's son, should be protected." said Chanakya, he also reiterated *"neighbouring country is an enemy which indulges in breaking the Kings Kingdom, will have his weaknesses, these must be exploited to tear apart this country by intrigue, deceit , spies and war, to have peace on the borders"*. Both the quotes are speaking of breaking a country which does not allow the nation to live in peace.

The present status of turmoil within Pakistan and its state of economy has put doubts in the mind of the many people around the world. The internal turmoil in the Provinces and within the Provinces is making Pakistan to engage it's military to bring the situation under control. The Provinces which are bordering Afghanistan has been cause of concern as the tribal war is common and in most of the part, the writ of the government is non existence, these Provinces were used by the tribal and terrorist organisations fighting in Afghanistan, Taliban also used these Provinces as their base and fought the Afghan War during USSR occupation and later against the US Forces, these two Provinces are Baluchistan and Khyber Pakhtunkhwa. In both the provinces Pakistan military is engaged in a big way to get things under control and facing the wrath of the people. The insurgency in Khyber Pakhtunkhwa, is an armed conflict involving

Pakistan and armed militant groups such as the Tehrik-i-Taliban Pakistan (TTP), Lashkar-e-Islam (LeI), Al-Qaeda and their Central Asian allies. The armed conflict began in 2004 when tensions rooted in the Pakistan Army's search for al-Qaeda fighters in Pakistan's mountainous Waziristan area (in the Federally Administered Tribal Areas) escalated into armed resistance. Pakistan's actions were presented to the world as contribution to the International War on Terror. Pakistan launched number of counter insurgency operations, this resulted in ceasefire agreements and peace deals. As of today the insurgency has been contained, but certain simmering still exists. Moreover, Taliban coming to power in Afghanistan will make a difference as the militant groups will be under the leash.

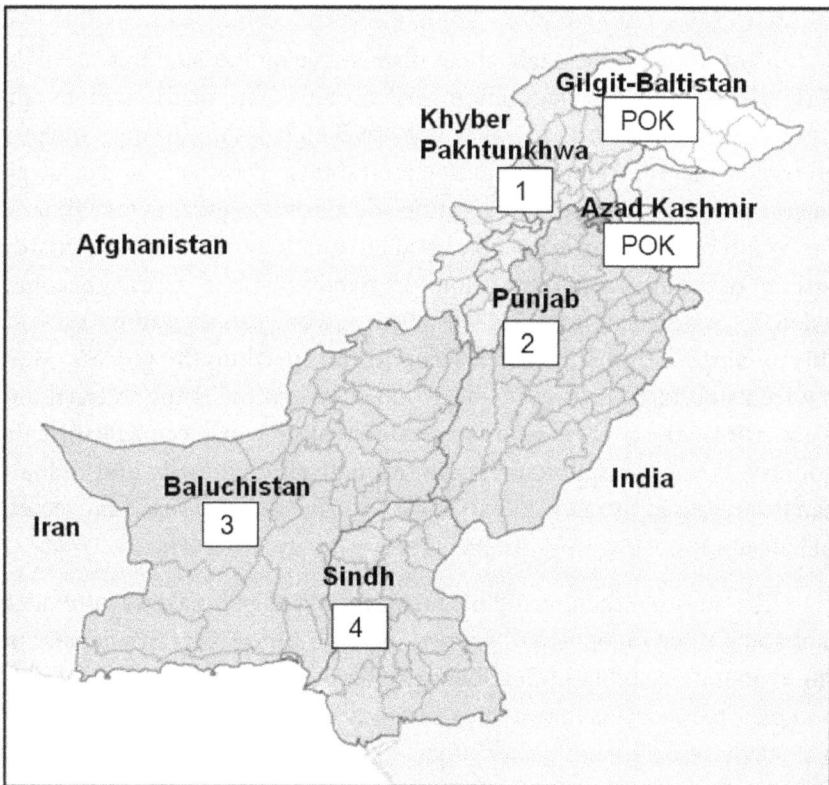

Map Showing Four Provinces of Pakistan

In Baluchistan, only about 37 percent of Balochi are in favour of independence and amongst the Pashtun population support for independence was even lower at 12 percent. Majority (67 percent) of Baluchistan's population did favour greater provincial autonomy. The Bugti tribe in the Northwest Baluchistan and the South Western areas supports the independence and separation from Pakistan, BLA (Baluchistan Liberation Army) and Baluchistan Liberation Organisation are fighting for 37 percent of Baluchi's demand of Independence, what is troubling Pakistan is that natural gas rich area and the Gwadar port falls in the affected area.

The Sind Province also has the issue of Muhajir movement even though the intensity is nearly negligent. It is Punjab and Punjabis who dominate the government affairs in Sind, which is an issue of contention. The Punjabi consider Sindis as second grade citizens.

Most of the Indians talk about dismembering Pakistan to resolve the Kashmir issue, and balkanisation of Pakistan is one of the options, the thought process is on the similar lines of Bangladesh. This very much is an option but will require extensive tactfulness, diplomatic and strategic manoeuvring. Complete balkanisation of Pakistan is going to take time, as the country to breakup is not an easy affair and there are many safe guards, just out of the atlas a country cannot be removed. Yes if Pakistan becomes a defunct State then breakup will be faster and one cannot wait for ages, for this to happen. India in such a scenario can speed up the process. More than outside force getting involved , in such case, it is the internal and forces within the country who can create situation which can balkanise the country, however support inclusive of political, diplomatic and military can be organised from outside to boost and give impetus to the movement of balkanisation..

The question then would be; *firstly,* the status of breakaway province, is it going to be independent or merging with India? This will depend on the economic viability of the liberated province to sustain independently. *Secondly, the* aspect is that all provinces may not breakaway or would form a confederation of independent governance; some will remain part of Pakistan thus ensuring continued existence of the State of Pakistan. *Lastly,* the issue of nuclear proliferation on breakup, the world will not support any breakup as it can lead to nuclear arsenals falling in the hands of terrorist organisations. The nuclear disarming of Pakistan will be an issue which will an area of concern.

Except for Baluchistan, the other provinces are well within the control of Pakistan. During partition Baluchistan had opted to join the Indian Union; however the Pakistan Army was inducted to takeover Baluchistan, from that day the people of Baluchistan has been in revolt and demanding independence, Baluchistan is the thorn in the flesh of Pakistan which it can neither pull out and throw but has to bear with the pain by suppressing insurgency. The other region which had dissented but were heavily suppressed, is the occupied Jammu and Kashmir i.e. Azad Kashmir and Gilgit-Baltistan, since 1948 the region has been denied the constitutional rights of the Pakistan, affecting the development and human resource initiatives. On the other hand in order to silence the indigenous population large scale population inversion by inducting Punjabis and tribals has been carried out to reduce the indigenous population to minority. Rest of Pakistan, whatever the uprising was there was effectively contained and the majority population composition ratio got changed by settlement from other provinces. As the provision on the lines of Article 370 and 34 A was not made applicable, Pakistan did not have any issue of population inversion and settlements in the areas of occupied Jammu and Kashmir.

Now the question comes what is the efficacy of this option and should India venture into breaking Pakistan? Following imperatives must be considered by India:-

❖ The Pakistan occupied Jammu and Kashmir will be freed, Northern Area of Gilgit and Baltistan to be merged with Union Territory Ladakh and the Azad Kashmir with Union Territory Jammu and Kashmir.

❖ What is going to happen with rest of Pakistan, will each of the Province be independent like Bangladesh or they should be merged with India as part of Greater India as was before partition.

❖ Liabilities of Pakistan Armed Forces, financial debts and defunct economy, will these be inherited and create burden on the Indian exchequer.

❖ Militant groups and organisations within Pakistan will be great cause of concern or they would takeover Pakistan under pan Islamic militant confederation like ISIS, Taliban and Al-Qaida.

❖ Pakistan Army will not be sitting duck and accept the fall of Pakistan as fait accompli, with support of Islamic Countries it will strike back and establish military rule, it will take support of pan Islamic militant organisation to quell all the uprisings.

❖ Interference from Taliban Afghanistan and likely takeover of North West Pakistan, FATA, Khyber Pakhtunkhwa and Areas of Tribal Baluchistan cannot be ruled out. This will create further problems of disputes after the balkanisation of Pakistan.

❖ China will not permit the breakaway, it will open the second front to keep India engaged and create strategic uncertainty along the borders or may open the second front with all out war. In worst case scenario Chinese takeover of Pakistan cannot be totally ruled out as its strategic and economic interest is equally affected. The occupied Jammu and Kashmir being given back to India, the question will never arise as it is of significance to China. Puppet dictator or political leadership will be part of the takeover tactics.

❖ Lastly, if Pakistan joins India and comes back to the status of before partition, this will be the win-win situation.

Breaking a country, that too which was created on communal lines of Muslim and Islam, is a difficult proposition, as it is part of confederation of Islamic Countries. The communal angle gives an identity of fraternity and thus the support of the fraternity. In case of Pakistan, perestroika - the restructuring or reforming the economic and political system with increased autonomy as was the case of erstwhile USSR is not going to happen, the balkanisation of USSR was due to this change which in case of Pakistan is difficult to happen.

In India there are many, who believe in this option and varied suggestions are advocated like making Pakistan bankrupt, failure of its economy, declaring it as terrorist country, making it a failed state or getting on board those who want to be part of India. These are the people who believe in 'Akhand Bharat' (Greater India).

Dismembering Pakistan is also not an easy task, and it cannot be done in jiffy, a long drawn process which has to be strategized on multitude fronts, as Chanakya says in his Arthashastra *"Intrigue, spies, winning over the enemy's people, siege, and assault are the five means to capture a fort"* and this would involve committed effort in the front of political, diplomatic, economic, intelligence, electronic media and military at strategic and tactical levels. First and foremost imperative is that , weakness is required to be created within Pakistan before dismemberment and as Chanakya say's *"exploit the created weakness to break the enemy's will , break the alley, break the people of the country, break its source of wealth and break its Army "*. In the present world environment the process will be a long drawn affair and more than Option –I Diplomatic Offensive.

Option -II will require continuity which can run into years and decades. The Other question is; will the 'political will' of India remain consistent with the change of power at the Centre. This option is best achievable in the scenario of the political party which initiates the option and who must see the end and this in Indian context is doubtful. The option cannot be out rightly rejected and has some merits, the only issue is how long can one wait and what is the guarantee that the option can give, of getting back occupied Jammu and Kashmir. The fall of Pakistan itself is not going to be certain and guaranteed, the involvement of power blocks of USA, China and Russia having strategic interest in Pakistan will interfere and put pressure on India, Middle East and Central Asian countries also have interest in having existence of Pakistan and thus pressure will be on India at varied economic and political front.

The next issue is the cost of investment in the venture, which will be rather very high, it is not the question of giving 1000 cuts and bleeding Pakistan or low intensity low cost Proxy War against Pakistan, dismembering will involve building up of the dismembered part of Pakistan. We cannot compare with balkanisation of erstwhile USSR, in this case Russia had retained its economic and military strength, and issue was independence of the countries which was brought under Communist Russia's expansionist ideology. In case of Pakistan, there is no country involved it is mere provinces and districts where some of the provinces are smaller than many Indian States. Therefore, context is totally different and it will have its own dynamics, which cannot guarantee that all of it will be in India's favour.

Yet the option is there which can be considered, it will require real political will, perseverance to have consistent continuity, diplomatic endurance, working up systems and set up deal. There will be requirement of having advisory groups and think tanks that would follow up the plan of action. It will involve composite, combined and multidirectional approach and focus. Plans have to be foolproof. Persistency will be one of the factors which need to be incorporated in dealing and handlings, as there are going to be many highs and lows, reversals and contingencies. Really very dedicated teams have to be formulated to be working in unison. The complete exercise will involve people's perception management, internal political manipulations, exclusion and castrating the leadership at various levels, psychological manoeuvring, resource executions, economic strategising and diplomatic strategy. There has to be total prudency in the plans and will need far-sighted implementations catering for unforeseen events. Yes India has to invest heavily in this endeavour and get the concerned players to its side favourably. Specialisation is the key word and one has to really work hard towards it. Once again reiterating the Option - II is going to be longer drawn than the Option – I.

Merger of India and Pakistan

Within this Option let us discuss the opposite that is merger of India and Pakistan on the lines of West and East Germany. If this happens then there will be permanent solution to all problems, it can also bring in league Bangladesh in the following years. This is very hypothetical case, as the partition of Pakistan and Bangladesh was on religious lines, irony is, these two countries were created on communal lines exclusively for the Muslim population but major part of this population remained with India. Another aspect which is of major concern is both Pakistan and Bangladesh are presently having radical Islam and fundamentalism has taken heavy roots, and both have declared themselves as 'Islamic Nation', there is only namesake minorities, whose numbers are negligible and are surviving under threat and intimidation. The ethnic, cultural and social identity is similar and is the only basis on which the grounds for the merger can worked upon or made to happen. There will be certain prerequisites which are:

❖ The Muslim population has come to consensus; it is this population which can bring the countries together. The fundamental elements and mullah's have to be kept at bay.

❖ The people to people contact has to be of very high order. It is the people only who can bring about the merger. It was the people of East Germany who brought about the merger.

❖ The political consensus has also to be there, as the partition was on religious and communal lines, the religious heads of Muslim of all three countries have also to be in consensus. This factor will be 'make or break' one.

❖ The militant, extremist and fundamentalist organisation have to be removed and neutralised, these elements will be the biggest hurdle and stumbling block. The sentiments of partition will be aroused to meet the ends of 'anti merger' philosophy of such organisations.

❖ The philosophy has to be 'peoples well being and better living'. The economy will have boost and equal development opportunities. Combined nation is stronger nation regionally and globally. 'Equal distribution of resources and development' is the key word.

❖ Lastly the concept of one nation must be acceptable at all and differences have to be buried, it is only then West and East Germany type merger can take place.

The merger for Greater India is very hypothetical and in the 'wish' stage. In actuality, there has not been any earnest endeavour in last 70 years by any of the said countries, there was a chance after 1971 War with Pakistan to get East Pakistan merge with India, this did not happen as Bengalis wanted a free nation, they had suffered badly in the hands of Pakistan, moreover it declared itself as Islamic country which created more distance and atrocities on Hindu Bengalis settled in the country. The Hindu refugees of 1971 did not go back. Getting two Islamic countries into merger is going to be tough proposition; in near future it is not possible as the difference in sentiments of Hindu and Muslim is too large. Only when, these nations become defunct states and volunteer to join back India, India must not give any pondering on the subject of merger. India must be more serious of coming out of developing nation to developed nation category.

In Option –II, there are going to be issues which have to be addressed with great deliberations and circumstantial build-up, over the years India has not been involved or made any endeavour in it at all since partition, the political 'will' has so far been lacking, moreover Congress which was responsible for the partition never gave any thought or attempted merging Pakistan with India, the question was never raised during its rule of over 60 years. The thought of dismembering Pakistan has come when the Indian generation got fed up of Proxy War, Pakistan's involvement in anti India stance and sponsoring of terrorism. Some schools have been advocating this especially hardcore Hindus. Those who have suffered due to Pakistan's adventurism has been the Hindus especially in Jammu and Kashmir i.e. the Kashmiri Hindu Pundits and the Hindu refugees who crossed over and settled in Indian Jammu and Kashmir.

Option – III

International Intervention and Mediation

So far the issue has been bilateral over last 70 years and no solution has come up as on date. Both countries are sticking to their stance and none is budging their grounds. India is fighting the Proxy War of Pakistan over Jammu and Kashmir and Pakistan on other hand is gradually increasing their interference in the Indian part of Jammu and Kashmir. Both the countries have denied any mediation and intervention. The UN Resolution of 1948 has become defunct as no terms of references has been honoured, thus plebiscite did not take place and now having plebiscite is out of question. The plebiscite is not the answer to the problem, as it was conditional i.e. Pakistan to withdraw its Armed Forces beyond the recognised borders of the State of Jammu and Kashmir.

❖ **Mediation.** First let us discuss the issue of mediation, here the question is who will mediate and will the mediation be acceptable to both the countries. The choice is UNO (United Nations Organisation) or Power Block countries or commonly selected country/countries:

➢ **United Nations Organisation (UNO).** The foremost concern is, the issue of Jammu and Kashmir which was tabled at UNO in 1948, when Pakistan's tribal and Army detachments invaded Kashmir in Sep 1947 immediately after partition, with the aim of annexing Jammu and Kashmir. Areas up to Srinagar, Poonch and Rajouri sectors was run over by the invading forces of Pakistan, whatever came in the path of the invaders was burnt, looted, women raped and men brutally killed. It was at this time the Ruler of Jammu and Kashmir acceded to India and Indian Army landed at Srinagar and war commenced for evicting the Pakistani forces. Before complete eviction could take place, cease fire was declared. It was decided that people of Jammu and Kashmir will be given right to choose the nation to which they wanted to be associated, thus plebiscite was ordered by UNO with certain conditions i.e. Pakistan will completely leave the areas which it is holding and withdraw its forces beyond the State boundary, the plebiscite will be monitored by UNO and Peace keeping contingent will be deployed to ensure vacation of the occupied areas by Pakistan and India to cease all operations. Till date neither the plebiscite happened and neither Pakistan vacated the occupied territories of Jammu and Kashmir. Presently UNO has no locus standi in respect of the resolution it passed in 1948, over 70 years have passed since then and in the present context is it non effective and the resolution is not valid. Again going through the procedure of tabling the issue, going through the debates and getting the approval of the Security Council will be a long drawn affair, till date Palestine has not been resolved so what will be fate of Jammu and Kashmir? India may take the initiative, but in case of Pakistan where loss of returning the occupied territories of Jammu and Kashmir, may make it hesitant to peruse the case. There is chance of making both countries accept the Line of Control as the border, thus keeping the region out of the purview of nuclear flash point and ease the tension stress points. This will not be acceptable to India which is of the understanding that their claim is legitimate and the occupied territories must be handed back. Factually speaking India will be at loss, if the case gets stuck in UNO and decision is against its interest. UNO has lobbies and these lobbies play an important role in deciding the sides and their veto does make lot of difference. Getting all of them into an agreement will be somewhat problematic, even if majority veto in India's favour but in Security Council one veto against, the case then will be kept hanging for ages. Getting tangled in the politics of UNO is not going to serve the purpose, however the forum must be used as an back up, as it would provide:-

- Putting the claim and proving its legitimacy, this will be in the back of the mind of all members and in any endeavour of taking back the occupied territories, it would be handy.

- India will be at the position of advantage, in countering any propaganda or actions by the countries illegally occupying the Indian territories.

- India will at safe side to define the attributably, in case of any misadventure is planned or actions undertaken by the China and Pakistan, from or within the illegally occupied territories.

- The nuclear issue will get addressed automatically as the pressure will be equal on Pakistan, China and India. The threat of nuclear black mail will thus get minimised. Here India will be in advantage, policy on nuclear retaliation on 'Second Use' will give more confidence to the members of UNO as compared to the policy of first use by Pakistan and China.

- Even though UNO cannot guarantee the return of occupied territories, but having the case pending, will keep the focus of the world on the issue and any development contrary to the Indian interest can be kept in hold and in status quo, thus making Pakistan and China either reconcile or withdraw. India has to use UNO to substantiate its claim and permanently stamp the claim.

- As the case will be with UNO, the Map of India thus will get the validity of inclusion of the occupied areas which otherwise is not shown in the world map of Pakistan or China and are included as part of its territory. This must also be contested in UNO and projected time and again. The reclaimed areas must be documented well and this must be made visible. Initiative taken by India in weather reporting of Gilgit–Baltistan is right step towards this end; here Aksai Chin must also be included.

➤ **Power Blocks Mediation.** Mediation by one of the power block is one of the options, actually speaking there is only one super power and that is USA. Even though in the power equation Russia, England and France is in lower order but can be considered for mediation. China to be totally ruled out, as it has own interest in holding on to the captured areas of Aksai Chin and the Shaksgam Valley handed by Pakistan. So far, the issue of occupied territories was left as a 'Bilateral Issue' between India and Pakistan. It has been bilateral issue since the UN Resolution failed and both countries did not give cognisance to it, number of agreements are there between the countries, here also Pakistan did not adher to these agreements and made these as a tool of convenience. Bilaterally resolving the issue of Kashmir so far has not been successful and Pakistan is not interested at all. Now the question is, mediator must be approved by both countries, the choice will or may vary, first the consensus has to be arrived and then only the mediator will be able to join, the mediation will have certain imperatives and these must be considered before coming to any conclusion:

- The dynamics and ground situation of issue have to be well understood. Awareness of the background, history and genesis is must. Here is the question of seriousness will matter, how seriously the mediator is going to get involved with the problem.

- The interest of the mediator and the guarantee, there must not be any partiality. Here the intent will also matter. This area will always be in doubt.

- Outcome of mediation is not compulsive, either of the party in conflict can move out. Perception differences will prevail. The question will be, coming to an agreement, signing it and implementation of the agreement. Here either both will be losing partially, one of the parties will be losing exclusively and one of the party will be the gainer. India losing partially or wholly will not be acceptable.

- In actual terms it has to be mediation with Pakistan exclusively as the occupied territories are to be returned back, that is doubtful. The next part will be compromise and coming to settlement, how much both the countries will be ready to accept, will remain a question mark.

- Whatever be the strategy, be it procedural or communication facilitation or agreement or meetings or accords or diplomacy, in case of India and Pakistan none has been effective because these all have been tried out bilaterally. Mediation with directives, which involves threat of sanctions, economic isolation or giving incentives, is the way out to get both countries on the negotiation table and to give out a solution to end the stalemate. Directive strategy will only be applicable to Pakistan, for it is the country which is occupying territory of another country illegally. Here the issue is not resolving conflict but return of forcefully occupied Indian territories of Jammu and Kashmir.

- Only country which can make difference will be USA, which has interest both in Pakistan and India. Issue will be either of compromise or outright decision, for India no compromise will be acceptable and for Pakistan outright decision of return of occupied Jammu and Kashmir will not be acceptable. This is mediation and not arbitration which is bounding, therefore any country can negate it and face the repercussion and live through it.

➢ Any mediation by power blocks/permanent member of UN Security Council or anybody else will not be the solution and will be wastage of time. Indian demand is explicit and there cannot be any deviation to it, which will be acceptable or negotiated. Mediation in this cannot work out for India and it will be futile to go in for the said option. The imperatives above clearly bring out two facets, *firstly* the issue is of return of the territory or vacation of the territories of occupied Jammu and Kashmir which is rightfully part of India and *secondly* is that, there cannot be any compromise about the Instrument of Accession signed by the ruler of Jammu and Kashmir Maharaja Hari Singh. If the mediation is not in favour of India, then it does not stand to logic and will be futility of efforts.

❖ **Intervention.** This is the second alternative in this option. Intervention has to be in form of 'War against Terrorism' and for this to happen in lines of Syria against ISIS or Afghanistan. The important imperatives here will be, firstly to get declare Pakistan as rouge nation and perpetrator of terrorism in the world, *secondly* India has to be the part of block which is committed in eradication of terrorism and declares war against terrorism, India has to participate in the war by supporting including employment of Military. It is only then the intervention can be expected, just desiring or without getting involved with a block, this will not be possible. Key word is – India has to be in league for 'war against terrorism'.

One thing which must be clear is that intervention is not without cost; interest of the block is an important imperative. Take the case of Syria and Afghanistan; USA had its strategic interest involving Middle East, Afghanistan and Pakistan, the NATO countries also got involved as the actions were against international terrorism and the NATO countries were affected by terrorist act from the said countries which were strong hold and bases of terrorist organisations. Moreover, intervention is a possibility when the state has failed and is in the hands of terrorist organisation or there is risk to nuclear proliferation to the terrorists, as same can be the case with Pakistan. Now let us examine certain scenarios taking that India is part of the block for 'war against terrorism':-

❖ In case Pakistan becomes a failed state, the power will in that case shift and Military Rule will come in. The regime will take all measures to ensure that no further deterioration takes place and will take support of the power blocks. World in this case will give chance to Pakistan Military Regime, as this would guarantee that the country does not fall in the hands of terrorist organisations. Moreover, the nuclear arsenal will be in safe hands for the time being. In this scenario the chances of intervention is not there.

❖ The second scenario is when the elected government of Pakistan Tehreek-e-Insaf party under Imran Khan is over thrown and alternate Party comes to power. In the present context alternate parties' political viability to over throw is doubtful, Pakistan Muslim League (N) and Pakistan People's Party which are out of favour or their leadership is involved in saving themselves from number of allegations, do not have support of the Pakistan Army. In such a situation the Mullahs under the sponsorship of the Army or through people's movement can take over the governance of the country. Then the intervention will depend on, how effective Pakistan Army is in controlling the Mullahs and the threat of nuclear assets falling in the hands of Mullahs and its proliferation to Islamic fundamentalist organisations. The question is can Mullahs be stronger than the Pakistan Army and instead of dictatorship why Pakistan Army will allow Mullahs to take over. Whatever be the outcome if Mullahs take over, here also the immediate intervention is doubtful as the situation will be under assessment and observation. The intervention will be there, when nuclear issue gets jeopardised and becomes untenable.

❖ The third situation will be total breakdown of Pakistan and becomes a defunct State, Pakistan Army in this case is ineffective and has suffered due to insolvency of the country. In such scenario, the ongoing insurgency and demand of independence by regions will become predominent and breakaway will be a possibility. Baluchistan movements will get intensified thus the probability of separation will be higher. The Insurgency in Khyber Pakhtunkhwa which has been brought under control with various agreement and accords may also again flare-up; this cannot be totally ruled out. In such a scenario the intervention from Afghanistan's Taliban Regime which is in close proximity to the insurgency prone areas of Pakistan, may take the advantage by liberating and annexing those districts which are bordering Afghanistan. Here India will be at an advantage to take back the occupied Jammu and Kashmir as part of Indian outstanding dispute which has been lasting over last seven decades. In such a scenario Baluchistan will gain its independence. The question then will be the issue of, what will happen to rest of Pakistan; does Pakistan remains with Punjab, Sindh and part of Khyber Pakhtunkhwa Provinces only? If such is the state and opportunity presented, India must intervene in totality by taking over Pakistan and merge it thus bringing the status of pre partition of India. Here what is going to matter is the support from the power blocks and the international community. This scenario is hypothetical but cannot be ruled out, the process will be long and will involve political and diplomatic game play of very high order, windows have to be created which must be exploited to make situation untenable and generate opportunities.

❖ The probability of weak Pakistan getting taken over by the Islamic fundamentalist militant Organisations, either by ISIS, Pakistan Taliban or Al-Qaida, cannot be totally ruled out. In that condition the neighbourhood and Kashmir itself will be in big turmoil, India in that case will get involved in a big way militarily controlling the affected State of Jammu and Kashmir, and safe guarding of its borders. Here intervention will become mandatory to bring back peace in the region.

❖ Another scenario where China which has strategic and economic interest, can takeover Pakistan either indirectly or directly, it already has presence of its forces for the security of CPEC. Pakistan has handed over the Skardu (Occupied Jammu and Kashmir) airfield to China, in order to ensure that there is no disruption or deep strike on the infrastructure of the economic corridor, more military installation are coming up in Gilgit-Baltistan and Baluchistan. Under the pretext of construction of Kohala hydro electrical project by China at 40 KM upstream of Muzaffarabad, there will be more induction of forces over and above the Chinese manpower in the Azad Kashmir region. China will be going in for more military infrastructure to make its footing firm. Pakistan by permitting Chinese in occupied Jammu and Kashmir is increasing the proportion of degree of difficulty, for any Indian attempt to reclaim the occupied territories, militarily. Pakistan is selling its sovereignty in return of alliance and financial bailout.

All the scenarios highlighted above will not warrant intervention, it is the very existence of Pakistan on which the intervention will depend, the country will remain and it cannot be obligated totally. The interest of the intervening forces/power block will also matter in 'war against terror' or the strategic and geopolitical interest. India can be part of this intervening force of reclaiming the occupied territories in the process.

Intervention is always militarily and this is the only effective way to control the situation or bring in normalcy. Intervention in Pakistan will be bloody:-

❖ The pan Islamic militant organisation will be actively participating and Pakistan Army may also be part of the opposing forces.

❖ Alternatively, Pakistan Army may be in support and create difficulties, it is a substantial Army and well equipped, having nuclear artillery and missile strike capability. It has effective Air Force which can be used in carrying out strike on intervening forces, nuclear strike here also cannot be denied. Navy is not that strong but will be used in deterring any landing and guarding its economic zone.

❖ The tribal areas are dominated by fundamentalist groups of Taliban, Al-Quaida, Hakkani Network, ISIS (Islamic State of Iraq and Syria), Lashkar-e Taiba sponsored militant organisation and Central Asia militant groups, the spread is from FATA (Khyber Pakhtunkhwa Province) to Baluchistan, all of these groups are battle hardened and are expert in guerrilla warfare and using asymmetric technique of warfare. All of these groups are mercenaries and if a cause of 'Jihad' is there, then they would unite and fight. Most of the groups are well armed and have their local manufacturing units; their dumps are full with arsenals of Afghanistan Wars.

❖ Chinese presence in Pakistan especially in the occupied Jammu and Kashmir raises certain apprehensions, any intervention by India (being part of intervention force) from the Line of Control will be heavily contested. Another aspect is that India's second front i.e. China Front can get activated; therefore, the question is how much support the intervention forces can give to India to tackle two fronts? It will be a logjam situation for the intervening forces.

The only intervention force which will be effective is USA (super power) and its NATO (North Atlantic Treaty Organization) partners. Russia is another power block, but ruling out Russia as the China factor involvement will make it difficult to commit for intervention, moreover it would not desire repeat of Afghanistan. India is not part of NATO, here the issue of hesitancy will be there, considering Pakistan as "partners across the globe by USA and Pakistan being designated as a "Major non-NATO ally" with its active participation in Afghanistan and Bosnia, also the fact which stands proven and have USA backing. USA wants that India should also be non-NATO ally and to be part of US and UN intervention force fighting in Middle East, the Indian dichotomy is its relations in the Middle East and oil. The second issue will be, declaring Pakistan as 'Terror State' by UNO; it is only possible by USA. India will be in 'catch 22' situation as going with USA will distance Russia which had been having strategic partnership with India for over six decades. India has to take tough decision on going in for intervention, here the tenacity of the political will and the political philosophy of the party in power will matter to a very large extent. Intervention can be a long drawn affair. These imperatives have to be considered by the Indian political party in power, there is hardly any party which can take tough decision. Here what matters, will be political continuity and people of India giving opportunity to the elected political party in the power, till the issue gets concluded. There are no other power blocks except for USA and Russia which will get involved. Any intervention by India in case of civil war in Pakistan or the liberation of Baluchistan will amount to full fledge war

This option viability exists but not very encouraging as the dynamics of strategic and geopolitical imperatives, will be at crossroad and may be conflicting. The *first* question will be how much importance is given by the international community in the bilateral issue between India and Pakistan? The *second* question will be how much Indian influence is there in getting a favourable outcome? The *third* question will be, India, Pakistan and China are nuclear States, and will international community take any risk? *Last* question is, how much can India depend on the mediation and intervention when there are so many cross-purpose dynamics acting uniquely?

Option III, I had discussed to examine the possibilities and deduction which comes out on probability of this option, this is rather very low. Indian analysts can take certain clues from the options to build on other options, where the possibility of success exists. It is Indian problem and India alone has to work the ways out within its ability and capability, supporters will be there but intervention, forget it. Mediation is also no go, what could not be achieved in seven decades, how can any mediation make a difference now? The only alternative in mediation will be negotiation and if India goes for it then issue of compromise will definitely come up, it will depend on the political strength, character and resolve, to give in or stick with the demand of return of occupied Jammu and Kashmir. Pakistan will never agree to part with Kashmir. Then the only answer is, to plug out the occupied areas from Pakistan. Option I and Option II in comparison to Option III is more viable and can be considered by India, everything will depend on creating the vulnerability and despondency and thereafter exploiting the windows of opportunities to achieve the determined objectives. Options discussed so far have their relevance and the Indian think tanks have to deliberate upon, moreover all the option can be concurrent and this would depend on the political will and the planned road map to achieve the objectives and degree of resilience of the political 'will'.

It is high time India must demand a seat in the United Nations Organisation Security Council. Prime Minister Modi has initiated the process and has spoken bluntly; the problem is that the world consensus does not exist. Literally a campaign has to be launched to break the lobbying. Moreover, India's contribution of elevating the world from crises has to be made to realise, in a large way India has to get into humanitarian aids, have to contribute both financially and participative involvement in UNO sponsored programme. Covid 19 Pandemic has opened a window of opportunity to show case India, the world campaign against China after Wuhan virus and Chinese hegemony in the region is another window which must be exploited. Being nuclear cannot be the only criteria of power, power has other dimensions also.

Option – IV
Taking Occupied Territories Militarily

This option is the direct and fastest one which can bring conclusive results, but will be costly. It is this option which both Pakistan and China is apprehensive about. In Pakistan's context the areas under occupation is considered as disputed and in case of China it is captured territory which has not been returned to India as per the international norms and conventions. Both give enough reason for India to wage war and reclaim the lost territories. Here the concern of the international community is that all three are nuclear, thus war remaining in the purview of conventional warfare is questionable. Therefore, there will be lot of international pressure and persuasion, and the war may remain localised. However how can one guarantee localise war if either of the country declares all front and all out war? In this chapter I will be discussing Pakistan and confine my views to the 'Pakistan Front'.

Before going into the battle for occupied territories, let us examine the situation and the terrain in the areas of Azad Kashmir and Northern Area of Gilgit-Baltistan:-

❖ **Azad Kashmir.** Azad Kashmir is 13,297 Square Kilometers, having 10 districts of Mirpur, Kotli, Bhimber, Muzaffarabad, Jhelum Valley, Neelum, Poonch Haveli, Bagh and Sudhanoti. There are three divisions of Mirpur, Muzaffarabad and Punch with total population of 4.45 million. Azad Jammu & Kashmir has total Muslim population. Most residents of the region are not ethnic Kashmiri. The majority of people in Azad Jammu & Kashmir are ethnically Punjabi and after the population inversion the Kashmiri, Gujjar, Bakarwal of the Jammu and Kashmir region are the minority population after occupation by Pakistan. Certain facts which need consideration for Option-IV are:

➤ The natives of Azad Jammu & Kashmir speak Urdu and Pahari, while the Kashmiri language is spoken by only 5 percent of Azad Jammu & Kashmir's population.

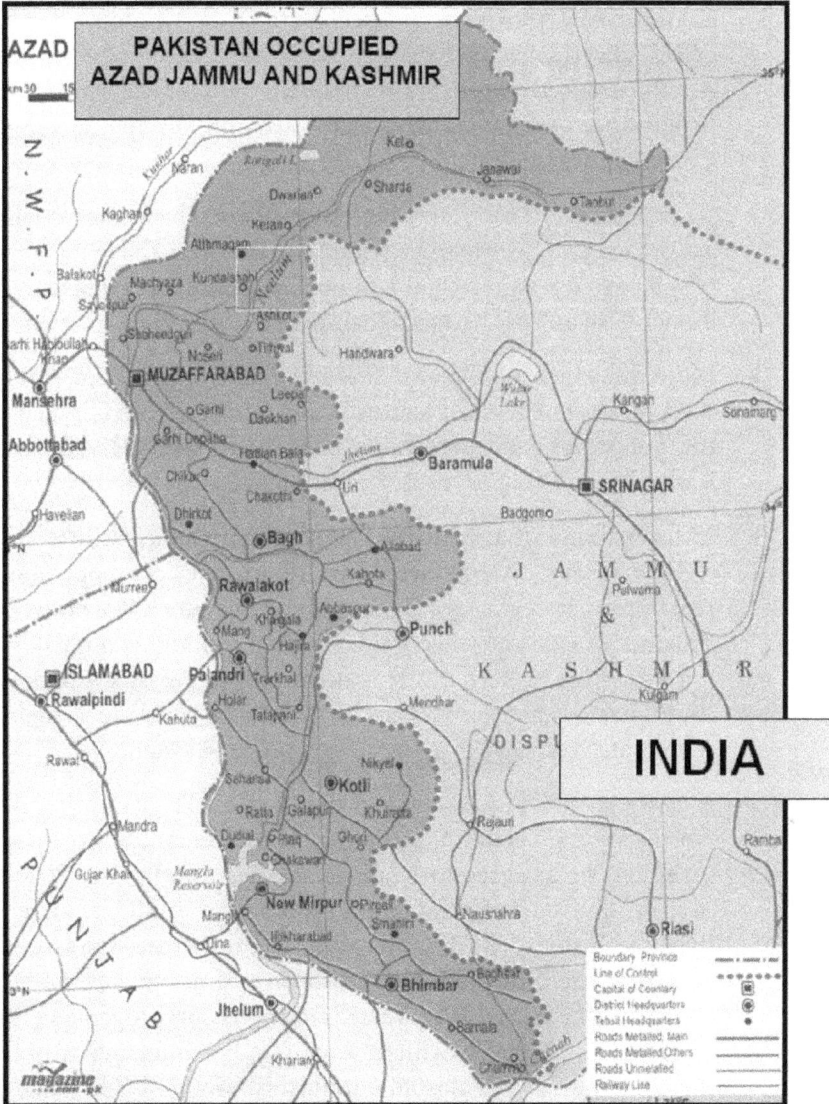

Map of Pakistan Occupied Azad Jammu & Kashmir

➤ Kashmiri in the Neelum and Jhelum Valley have been made to come to the status of minority population, due to large scale settlement of Punjabi population. The population inversion ratio by way of settlements of non Kashmiri, in a big way has changed the equations in the Kashmiri dominated regions.

➤ Azad Jammu & Kashmir in Pakistan does not have any constitutional provision of special status or freedom, the so called governance is totally under the control of Pakistan Administration, without any freedom in political sphere or people's representatives' associated decisions by the so called Constituent Assembly.

➤ Azad Jammu & Kashmir as such is dominated by Punjabis, who are radical and believe in hegemony of Pakistan, the percentage of subjugated Kashmiri and Jammu population is negligible thus do not have any power to stage protest.

➤ Moreover, most of the anti India militant organisations have their camps in the Azad Jammu & Kashmir, they also influence the politics and no anti Pakistan activities are allowed, thus Kashmiri are living only for their existence.

➤ The possibility of any justified referendum or plebiscite as per the UN Resolution will never be possible as the basic population structure has got changed in the disputed territory. It is not yet a Province of Pakistan since 1948. Pakistan is thinking on making it a Province or alternatively make it part of Pakistan Province of Punjab. Whatever Kashmiri Muslims who are people's representatives, have to swear allegiance to Pakistan.

➤ In 1993, a case was brought to the high court saying that the Northern Area administered by the Federal Government separately be annexed to Azad Jammu & Kashmir. The verdict of the High Court of Azad Jammu & Kashmir was in favour and the Azad Jammu & Kashmir Government was ordered to assume charge of the Northern Area. The case came up to Supreme Court of Pakistan, which reversed the high court judgement, the contention was that Northern Area was being looked after by the Government of Pakistan administratively on being handed over by the British and is disputed. It was further argued that the High Court of Azad Jammu & Kashmir lacked jurisdiction in this matter and could not issue a writ to the Government of

Pakistan, it stated that " *the Northern Area are part of Jammu & Kashmir State but are not part of "Azad Jammu & Kashmir" as defined in the "Azad Jammu & Kashmir" Interim Constitution Act, 1974"*. The idea was to keep the issue of Northern Area separate as it was part of the dispute and that it would jeopardise its demand for the whole of Jammu & Kashmir, if the issue is to be resolved anytime according to UN Resolutions. Pakistan always claimed that Azad Kashmir was liberated by its forces, thus it has exclusive rights to retain it. This is a wrong presumption which India does not agree. Azad Jammu & Kashmir and Northern Area which otherwise is part of Jammu & Kashmir is considered separate by Pakistan.

➤ The population affiliation with Indian Jammu & Kashmir and Kashmir Region is virtually nonexistent, neither there is any domination due its status of minority population and there being total polarisation in favour of the Pakistan held Azad Jammu & Kashmir. Some school of thought are of the view that there is similarity in socio-cultural fields with Indian Jammu and Kashmir, the fact is, it is not so. In last 70 odd years, lots have changed in Azad Kashmir with total polarisation towards Pakistan, differences are existing between the two parts of Jammu & Kashmir's on either side of the Line of Control. Therefore presuming that the population of Azad Jammu & Kashmir will be in favour of the total independence of whole of Kashmir i.e. not being part of Pakistan or India, as being propagated by some of the factions of the separatist organisations in India, is a big question mark? Moreover, whole of Jammu & Kashmir to be a party to such view is also doubtful?

➤ The indigenous population of Jammu and Kashmir cannot organise protests, voice for freedom is suppressed by force, and the domination of Punjabis in the political and economic arena makes the position of original people of Jammu & Kashmir weak.

➤ Pakistan will gain if the Indian Kashmir gets annexed and it is brought in the ambit of the present Azad Jammu & Kashmir governance system, Pakistan for this very reason is trying to bring radical Islam in the Indian Kashmir and change the religious sensitivity from moderate Kashmiri Sufi culture to fundamental Islam, so that in case of merger with Azad Jammu &

Kashmir religious amalgamation with Punjabi radical Muslims who have settled there. Thus Azad Kashmir will be said to be part of Islamic Pakistan.

➤ Azad Jammu & Kashmir is sensitive as it acts as buffer to the strategic depth to Pakistan and has now become more critical due to the China Pakistan Economic Corridor's (CPEC) proximity to Abbottabad and Muzaffarbad, thus the issue of Azad Jammu & Kashmir getting annexed with the Indian Jammu & Kashmir does not arise. It is for this reason that Kashmiri have been brought down to minority population through gradual population inversion and settling down of Punjabis from Pakistan Punjab and deny 'Kashmiri Azadi' (freedom) syndrome cropping, in Azad Jammu & Kashmir.

➤ Pakistan would never like to part with Azad Kashmir that easily, it would fight tooth and nail to retain it. Azad Kashmir acts as a buffer and provides strategic depth to its sensitive strategic road and rail communication artries from Lahore - Gujranwala – Jhelum - Mangla to Islamabad and Lahore – Shekupura – Rawalpindi – Abbottabad to Frontier Province; these are the life lines of Pakistan. Military installations are stationed on both of these road arteries. The sensitivity of these areas and the depth which is provided by the Azad Kashmir thus will be making Pakistan to hold the area strongly. The Mangala Dam over Jhelum River is another sensitive structure which Azad Kashmir provides depth. On this dam the agriculture and irrigation canals of Punjab Province is dependent.

➤ Islamabad capital city of Pakistan and Rawalpindi Headquarters' of Pakistan Army is echeloned immediately behind the Azad Kashmir. Any threat to these two cities, Pakistan will react vehemently. It is for this very reason, the Azad Kashmir has been held in strength militarily and will be proactively offensive to deny any ingress. Both in 1965 and 1971 wars Pakistan had held the India forces by going offensive and putting pressure on Indian forces. Here I am not discussing the tactical battle, however for inferring of the strategic and tactical importance and understanding the gravity, it is pertinent to know that Pakistan is very sensitive if Azad Kashmir is captured by India.

➢ The heights of Azad Jammu and Kashmir in the North are dominating the areas of Uri and Punch salient. These heights are held strongly and dominates the Indian defences on the Line of Control, Hajipir being the fulcrum point linking Punch and Uri, which saves 200 Kms for Indian Forces to reach Uri from Punch but due to Line of Control circuitous route have to be taken. In 1965 Indo - Pak War, Hajipir was captured by India but was given away to Pakistan after Tashkent Agreement. Giving away such a strategic feature was one of the blunders of Indian. These heights have now been reinforced heavily with concrete defences, since 1965. More over these heights on the Pakistan side gives good observation into Abbottabad, Manshera, Muzaffarabad, Bagh and Rawalkot , the strategically sensitive areas of Pakistan.

Physical Map Azad Kashmir and Jammu Region

> The terrain of Azad Kashmir one must understand, to fathom the military effort required in capturing Azad Kashmir. In the North Azad Kashmir Line of Control is in the alignment to the Shamshabari Ranges, on the West from Uri is the part of Pirpanjal Ranges which then goes towards Banihal at North East direction, this separates the Kashmir Valley in the South with Jammu Region. From Punch runs South Eastward Punch –Riasi Hills and further down South is the Shivalik Range. The Azad Kashmir thus is having hills and ranges up till Mirpur – Bhimbar. Both sides of the Line of Control are having defences on these hills and ranges and over last 70 years these have become formidable.

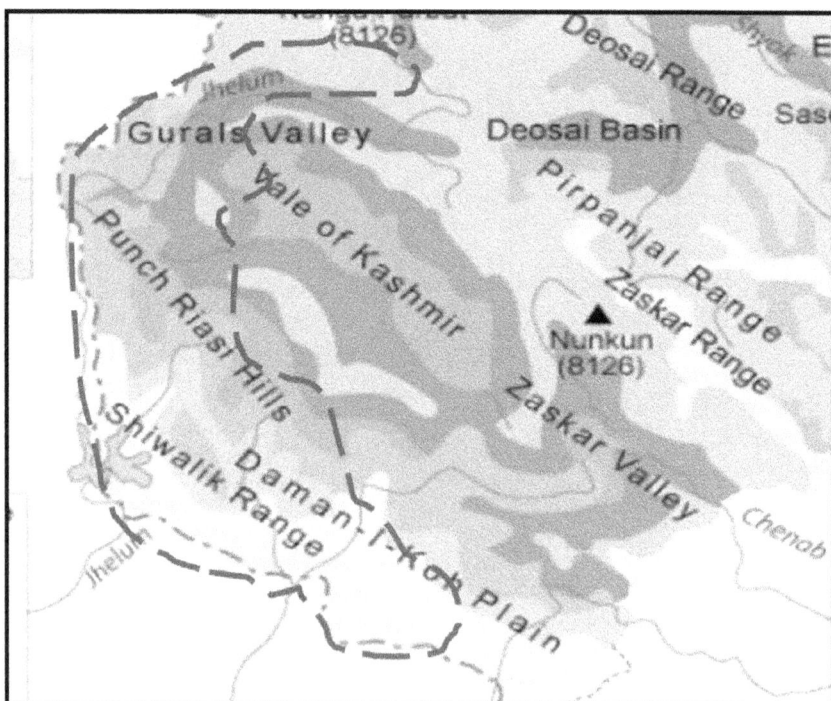

Map: Terrain Azad Kashmir and Jammu Region

> 1965 and 1971 war minefields are still active on the Line of Control, these are very old and some have deteriorated, but the risk still prevails.

> ➢ South of Azad Kashmir is the plains of Pakistan Punjab. North Azad Kashmir is the gateway to Northern Area and Gilgit – Baltistan. Thus, capture of Azad Kashmir will give India the option of limited war or in case of total war turn the flanks of Pakistan. War will be heavily contested as both sides have substantial forces deployed along the Line of Control and in depth. India will be in advantage once the front-line defences in Azad Kashmir is neutralised, thereafter going will be easier as lay of the land provides Indian forces faster roll down.

❖ **Gilgit – Baltistan.** The people of Northern Area to include Gilgit-Baltistan- Skardu Regions were part of the Jammu and Kashmir State of Maharaja Hari Singh. The British Officers who were part of the Maharaja's Army staged a coup; Gilgit Scouts under the command of Major William Brown rebelled on 1 November 1947 and imprisoned the State's Governor Brigadier Ghansara Singh. Brigadier Ghansara Singh was appointed by the Jammu and Kashmir Government to take over charge of Gilgit from the British Government to which it had been leased by Rulers of Jammu and Kashmir for 60 years. On the eve of culmination of the British rule in India, the Brigadier Ghansara Singh flew to Gilgit on July 31, 1947 but was taken prisoner in a mutiny jointly planned, executed and sponsored by British officers and some Muslim officers. Governor Brigadier Ghansara had said *"British officers were involved in Pakistan's plan and that the loss of Gilgit was the result of 'piratical action'."* The ethnic population thus came under Pakistan's Administered Region of Northern Area. Moreover, the people of Northern Area did not want to be under the Maharaj's rule and Kashmiri's hegemony, thus there was no opposition. Pakistan on assumption of administrative authority had created a constitution assembly but had not made it part of Pakistan Provincial Constitution. As the area was declared disputed by UN Resolution 1948, Pakistan kept the constitution of Gilgit- Baltistan separate. The area is still termed as disputed by Pakistan and have kept it in suspended animation. There are certain factors which would need consideration in case of Option –IV:-

> ➢ Ethnically, the Northern Area has population consisting of Tajik, Uzbek, Mongol, Turkmen, Baltees, Shins, Yashkuns, Kashmiris, Pathans, Ladakis Shias and Sunnis. The Shias are sub-divided

into Asharis, Ismailis and Noor Bakshis. The population of Gilgit-Baltistan is totally Muslim and is denominationally the most diverse in the country. The Northern Area remains a neglected area, with no educational and economic infrastructure. There are no industries and subsistence is largely on tourism, animal husbandry, horticulture and timber trade. While people from POK can emigrate, those from Northern Area need an exit visa, adult franchise is also a distant dream in the Northern Area. No person or party can call for self-determination, even though the Pakistan government has itself admitted to the courts that Northern Area is not part of Pakistan.

➢ The region is also the only Shia majority area in an otherwise Sunni dominant Pakistan. In 1948, the Shias and Ismailis constituted about 85 percent of the population. The demographic change was made by encouraging the migration of Sunnis from other provinces and the Federally Administered Tribal Areas (FATA).

➢ The remoteness of the area and sparse population has kept it underdeveloped. Total population is approximately 1.8 million; the Northern Area remains one of the most neglected and poorest parts of Pakistan. Sectarian differences exist between communities especially Shia and Sunni Muslims. The population is subjugated to strong hand handling by the Pakistan Administration and the Army.

➢ Pakistan claims full rights over Northern Area, as it was handed over by the British after the Gilgit Scout mutiny and when the people revolted against the Maharaja's rule. An independence movement currently exists in Gilgit-Baltistan (called "Balawaristan" by its supporters) but the intensity is lukewarm. Balawaristan National Front (Hameed Group) led by Abdul Hameed Khan was active group and demanding independence of Gilgit-Baltistan from Pakistan, however, Abdul Hameed Khan unconditionally surrendered to Pakistan security officials on February 2019, following his surrender the group lost its entity and its members got arrested. Another organisation by the name of Balawaristan National Front led by Nawaz Khan Naji is demanding Northern Area as fifth province of Pakistan;

this is more of an internal issue. Sardar Arif Shahid, a Kashmiri nationalist leader who advocated for independent Kashmir from both India and Pakistan's rule, was killed on May 2013 outside his house in Rawalpindi. It was the first time any pro-independence Kashmiri leader was targeted by Pakistan.

➤ People now seem to be fed up due to poor economy and subsistent life due to lack of development. Chinese settlements due to the CPEC have also become an issue. Moreover in the attempt of changing the majority dominance factor, Sunni Muslims have been made to settle in the area, which have resulted in Shia–Sunni communal differences; most of the ethnic tribes are either follower of Shia or Sufi cult. With abrogation of Article 370 and 35 A by India and dividing the State into two union territories. People have desired to join Ladakh Union Territory (UT) which meets their aspirations and abhorrence of Kashmiri hegemony, which was an age old mania among the various ethnic populations of Gilgit–Baltistan.

➤ Agitations have started against Pakistan and demand of freedom has gained grounds. Strong hand handling by the Army and police is not affecting the spirit of the agitation. People are not hesitating in conveying their feelings of being part of India and that of Ladakh UT.

➤ Concern of China in Northern area is evident by its consolidation of China Pakistan Economic Corridor (CPEC). Induction of Chinese Army is also a cause of concern. Pakistan has handed over the Skardu airfield to Chinese, moreover number of military infrastructures have come up. CPEC provides faster induction of forces from Chinese Autonomous Region of Tibet and Xinjiang. The increased rise in Chinese population and settlement is disturbing and is not being welcomed by the local population.

➤ If India takes back the occupied territories of Northern Area, it will throttle China and make it lose the strategic advantage as also deny access to Gwadar Port; this will hit the strategic economic interest of China. Moreover, China itself is occupying illegally the Indian territories of Ladhak at Aksai Chin and Shaksgam

Valley, thus China cannot hold on to the captured and ceded areas and as per international convention is liable to return.

➢ The terrain is mountainous and the road communication is poor. Area is underdeveloped and population spread is sparse, only major communication centres of Chilas, Gilgit, Skardu and Hunza have settlements and are commercial hubs. Barren mountainous areas where survival itself is difficult, accessibility is poor, harsh cold weather and barren unproductive terrain made Pakistan to cede the Shaksgam Valley and part of Karakoram Tract to China in 1963. The realisation among the Pakistanis of the strategic importance came, when India occupied the Siachen Glacier, the un-demarcated portion of the areas from NJ9842 and North (Line of Control is only up to NJ9842; this line is also called the Cease Fire Line). Siachen separated the direct link between the Shaksgam Valley and Chinese occupied Aksai Chin. This tactical debacle is still repented by Pakistan.

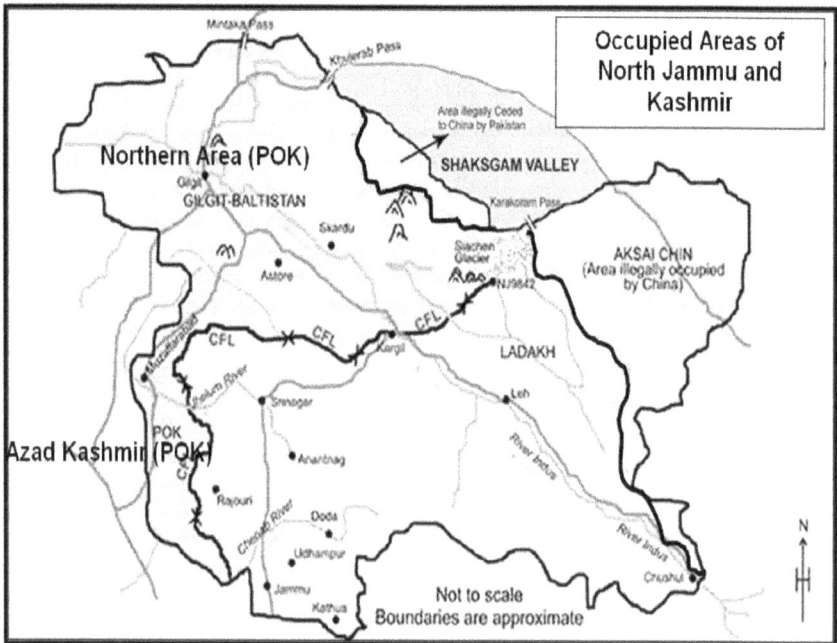

Map of Northern Area and Ladakh

➤ The terrain is high altitude in the Northern reaches and glaciated, the Great Himalayan Ranges are running, South-Northwest direction. Indus is the main River and flowing in the same direction of the ranges and from Gilgit it flows South and enters Pakistan, there are number of tributaries emanating from the glaciers in the North and Northwest and meeting Indus River. Terrain is nightmare for any form of operations; it will consume lot of troops and logistics. The strategic value of the area has been discussed in Significance Chapter, however one must understand the strategic and geopolitical importance of the region, in earlier times it was the gateway to India from Central Asia, Tibet and Afghanistan, and same is also applicable today. It is for this reason China is holding Aksai Chin and Shaksgam Valley. Moreover threat from India to Xingjian and Tibet Autonomous Regions of China and the Khyber Pakhtunkhwa Province of Pakistan has made these two countries apprehensive, thus will not like to vacate the areas which act as buffers with India. The other strategic value of the Northern Area is the river water, Indus flows right through this area and is fed by number of tributaries, Jhelum River also has source in the Ladakh region and flows through occupied Northern Area and Azad Kashmir, thus loss of the Northern Area will be very costly for Pakistan, India can anytime walk out of the Water Treaty with Pakistan, this would make Pakistan desperate as the agriculture, power and canal/distributaries are dependent on the water of Indis and Jhelum and will get dried up . Like the erstwhile Prime Minister of India J L Nehru one must not say *what use is of the land where not a single blade of grass does not grow*", when Aksai Chin was not returned by Chinese after 1962 war and neither it was pursued both politically and diplomatically by the governments of India in power with China and in the international platforms for last 68 years since 1962, it was clear that strategic and tactical realisations among the political heads were not there and neither they were farsighted.

Map: Terrain Ladakh UT and Northern Area (POK)

The above prognosis was to give insight into the prevailing status, imperatives and importance of the occupied territories. This prognosis will be of help in understanding the Option -IV. Military appreciation is done with lot of deliberations and in-depth analysis of various factors; I will not be discussing the military appreciation but just giving out a suggested general broad outline plan of action in this option. Inputs will provide insight into the magnitude of operation, possibilities, what all operational option India has and what will be Pakistan's reactions. Before going into the offensive options, it would be prudent to understand the imperatives and the ground factors:

❖ **Azad Jammu and Kashmir and the LOC.**

➢ Both sides of the LOC are heavily defended and have reinforced bunkers and pillboxes. Domination is on both sides, at places Pakistan is dominating Indian posts or defended localities and also India at many places is dominating the Pakistani posts. The

Pakistani posts are used as launch pads for militant infiltration thus there will be certain concentration of trained militants in some of the posts which will add to the fighting potential of Pakistani defences.

➤ Border fence on Indian side and vintage minefields are obstacles. The hilly terrain is interspersed with ravines, river and rivulets. Going will be against the grain of the country.

➤ Indian Army is holding the defences based on Key Defended Locality and in anti infiltration out post concept, these are heavily fortified on the LOC (Line of Control). On the International Border (IB) the border posts are manned by Border Security Force (BSF). Defences on the Indian side of IB is based on Ditch Cum Bund and anti flood bunds. In the Pakistan side LOC has defended localities and on IB are the Rangers Posts, it also has defences in the depth base on canals and bunds, Pakistan has two sectors opposite Indian Jammu and Kashmir these are Azad Kashmir and Punjab, the LOC is up till Bhimbar/Akhnoor and balance southward is IB. The defences and contingency positions are in ready to occupy state on both sides.

➤ In Pakistan, near vicinity of the LOC sector of Azad Kashmir, it has three Infantry Divisions located at Jhelum, Mangla and Murree. In the North it has FCNA (Force Command Northern Area) a brigade of this force deployed at Kel. In case of war these forces can mobilise and occupy defences at a very short notice. The battle of Azad Kashmir and the progress of operations give Pakistan the advantage to read the battle and place its forces accordingly or go in for the option of counter offensive in Akhnoor – Chamb - Jouria sector or Uri – Kupwara sectors. In case operations in the Azad Kashmir gets stalled ,it will affect the overall plans , then India cannot restrict the war to 'limited war' but go for all out war, all along the western front. Therefore, chances of limited war escalating into full fledge war cannot be ruled out, which can be either by compulsion or design.

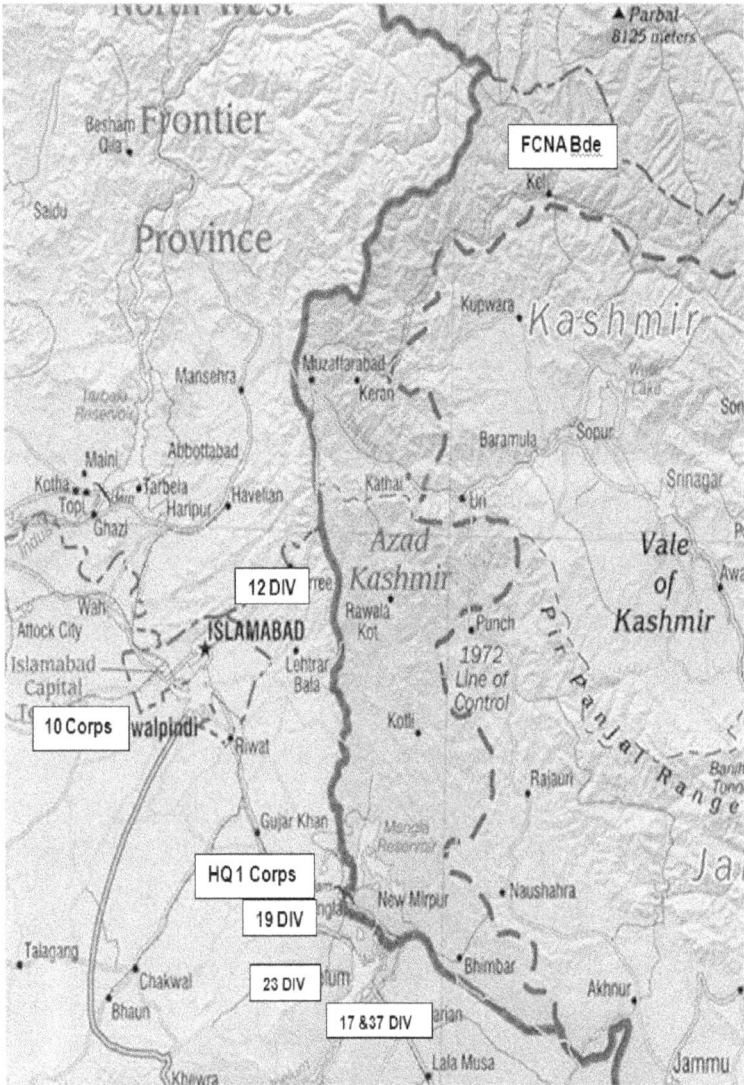

Map Showing Pakistan Formation Deployment

➢ Pakistan has both defensive and offensive formation in the plains of Punjab, 4 Corps is at Gujranwala with Divisions 8 and 15 and Strike Corp i.e. 1 Corps at Mangla. At NWPA (North West Frontier Province, now called Khyber Pakhtunkhwa) have the 11 Corps with Divisions 7&9 at Peshawar and Kohat respectively. Pakistan's 12 Corps with Division 41 & 33 located at Quetta, this is the reserve Corps and was deployed at NWFP and FATA (Federally Administered Tribal Areas) to contain insurgency in the region and thus is trained for operations in the mountainous terrain. Moreover, for protection of CPEC (China Pakistan Economic Corridor) Pakistan is having Special Security Division consisting of 9 Infantry Battalions and 6 Wings of Rangers, these can also get deployed to improve the defensive posture. Thus, Azad Kashmir is well covered by Pakistan's deployment of formations; and the build up time is shorter due the better road communication network.

➢ Pakistan is very sensitive in the area of Azad Kashmir, some of its offensive and defensive formation localities are bordering the Azad Kashmir boundary and any threat to Azad Kashmir, threatens these Military Stations. Actually, Azad Kashmir is the buffer and gives depth to the vulnerable strategic depth of Pakistan. Pakistan will not give Azad Kashmir just on a platter; it will defend Azad Kashmir very strongly.

➢ Most of the terror militant organisations are located and operating from Azad Jammu and Kashmir. The armed militant cadre strength is available and can supplement the Pakistani defence's strength, they will be used for disruptive tasks, reinforcing the forward deployments, and alternatively they can be used along with the Battle Action Teams to interfere with Indian operations.

❖ **Northern Area of Gilgit-Baltistan**

➢ Totally mountainous terrain and with tough going, the prominent ranges are Karakoram Ranges, Greater Himalayan Ranges, Ladakh Range and Zanskar Range. All these ranges run South–Northwest direction. The rivers are flowing in the same direction, between the ranges into Northern Area and then flows North - South direction into Pakistan. The degree of difficulty is high as the region is interspersed with Indus and its tributaries, the altitude is between 7000 – 17000 feet and weather is extreme. Operations here are nightmare for both defender and attacker.

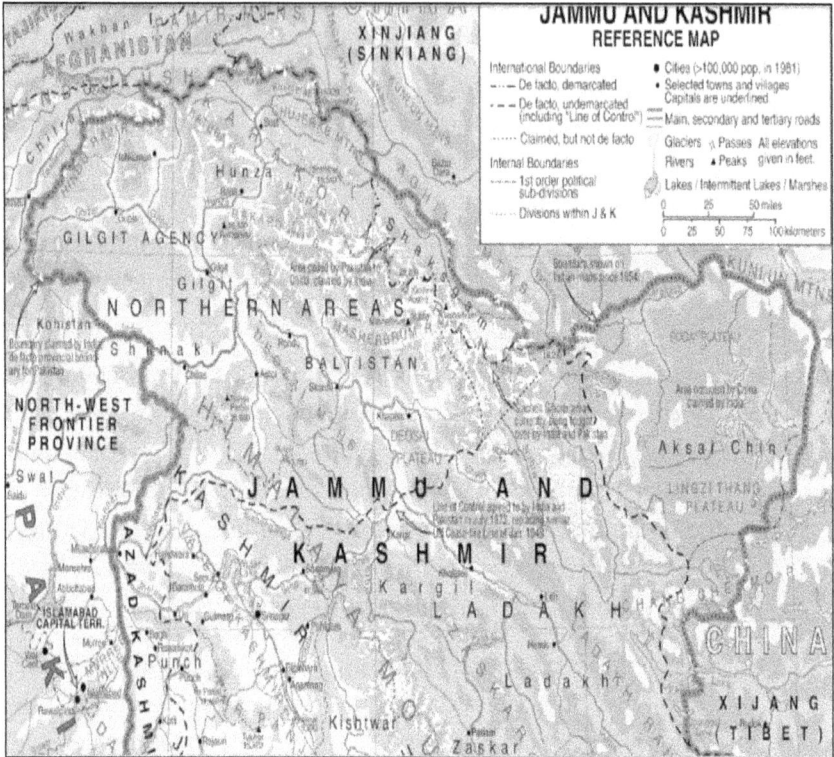

Map Showing Terrain of Northern Area and Ladakh

➤ Build up of forces and logistic maintenance is difficult, communication network is poor thus dependency of forces is on air maintenance. Both sides of the Line of Control are well defended. The Kargil War with Pakistan is the proof of ratio of forces required to evict the defender entrenched in bunkers and sangarhs (locally made bunker of stones), usually the force ratio in mountains is 1:12, minimum required ratio cannot be below 1:9 (i.e. for one defender 9 attackers). It is said mountains 'eat away troops', operations are infantry based and is time consuming, the capture is from bunker to bunker and during attack close support of artillery and air is problematic.

➤ In mountains the fire support either by air or from artillery is not very effective, problem of crest clearance and defensive deployments based on ridges lines and spurs which makes the target small and unobservable. In offensive operations for neutralisation of advancing forces mountains provide good cover where the support fire of defender is not that effective. Concentration of fire support has to be very heavy to be effective, thus large support force will be required for both defender and attacker.

➢ FCNA (Force Command Northern Area) is deployed in the Gilgit-Baltistan. It has five brigades and each brigade has three to five battalions. Special Security Division comprising of 9 Infantry Battalion and 6 Wings Rangers (equivalent to infantry battalion) is deployed for security of CPEC; these forces will also be employed for defences of Northern Area. Peshawar and Kohat Divisions are echeloned behind the Northern Area in the Khyber Pakhtunkhwa Province in Pakistan; these Divisions will definitely join the battle if not engaged elsewhere.

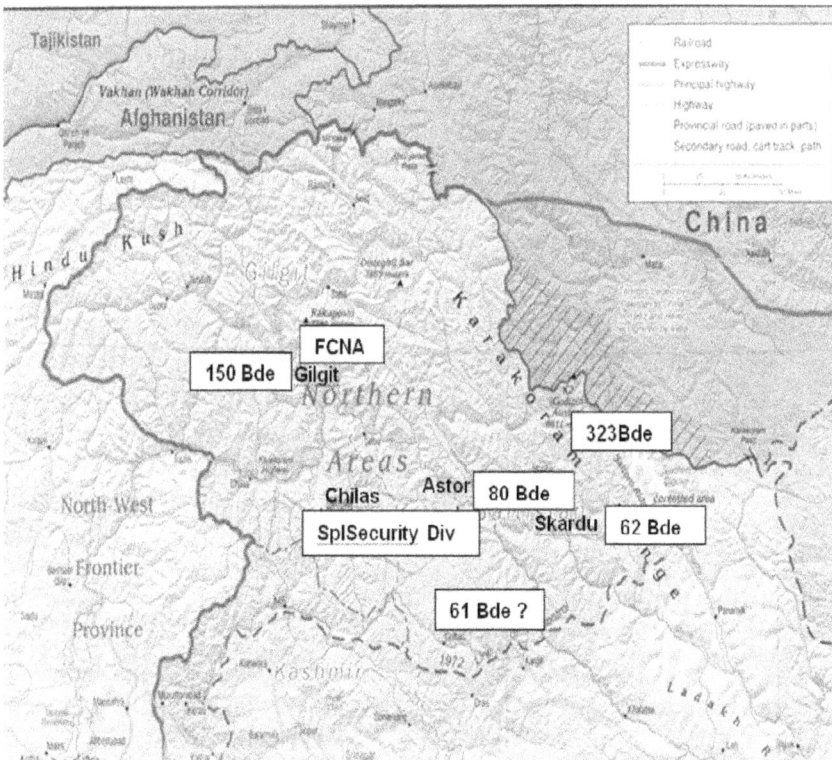

Map Showing Pakistan Formations in Northern Area

> ➤ The reserve forces which have exposure in counter insurgency warfare in mountainous North West Frontier Province and FATA can be employed to reinforce or for counter attacks. Most of the troops are from Northern Light Infantry; they are locals and are well acclimatised.

> ➤ Acclimatisation is an import aspect of any warfare in mountains with the altitudes which at places goes over 17,000 feet. Mountains require special training and warfare techniques.

> ➤ Population of Gilgit – Baltistan have been facing certain issues which have made them raise their voice, *first* is the Pakistan's autocratic administration, *second* settlement of Sunni Muslims from other provinces and sectarian clashes, *third* Chinese Army dominance in China Pakistan Economic Corridor infrastructure development and the Chinese settlement, *fourth* is exploits of timber mafia from Pakistan and *Lastly* lack of development of the area, these have made the people to go against the establishment. The region has a typical cultural and ethnic living style which are different between the sects and the tribes, in spite of modernisation the people do not want to lose the identity, Pakistan's action have created apprehension of their ethnic survivability, thus looking for freedom. Such sentiments are favourable and can be of use in operations to liberate Northern Area from occupation.

> ➤ Major part of the occupied territory of Northern Area the economic corridor is passing through, China is very sensitive and will interfere in case of any Indian attempt to reclaim the occupied territory. Akashi Chin is also case in point for reclaim which China cannot let go as the very concept of CPEC will die its own death and make heavy loss on the huge investment it has made.

❖ **China Factor.** It will be a factor which India has to reckon in its consideration, as explained earlier China has vested interest and will not like to be interfered or disturbed. Managing China will be an exclusive priority before India ventures into the option of military action against Pakistan, the ramifications which require considerations are:

➢ The 'Johnson Line' in 1865, which put Aksai Chin in Jammu and Kashmir. This was the time when China did not control Xinjiang, so this line was never presented to the Chinese. Johnson presented this line to the Maharaja of Jammu and Kashmir, who then claimed Aksai Chin within his territory. Aksai Chin thus is not disputed but was captured by China in 1962 and was not returned, and being retained illegally. As per the Article 49 of the Fourth Geneva Convention, captured territory after cease fire must be returned. Now the issue with China is the recognition of the McMahon line and the claims by both countries. The British India border with Tibet, Maps clearly indicate the Aksai Chin as part of Jammu and Kashmir kingdom.

➢ The McMahon Line was part of the 1914 Simla Convention between British India and Tibet; India recognises this line as the border. China is not in agreement with the McMahon line and does not recognise it as border. In this context China claims Arunachal Pradesh as part of Tibet on the pretext of its claim on the argument given is that, historical ties existed between the Tawang monastery in Arunachal Pradesh and the Lhasa monastery under one Dalai Lama. Hence, the Chinese logic is that given Tibet is now part of China, Arunachal Pradesh should form a part of it as Dalai Lama had his area of influence in North East region of Tawang. This claim can be made a negotiating counter claim for reclamation of Aksai Chin. Thus, for both China and India it is going to be catch 22 scenario.

➢ How China is going to react if it's CPEC is threatened. Will it open a second front or take posture to deny India the advantage of offensive strength against Pakistan, by making India deploy on Chinese front. This contingency has to be catered in the planning stage.

➢ Chinese providing military support to Pakistan both covertly and overtly to sustain the war and face up to the Indian threat, thus delaying the progress of operations and denying capture of the occupied territories. Therefore, gaining time for UN and international intervention to stop the war by compulsion and pressure on India.

> In case of a limited and localised war with Pakistan, with the aim of reclaiming the occupied territories. What would be the posture of China? Will it still give the military support and open up the second front or will go in for offensive to join the Shaksgam valley and Aksai Chin by attacking and capturing Siachen, thus making its defensive posture stronger.

> As per the agreement on Shaksgam with Pakistan when it was ceded in 1963, being part of disputed territory was returnable and it was not a permanent transfer, Pakistan did not have any locus standi over the said ceded territory, nether it had the rights over the said territory. If so, the China in this case has to return the ceded territory to India and cannot illegally occupy it as its own territory? Shaksgam and Aksai Chin are the bone of contention and do not fall under the purview of border (Line of Actual Control) dispute or claims.

> China is the permanent member of the UN Security Council, it carries weight and the veto can make difference. Chinese interventions in the UN thus can change the dynamics of developing situations. Thus, pressure can be mounted on India to make it refrain from taking recourse of application of force to reclaim the occupied territories.

Having analysed the considerations, the question now is how India is going to go with Option IV, the military recourse. Here I am not discussing the Indian plans but giving out the scenarios which India can attempt to ensure reclaiming the occupied territories through military actions. India stands very strong with active forces , reserve force and paramilitary forces, therefore there must not be much apprehensions that India cannot bear two front war, figures are available in internet, what is important is how India is going to prioritise and apply its forces in achieving its objectives. The important issue which is going to matter in the decision is that all three India, China and Pakistan are nuclear state, it is here where the political will matter, how not to carry the war beyond nuclear threshold or take the risk of taking on nuclear strike and retaliation will be the questions which must be answered. In this option both political and diplomatic front has to be equally effective and will be an important part of the Option IV. Before going for Option IV, the Options I to III have to be in place to an extent that it supports the Option IV; terms of reference of the Option IV will depend on the political will and determination of Indian leadership.

It is going to be difficult decision at political level and will depend on the political party in power, time and when. The Bharatiya Janata Party under Prime Minister Narendra Modi has initiated the process of reclaiming the occupied territories. The three actions which substantiates the political 'will' are *firstly* abrogation Article 370 and 35 A of Jammu and Kashmir, *secondly* dividing the State into two union territories of Ladakh and Jammu and Kashmir thus negating both Pakistan's and China's contentions of claims in Jammu and Kashmir, *third* is the step towards reclaiming or getting back the occupied territories of Jammu and Kashmir. Considering that the political and diplomatic efforts have been attuned and military option is decided, what are the military strategic and tactical options which are available? These I am discussing as scenarios:

❖ **Scenario - I Limited War in Pakistan Occupied Kashmir.** In this scenario the objective, is reclaim only the Pakistan occupied Kashmir which includes Northern Area consisting Gilgit – Baltistan regions and the Azad Jammu and Kashmir. The offensive here is localised and is restricted to the confines of the actual border between erstwhile Jammu and Kashmir before partition and Pakistan. This option will have certain ramifications which will need consideration:-

➢ Pakistan is more sensitive with regard to Azad Jammu and Kashmir, the capture will threaten its strategic depth and sensitive communication centres of Jhelum, Mangla, Kharian, Rawalpindi, Islamabad and Murree which are housing various Army formations, Political and other institutions. These areas will be under observations and perpetual threat of Indian actions, once Azad Kashmir is captured. From the Azad Kashmir border to the Afghanistan Border Pakistan is having the narrowest depth, actually Azad Kashmir is the buffer and Pakistan will not like that the buffer is removed, so it will put all its might, to hold on to it.

➢ How much limited will Pakistan keep the war of reclamation, even though Pakistan is at an advantage of concentrating its forces if it is a limited war, concentrating and increasing the force ratio by employing its reserves and side stepping formations, it can give a tough fight to India. Pakistan will not take the chance of keeping the International Border vacant, it has the capability to maintain balance defensive posture and keep counter offensive options open.

> Northern Area being mountainous and high altitude would entail having acclimatized troop deployment. Pakistan Army has local NLI (Northern Light Infantry) Battalions in its FCNA Brigades which are acclimatized and familiar with the terrain. Pakistan has acclimatized formations which are deployed in North West Frontier Province. Formations from the plains cannot be directly inducted for the battle and acclimatization is a time consuming process.

> Chinese covert support to Militant Organisations for rough actions and direct support to the Pakistan Army in terms of preparedness and subsequent battle backup will be there. Chinese interest is too heavy, due to the economic corridor and the risk to its Aksai Chin and Shaksgam Valley under belly of Xingjian and Tibet Autonomous Regions.

> To make the war limited, it has to be within the boundaries of Jammu and Kashmir and Ladakh, and confined to the occupied part of the territories. The terrain does not permit clean sweep operations. The operations have to be progressive fighting ridge line to ridge line and capture of heights, it will be more of creeping operations as the opposition will be tough due to application of higher strength ratio, and the war being confined and localised. Effort will be to create position of advantage in each phase line and capture important road communication and intact bridges, military infrastructures of air fields and helipads/helidromes, logistic dumps, population centres and secure defiles to progress operations at faster pace. High altitude and mountains will require acclimatised troops and reserves to maintain the momentum, so as to speed up the operations

> Surprise will be the main factor, as time will be of India's choosing.

This scenario is having three options for operations; *firstly,* addressing Azad Kashmir and Northern Area simultaneously, *secondly,* operation in phases, tackling first Northern Area and then rolling down to Azad Kashmir and *thirdly,* the opposite first address Azad Kashmir thus cutting off Northern Area and blocking the Pakistan Army, then subsequently address Northern Area.

❖ **Option- I Simultaneously Address Northern Area and Azad Kashmir.** In this operation the, commitment of forces will be maximum, however on Pakistan side the forces will get divided as two areas are getting address simultaneously, the focus and the concentration will be divided. Moreover, India in order to ensure Pakistan does not move its forces from other Commands will mobilise and deploy its own forces all along the border in such manner to keep Pakistan committed. This Option is workable as the operations will get completed at the shortest time frame, the speed in operations is going to outbalance the Pakistani forces, both land and air will play an important role however as the area is constricted to the borders of the claimed occupied Jammu and Kashmir, forces will remain within the boundaries. India might go into the operation with the aim of not escalating the war into an all out war, but the same cannot be guaranteed from the Pakistan side, thus all contingencies have to be worked out. The operations envisaged will be somewhat as shown in the map below.

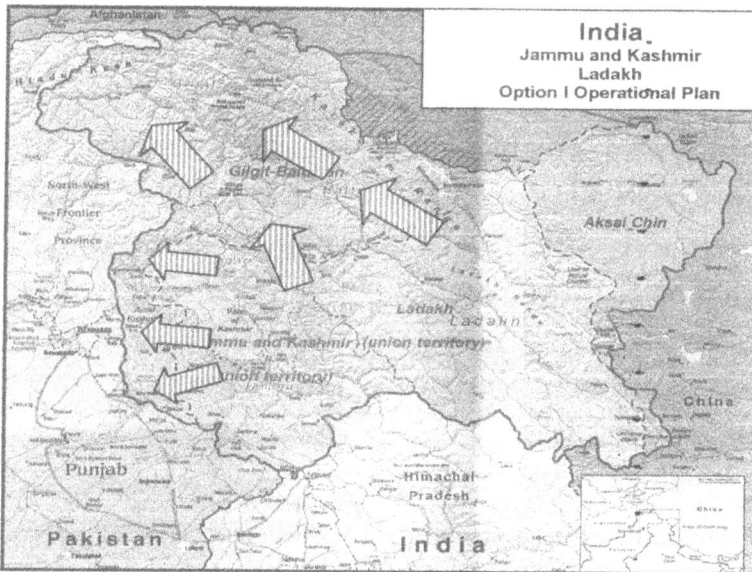

There are certain imperatives in this option which will require considerations on part of India, these are:

> Surprise will be an important factor, followed by speed in operations; aim will be complete reclaiming of occupied

territories before any intervention takes place. Limit must be the erstwhile borders of the State and not beyond.

➤ The Pakistan's deployment and force application will be spread. India in this option has to ensure that whole of Pakistan Army does not get committed to restore the status quo or opens other fronts to suck in the Indian forces.

➤ As the limits are within the boundaries thus the territorial integrity of Pakistan's main land is intact, the aspect of nuclear flash point is minimal.

➤ China can in this scenario open its front by aggressive posturing; India has to cater for the same in their plans.

➤ Indian force application has to in proportion to the degree of difficulties in terms of ratio, terrain, three dimensional force application of land and air forces, composite warfare systems, more reliability on air land battle concepts as applicable in mountainous terrain and robust logistical support. It is only then India can assure there are no stalemates or operations get stalled due to resistance. Once in battle the end result has to be achieved because war after war cannot be fought over the issue.

➤ India has to keep Pakistan on tenterhooks by making it deploy its forces on ground and keep the apprehensions lingering thus building up tension and fatigue among the ground troops. As the time is dependent on India's choosing, this will give advantage of engaging political diplomacy to create uncertainty and anxiety in Pakistan. Making Pakistan weaker in all facets of survival will give better dividends.

❖ **Option-II Reclaim Northern Area and then rolling down to Azad Kashmir.** In this option major chunk of the land area is reclaimed and the position consolidated, before addressing the Azad Jammu and Kashmir. This option will open up many avenues of addressing Azad Kashmir subsequently. In this option China will be most affected as its occupied Aksai Chin and ceded occupied area Shaksgam Valley and part of Karakoram Tract by Pakistan is equally threatened. The economic corridor will get cut off and this is going to affect both Pakistan and China. In this option consolidation and linking will be an important part of operations, as road communication is limited operational tracks have to be constructed from the Kargil and Drass sectors for link up. Use of Siachen as firm base to launch operations into the interior and towards Karakoram Pass must be exploited to speed up the operations and cut off Chinese interference. The only disadvantage will be that reclaiming Azad Kashmir subsequently will be more difficult as Pakistan will by that time reinforced the area and will be better prepared for the battle of Azad Kashmir, more over the intervention will be forthcoming from various international forums thus the reclamation of Azad Kashmir will be getting relegated and delayed. Thus, the wait period will be longer and this in turn breaks the momentum. However seeing the positive side, after consolidation of the Northern Area, two aspects emerges, *firstly* the land route to Afghanistan and Central Asian Countries opens and *secondly* NWFP i.e. Khyber Pakhtunkhwa Province of Pakistan will be bordering Indian Ladakh Union Territory and this will be of concern for Pakistan. Pakistan must be made to reconcile to the fact that Azad Kashmir will have to be returned, thus it should move its formations from the vicinity or from the occupied areas. If this is made to happen at political and diplomatic levels, then in order to avoid any further war on Azad Kashmir Pakistan can be made to hand over the occupied territory, even though in the present context it is less likely but chances can be explored. The hypothetical operation plan of this option may be something as given out in the map:

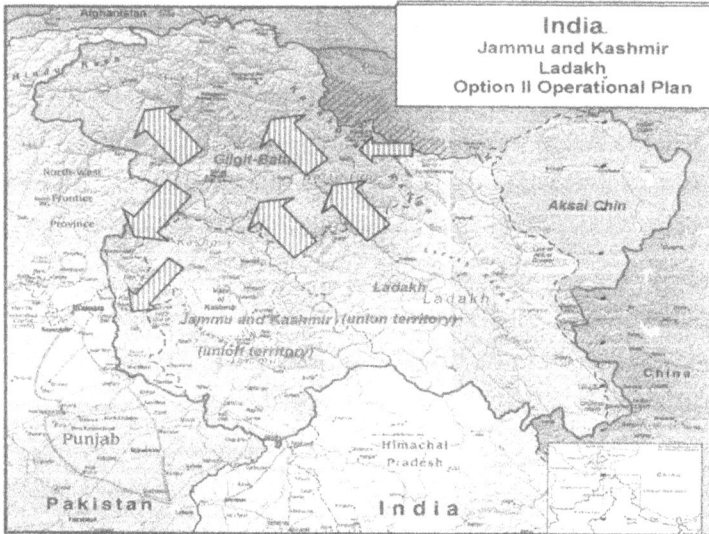

There are certain imperatives in this option which will require considerations on part of India are:

> Operations have to be multi prong and after capture, consolidation is must. In mountainous terrain important geographical features, ridges and communication lines have to be tackled in series thus operations have to be phased out.

> Imperatives of Option-I are equally applicable when addressing the Northern Area and the mountains.

> As operations will be at the near vicinity of Shaksgam Valley, Chinese interference from North cannot be totally ruled out, similarly as the operation progress towards the CPEC there will be heavier resistance as Chinese forces may be deployed. The economic corridor it is an important link within Northern Area, i.e. linking Karakoram- Gilgit- Chilas, this link will be used by Pakistan for faster induction of the reinforcement and counter attack forces. Thus, with air operations, it must be captured intact.

> Denying the use of economic corridor will be an important imperative of Indian offensive. If the corridor it taken intact it

will facilitate India in establishing the link and in consolidation of the defences of the captured areas. India has to plan accordingly.

➢ Concentration of forces for the offensive and maintaining of surprise will be an important imperative. The mountains are barren and any movement are detected, it is easier to have clear satellite imageries.

➢ If the windows of opportunity are available along with consolidation, then addressing of Azad Kashmir from North and East in a blitzkrieg operations will pay very good dividends and out balance Pakistan. It will be better to finish operation in one go, rather than phasing out Northern Area and Azad Kashmir as separate operations.

❖ **Option- III Address Azad Kashmir thus cutting off Northern Area.** In this option first take Azad Kashmir and then progress operations to Northern Area addressing it through north of Azad Kashmir and from the Kargil-Drass sectors. The force applied for Azad Kashmir has to be substantial so that Pakistan gets constricted within its own territory and create threat perception to the level that forces are made to remain deployed for the threat to its mainland. The advantages of internal disturbances in Pakistan have to be exploited, to engage the Pakistan's armed forces in containing the internal disturbances. All the options which are being discussed have same interpretation i.e. limit of the war is constricted to the occupied territory only and not infringing crossing over of the borders, therefore the warfare will be very tricky, keeping the Pakistan forces engaged, deployed and restrict moving of its reserves to reinforce any of the sectors will be a challenge. In this option capture of Azad Kashmir will make Pakistan react violently and will use the NWFP to reinforce the Northern Area before it is cut off, however due to restricted lines of communications the build up will take time and this has to be exploited. The option is when there is restriction of forces thus first address Azad Kashmir regroup and the go in for Northern Area. This time lag can be costly as there are chances of intervention and obstructions which can put pressure and thus the chances of postponing or waiting for next opportune moment will become a factor. The hypothetical plan is as given in the Map:

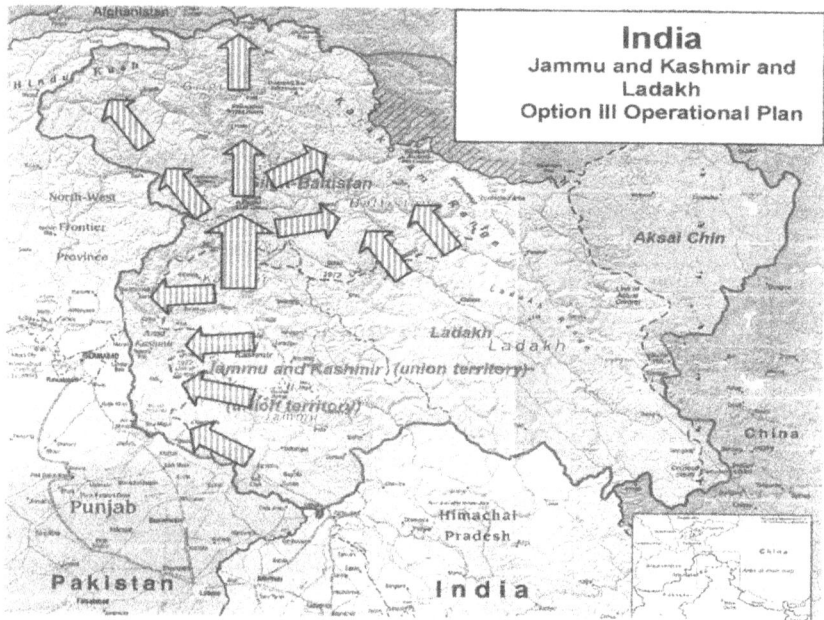

There are certain imperatives in this option which will require considerations on part of India will be:

> For the initial phase of addressing Azad Kashmir acclimatisation of troops will not be necessary. But for Northern Area troops have to be acclimatised. Therefore, two separate set of forces will be required if operations has to speed up.

> Land Warfare, Air Warfare, Disruptive Warfare and Standoff Systems War & Artificial Intelligence warfare, all inclusive will be the requirement and must be worked upon. But as the war will be constricted by the borders any fall outside the borders of Jammu and Kashmir will lend to aggravate the war into all out war.

> Most of the imperatives of other options are equally applicable here also in terms of terrain, time and space and force applications.

❖ **The Scenario - I** is very typical and cautionary approach. Where the risk of nuclear flash point gets avoided and expectation of international intervention is there to rein in Pakistan, as the occupied territories are not part of Pakistan and it has no rights over it as per the Instrument of Accession 1947 legally the occupied areas are with India. If the war does not spill over to Pakistan parse, then the chances are there that limits are not crossed and reclaiming war is under monitoring of the international forums, obtaining the support of the international community is must for this scenario. Safer option but intricacies are many as it will be disturbing the Militant Bases and Terrorist Organisation Headquarters, due population inversion and changed ratio of local population in the occupied areas resistance will be there from Pakistani settlement populations, Chinese use of the occupied areas for its economic corridor and strategic importance of holding on to ceded and captured areas since 1962 and the Chinese's support to Pakistan as strategic alliance partner are the issues which will make difference and matter.

Day, Date and Time will be as per India's choosing but how long it is going to take place will depend on the political will and determination of the party in power and consistency in the claim and efforts to win over support of the world. The Indian think tank and strategic planners have to work out the ways and modus, with pragmatism and sequencing of the efforts to obtain total success. Let us wait and see.

❖ **Scenario - II All out War with Pakistan.** This is the scenario which is obvious, the question will be who is going to start and be aggressor. For India it can be reclamation of the occupied territories of Jammu and Kashmir or going in for the liberation of Baluchistan as Bangladesh style. Both have different connotations. In reclamation the Pakistan's combined Armed Forces have to be engaged and defeated, so that occupied territories are reclaimed and consolidated, thereafter ceasefire can be declared. In the operation to break Pakistan and liberate the provinces which are in revolt all out war with deep strike operations need to be launched to defeat Pakistan, make it recoil and the Provinces which are in revolt will get liberated and declare independence. There are certain imperatives which will need in-depth analysis and have to be taken into considerations in this scenario:-

➢ The mistakes in Chamb-Jourian in 1965 and 1971 cannot be repeated as it will turn the Indian flank and reclamation will then become a difficult proposition. Whatever the General's may claim, it was a failure and very poor Generalship on the Indian part. If such reversals take place, the basic aim of the all out war will be defeated, this war has to be the only war on Pakistan and has to be decisive one, so that India need not keep fighting war after wars or bear with any proxy war year after year.

➢ No windows of opportunities can be wasted as it happened in Lahore sector when Ichogil Canal was crossed. India takes pride in deep penetration of 48 hours and 72 hours, but any stalling of operation is going to cost dearly. Resolute Generalship is required. It will be matter of total annihilation of the Pakistan forces and there cannot be any two way about it. Maximum potential have to be achieved before venturing with the all out war, be it force or equipment increments in all fronts of land, air and sea. Enemy is to be made to realise the futility of battle and must succumb to the pressure.

➢ If Pakistan is made to go for war on India, this must be exploited by series of strong counter offensive all along the front to create a situation of instability in all the fronts of the offensive and destroy the fighting capability of Pakistan. Reclamation of occupied territories must be supported by total annihilation of the terrorist organisations; a separate operation on these targets will pay good dividends and end the proxies, state actors and non state actors.

➢ War will be five dimensional and thus coordination will be of high importance. Missiles will play an important part to make Pakistan incapable to use its weapons, bases and communication, technological advantage have to be taken to decapitate and kill all the options including nuclear strike by effective application of multiple dimensional warfare

➢ The strategy of Cold Start will be on the test bed and on it will depend how the surprise is going to be maintained, war of this magnitude will have large scale mobilisation. This is more applicable when India has the choice of time and place.

➢ Operations have to be really fast before Pakistan contemplates use of nuclear weapon. Alternatively, all launch sites need to be neutralised simultaneously with the offensive. This is going to be an important factor for consideration, which will make India, to think twice before venturing into any battle with Pakistan. Short and intense war is the only answer. War cannot be kept lingering, there will be reversals but these have to be overcome, the preponderance has to be in superiority to change reversals into annihilation of the opposing forces.

➢ All will depend on the political will and ability to withstand nuclear assault if it ever occurs, even though in retaliatory action Pakistan will be non-existent, which it is well aware. Nuclear diplomacy will play an important part, as disarming nuclear Pakistan will make a difference, support of international community in achieving this will be an issue of concern, and thus it will be part of the integral planning for the war.

➢ An all out war is going to create reactions from pan Muslim world and support will be forthcoming to Pakistan. Involvement of the pan Islamic militant organisation like ISIS and Taliban cannot be ruled out in totality, rough action on Indian advancing forces will be there or fighting alongside the Pakistan Army the possibility will be there, thus this aspect need to be catered in the planning.

➢ In case the liberation of Baluchistan is part of the aim, then the situation in Baluchistan has to be pitched up to the extent of revolt against the establishment and get Pakistan Army fixed in controlling the situation. Support by the Baluchistan Liberation Army will be an important imperative in terms of assistance and coordinated joint operations.

➢ With CDS (Combined Defence Services) in place and the concept of integrated battle groups, the application of forces and the integrated battles will be the predominant factor. Efforts has to so planned that the opposing enemy is made to commit its forces and the reaction capabilities are negated, thus denying shifts and sidestepping to upset own offensive. Offensive air support has to be at a larger scale to deny the enemy use of the air space both at conventional and nuclear scenario. The Battle will be more reliant on domination of the air space and destroy enemy air within first 24 hours of the battle; the dedicated Air Defence Command of CDS will make lot of difference. Land Air battle option must also be kept open; however, formations have to be extensively trained for the said battle. Option of amphibious operations on the coastline of Pakistan must also be explored and must be considered to turn the flanks in Baluchistan Province. In all out war all possible options have to be applied so as to make it the last war with Pakistan, it has to be total annihilation. All spectrums and dimensions of warfare have to be explored and applied, to gain position of advantage and throttle Pakistan. Therefore, integrated battles will be the order in all Commands and Regions.

➤ Domination of Indian Ocean Region will be another factor which has to be considered, just sealing the Arabian Sea and enemy's Exclusive Economic Zone (EEZ) will not suffice, China factor will play an important part as it may support Pakistan or commit own resources to keep the sea lanes open. As the China Pakistan Economic Corridor will be under the war zone, the use of the same will be denied, only source of supply will be the Pakistan ports. This will have dual impact; *firstly,* deny all the ports and *secondly,* launch amphibious operations without any interference as this would achieve dual aim of liberation of Baluchistan and operations behind the enemy front line.

➤ Lastly, getting the power block less China in favour and support the Indian cause. This is must if the battle is to be fought to its conclusion. Both China and Pakistan factor will play an important role, China for its COVID-19, human rights (Hong Kong and Uighur Muslims) and expansionist attitude and Pakistan for sheltering pan Islamic terrorist organisations. Present geopolitical scenario of 2020 is in favour of India and this bondage has to be maintained and made stronger.

The outline plan of the operations which I am giving out is hypothetical in order to just giving the idea what is required to conclude the war in favour of India:

© 2005 Encyclopædia Britannica, Inc.

As compared to all other options, all out war is the easiest option which will give faster dividends and straight out accomplishment of the objective. The superiority of military power over Pakistan has to be exploited to its maximum potential and Armed Forces have to be made further stronger. The modernisation and force potential increase must not be exclusively for Pakistan, but also to tackle the second front of China. I am of the opinion that until the muscle power of the country is not enhanced, then we must forget about being regional power or for that matter one of the world power, India cannot repeat the mistake of First Prime Minister Jawaharlal Nehru who had openly flaunted that '*India does not require Military Muscle*'. Alone democracy, economics, business, trade and foreign reserves cannot make a country powerful and to keep the country's sovereignty intact military is also one of the important imperatives of powerful nation.

All out war to reclaim the occupied territories held with Pakistan over last seven decades since 1947 will have its ramifications, there will be two worlds divided one each 'for' and 'one' against , this will be having pulls and pushes. The all out war has to be swift, short with definite result and under the nuclear threat. For this India has to prepare and consolidate its position before taking the decision to reclaim the occupied area, by force. The plans have to be worked out and war gamed, all dimensions of warfare with the land operations, amphibious operations, air land battle, air battle and sea warfare, have to be looked into to make the war swift and short. Prolonged war will create number of stalemates and interferences, even though this will kill Pakistan economically and exhaust its war sustainability which is about 10 days. This alternative is also one of the possibilities which the Indian think tank must ponder upon and can work on the plans and phases of operation.

Keeping the nuclear first use by Pakistan scenario in view and taking the nuclear assault and retaliation factors when the Indian forces will be deep inside Pakistan, have to be considered. The issue of making Pakistan incapable to launch any nuclear attack low or high intensity in magnitude, will be more important in the first few days of the war, this has to be planned by immobilising Pakistan air force, missile and launch sites, artillery posts and other means of delivery. Another factor which must kept in view is that nuclear arsenals falling in the hands of terrorists and prepare plans to neutralise have to be worked out, here the international intervention is expected which must be taken to advantage.

Possibility of all out war is very much workable and will depend on the political will, continuous modernisation and build up of capability of all three arms of its armed forces, enhance economic stability and foreign reserves. This war must be the last war and thus has to be planned accordingly, for there cannot be perpetual war on reclamation of the occupied territories, India cannot keep living with potential enemies along its borders.

Indian politics is very unique, a political party is very proactive and domineering, the second party will contradict the party in power and when it comes to power undo what the other party has done and will be reluctant to continue with the initiatives, thus the matter of continuity may exists but the 'will' may not be existing, the parties which matter are BJP and Indian Congress, rest are not of much consequences. Today Bharatiya Janata Party (BJP) has taken the initiative, both at Pakistan and China front, it has shaken them, but both the countries will be looking forward to Congress coming to power as the things will be changing and easing out, the wait is of five years. By the time the first party comes to power the equations would have changed. This game, will keep delaying the execution of the plans for reclamation of occupied territories. Coming to decision is time consuming and requires continuity, if BJP continues to be in power, the possibility will be existing of reclamation of occupied territories by force. I have my reservations about other political parties unless there is a dynamic leader.

Pakistan is having standing armed forces since independence and is rather well equipped in the present context. With the support of China and Chinese supply of military hardware Pakistan is adequately armed. Earlier military hardware from USA, Strategic Alliance organisations such as CENTO etc and two Afghan Wars, one against Russia and another in support of USA against Taliban and Al Qaida, the arsenal dumps are well stocked. Thus, for India it will not be a 'cake walk' in case of all out war. The prudency of the decision will depend on preparedness of the armed forces, sound economy of the country and time of own choosing which will require looking into the perquisite of creating right opportunity.

❖ **Scenario - III Two Fronts War.** In this scenario both Pakistan and China front gets open. It would be facing two enemies simultaneously. The contingencies which must be considered in this scenario are, *first,* all out war against Pakistan and against Chinese, offensive posturing in case China supports Pakistan along the Northern front (can result in limited offensive at number of places (from Ladakh to Arunachal Pradesh), *second,* have limited war with both China and Pakistan restricted to the occupied territories and *third* is to have both the front open with all out war to regain the occupied territories and capture areas of both China and Pakistan as negotiating bargains and barter and *Lastly* take the all-out two front war in liberating Xingjain/Tibet and Baluchistan respectively. Now in this scenario, lot will depend on the capability to take on both the fronts. Each of the contingencies have its pros and cons which the Indian political heads and the military planners have to consider before coming to a decision :

➢ **All Out War with Pakistan and Offensive Posturing Against Chinese in case it Supports Pakistan.** In this option the major factor is China as it will hold large quantum of forces along the LAC (line of actual control) in the North and North East fronts.

This is going to impact the force equation in the all out war with Pakistan especially when mountains and hill sectors and plain and desert sectors have to be address and where the concept and technique of warfare are different. India has to defend the Northern frontier with China with strength and retain capability for counter offensive, at the same time employ full strike capability against Pakistan. The duration of the war would depend how fast Pakistan is made to capitulate, so that the war can be brought to an early end. Nuclear threshold will be an issue, as both China and Pakistan are having nuclear capability, and in 'all loss' or 'no go' situation at both the fronts, this factor India has to reckon with and take the risk, when deciding to go for war in order to reclaim occupied territories. In this option India has to consider:

• In the China front, have well coordinated and defended localities which can withstand the Chinese onslaught. Logistic support has to be of very high order and infrastructure available to move troops and equipments as forward as possible and having all weather road connectivity.

• Capability enhancement of the forces and equipments to withstand extreme climate and ruggedness of Himalayas. There will be need of having additional Mountain Divisions and Mountain Strike Corps. Any holding operations without counter offensive capability are useless and in case of reclaiming Aksai Chin and Shaksgam Valley, this is very much required. China must be kept threatened and be apprehensive, with respect to Tibet/Xingjian.

• India cannot repeat the follies of 1962 War, with near equal deployment in battle ready state having integrated battle group warfare concept on ground, China understand it cannot overthrow on weight of strength, the Indian Army as it did in 1962. Therefore, the efforts have to be equally distributed at both the fronts. One thing which India must keep in mind is, that war with China is going to be different ballgame, thus equilibrium has to be made in the military power, and one cannot take China head-on with scanty resources, even if it be a defensive battle.

- In order to keep Indian forces contained in the Northern frontier and keep the Western front force application in par with Pakistan, China will go in for capture of disputed areas all along Line of Actual Control (the McMahon Line) in its posturing, thus keeping India on tenterhook and hesitant in applying its full combat power in the Western front. Indian think tanks and military planners have to really work on the ratio factor of combat potential at both the fronts; this is going to be a tough decision. Problem is that the fronts have varied terrain configuration and the distance involved is large, both front have to be fought separately without any scope of shifting or sidestepping of forces.

- India have to be heavily dependent on Russia, Central Asian and South East Asian countries bordering China, to get Chinese forces committed, otherwise it will have sufficient forces to upset the combat equation ratio and the Indian plans. Western Block will have a big role to play. Diplomatic initiatives will play an important part in getting commitment from these countries. Stage therefore is to be set in a way, that Chinese battle capability does not cross beyond the limit of posturing or limited offensive.

➢ **Have Limited War with both China and Pakistan, Restricted to the Occupied Territories.** This would be the most ideal option, where the war is not at escalated level. However, if Pakistan and China, find themselves losing their ground, it may escalate the operations to all out war. The war will depend on the limit of tenacity of each of the participants; it will carry on till no ground is lost. When targeting only the captured area and the occupied area, the operations have to be really fast, but mountains consume time and troops. Therefore, the best option is to have massive infiltration operation both vertically and horizontally to occupy areas behind the enemy deployment and hold it strongly thus denying reinforcement and deployment of additional forces. If the area is heavily reinforced and defences held in tiers, then capture of a reinforced locality and withstanding an intensive counter attack are two aspects which is required to be considered, especially in case both China and Pakistan are able to concentrate their forces in the restricted areas well before the operations, on anticipation. It will be a real head bashing against the wall. This option will not stand to confined areas but will escalate to two front wars. In case of Pakistan, it will definitely employ the fifth columnist of Jihadi Organisations in Jammu and Kashmir to disrupt and carry out sabotage behind the Indian forces and in the hinterland; this will tie down large quantum of Indian forces. In case Pakistan is able to create a dent here, then it definitely will open up the war and attempt capturing Kashmir, this option of counter offensive will always be there to tie down India or can go in for a pre-emptive strike to upset India's calculations. Certain issues which would require consideration will be:

- The escalation level and breaking point, it will be different for China and Pakistan. The confinement of operation will remain limited and localised, till such time Pakistan is able to hold India. In case of China the crossing of the Line of Actual Control, can result aggressive posturing but any threat to Karakoram pass and the economic corridor will bring violent reaction not only in Aksai Chin but at other areas, thus opening the complete front.

- Till such time the people of Northern Area of occupied Kashmir goes against the Pakistani establishment and openly support merger with India, localised war of liberation will not be fruitful as there will be opposition this will hamper the operations. The ethnic population must have the will to separate from occupation and join the erstwhile State which is part of India. In case of Azad Kashmir where the population inversion has totally taken its effect, Kashmiri's are presently in minority, here forceful reclamation is the only alternative.

- In case of China, the best would be if by any chance like USSR it breaks, it will be appropriate time to reclaim the captured territory of Aksai Chin and ceded Shaksgam Valley. The other alternative will be to get Tibet 'rise to arms, revolt and seek independence'. India had supported China and raised no objection to Tibet being captured and being made part of China. India's strategic interest was a concern for the Congress political party at helm of affairs at that time, India at that time did not want to go against China, as its border issue was disputed and China was a growing power. Now this requires introspection at the political level and there is a need of rethinking on this aspect. One thing one must not forget that China had its hand full in instigating insurgency in North East India and the Naxal movement in India, Chinese support was very much evident from the recoveries and interrogations. Tibet is looking up to India for the support? India has to play its cards well. This is the opportune time especially when after the COVID 19 and Wuhan Corona virus episode, the world is against China. It is high time that India becomes self reliant and be part of world lobby, it will make hell of a difference.

- The concept of localised war, there are issues which create constraints and at times becomes difficult to take decision:

  - Take the case of Kargil War in the battle of eviction of Pakistan Army from occupied strategic heights across the Line of Control (LOC) in Drass and Kargil sectors in India. India maintained the restrain of eviction up till the LOC and not crossing the LOC in pursuit of withdrawing rooted Pakistani Army. In this option such guarantee cannot be expected from Pakistan and China. International pressure will be there as the nuclear threshold is a factor which makes the International Community nervous, pressure will be from the start. Answer lies to the question of the political will and the preparedness.

  - Escalation will be an existing factor and has to be catered as contingency. India has to be prepared.

  - Option of staging the offensive need to be pragmatically considered, Phase out the operations, first tackle Pakistan, at later stage go for China, first diplomatically and if talks fail then by force reclaim the 1962 captured territory and the ceded areas. The fact that once force is applied on Pakistan, as Chinese strategic interest will be at stake it can get involved by attacking India.

- Lastly how much India can contain the limits of the occupied territories, it must keep its options open of all out war in both the fronts.

> **Both the Front Open with All-Out War to Regain the Occupied Territories and Capture Areas both in China and Pakistan, for Negotiating Table Bargains.** This option will be the trickiest and difficult one; here the issue of Indian reach and potential will be main concern, when it comes to deal with two fronts simultaneously. Pakistan may not be that tough an issue but China is going to be tough nut to crack. In my opinion India must not thrust war on China, it is when China declares war on India, it is at that moment India can think of taking back Aksai Chin and Shaksgam Valley. The vulnerability of Tibet and Xingjian is going to play an important role in the Chinese offensive as the apprehension and anxiety will be prevailing, that if India turn the flank and in the process goes in for Tibet and Xingjian, it may result in revolt and liberation, thus China has to cover its vulnerability which will take away substantial quantum of force. India will require support from Russia and Central Asian Republics, South East Asian Countries and Magnolia which are having border disputes with China to tie up partially some quantum of forces. All these will require astute diplomatic initiatives. In such a scenario, at the Pakistan front India cannot get involved in prolonged battle, it has to swiftly conclude the operations either by dismembering Pakistan or reclaiming the occupied part of Jammu and Kashmir and cease the operations. Before contemplation of two front addressing, India has to be militarily strong, be self reliant and have sound economics to sustain long battle especially with China. India will require international support and as all three are contemporary nuclear power states, this will be a big concern for all three participants and the world. Indian nuclear doctrine will also require introspection and change from the status of second strike concept; it should not so happen that the opportunity of retaliation will not be there at all, as the conflict gets terminated

due to aftermath of immobilising first strike. So far world has not seen any war between nuclear power states, last was World War II where nuclear state strikes a non nuclear state!

In this chapter various options has been discussed. The best in my opinion is to make Pakistan declare war on India in desperation, this will make Pakistan the aggressor. All the tact of compelling has to be engineered whereby Pakistan must not have any options left rather than declaring war against India. This will give opportunity to retaliate with swift counter offensives as the Pakistan's offensive forces would be committed in the battle and will be in the perplexity of employing the reserves. If the war is started by Pakistan then the involvement of China will be in doubt and it will not open the second front by declaring the war in support of Pakistan, this will make the world powers take an stance against China and can become another front for China which would go against its own calculations. India must be prepared for this and the capture of the occupied territories.

Pakistan of late has started falling in the trap, Prime Minister Imran Khan has unveiled a political map in which it claims whole of Jammu and Kashmir and Gilgit – Baltistan up till Siachen Glacier, balance it seems Pakistan has left it for China, it has also claimed Sir Creek and Junagarh in Gujarat, have a look at the map:

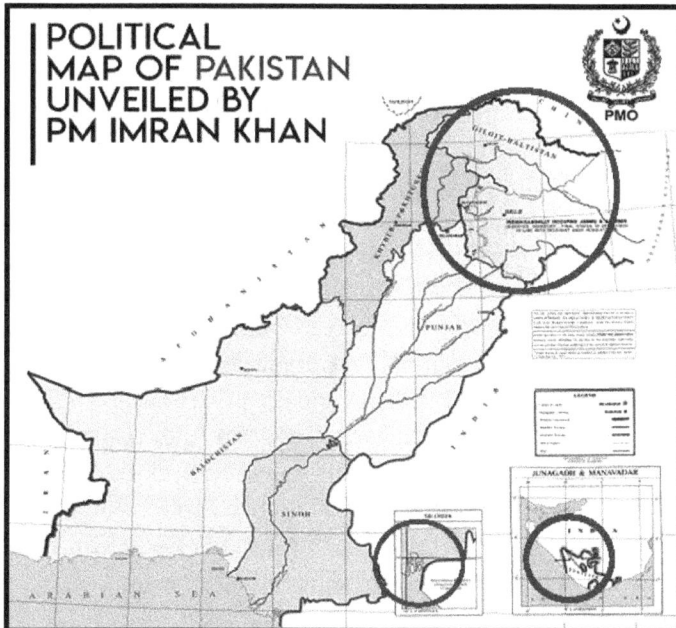

Pakistan by making the Map of occupied territories as part of its own integral part, thus claiming it to be liberated Azad Kashmir and accession of Gilgit-Baltistan to Pakistan is a great game play. Pakistan is planning to make the Northern Area as its fifth Province. Merely making it the province when the land held is disputed and forcibly occupied by coup from the states, to which it belongs, do not hold ground legally in the international forums. Moreover, when International fraternity is claiming as disputed, then it cannot be made part of Pakistan by putting dotted lines on the Map.

Both China and Pakistan have taken the map to UNO and the Security Council where it has been rejected and in turn reprimanded. Apprehensions and anxiety is prevailing in the minds of Pakistanis, after Prime Minister Modi of India had reclaimed the occupied territories which is legally belongs to India. Such gimmicks have purpose to keep at bay Indian adventurism. So far the map of Pakistan has been showing Gilgit – Baltistan and Azad Kashmir as disputed and its courts have also accepted the same and had been highlighted in the agreement of ceding Shaksgam Valley of Karakoram Tract with China. Now merely by changing the Map, Pakistan is trying to claim the occupied territories as its integral part. Instead of averting Indian actions, it is digging its own grave, yes the repercussions may get delayed as India will take some time to make the world realise the game plan, but ultimate seal will be put, which will break Pakistan. The bells have started tolling on Pakistan and this is making it nervous and apprehensive. China is also reacting, it has started LAC (Line of Actual Control) domineering and bullying tactics, Galwan Valley in Ladakh was one such act in the series, there is more to come to keep India in tenterhook, it is sensitive to Aksai Chin, Karakoram and the China Pakistan Economic Corridor, any reclamation by India is going to cost China heavy, it is going to make India commit heavy deployment on the LAC and burden the Indian Forces logistically and economically. India at the Chinese front has to act proactively and check mate its intensions aggressively, it is the only way out to keep China at bay. It is high time that India starts acting as the Regional Power and makes way forward of being one of the world powers, the military muscle power has to commensurate with the stature of India, in this regards Congress 'Antony syndrome' which took Indian Armed Forces more than a decade back due to scams and paybacks for no modernisation of the Armed Forces took place. Indian politics has to come out of this syndrome, otherwise it will make India lag behind, it is time to become strategic military power and increase the military potential.

The Indian think tank and strategic thinkers have to really work out a pragmatic and affordable plans, in this chapter various ways, options and pros and cons have been highlighted which will give some ideas and the contemplated actions, which have to be undertaken to make Indian politics take the initiatives and resolve the issue of occupied Jammu Kashmir and Ladakh permanently, which rightfully belongs to India, it has to be reclaimed if require by force and amalgamated. If one thinks rationally, Pakistan rightfully belongs to India, it was only few interested parties and personalities who had opted for partition and created the religious divide, which in the present polarised world affairs does not stand its ground, thus divided country becomes one country like Germany or Republics in case of breakaway as was the case with USSR and Russia. This polarisation within a country and between countries will have its influence in determining the geopolitical and socio economic consequence, even India is not outside its purview, this factor is going to bring changes in constituents of the federation or union or association, which would change the status of the said region or country, and China and Pakistan is also very much on the road towards this happening. What is required on the part of India is to consolidate its own internal affairs and wait for the opportune moment to strike for the reclamation of its lost territories. The political ambiguity has been going on for decades and behind the ambiguity shield, the indecisiveness of the political leaders were kept, public also had no interest in future of the country as nothing was of concern but their living and 'Roti, Kapda aur Makan' (bread, clothes and home). It is the duty of politician to give a future to the country of peace, prosperity and strategic survivability, political vision has to be beyond personal or party gains.

"*The attacker should know the comparative strengths and weaknesses of himself and of the enemy, and having ascertained the time of marching, the consequences, the loss of men and money, and profits and danger, he should march with his full force; otherwise one should keep quite*"

–*Chanakya*

Chapter – V

China and Reclamation

"Every relationship has one or the other motive behind it. Friendship or enmity is not purposeless. Oneness of motive is turned into friendship. Diversity of motive causes enmity. Royal relationships also depend upon one or the other purpose. But such relations are mainly for the welfare of the state"

- Chanakya

What can be achieved with Pakistan, it is not so in the case of China. The ball game is different. It would be better first to understand the history and the psychological tendencies. China as a nation has always been at war with its neighbours, right from the monarchy days to the present day of communist dictatorship. The population basically consisted of ethnic nomadic tribes, the majority being the Hans. Number of dynasties has ruled China each believing in centralisation of the rule and in expansion of the empire, this got factored into the psyche of the people's communist party coming to power after great revolution. By the cumulative efforts of the monarchy and the communist China, nearly seventy five percent of the territories of China are occupied militarily or by subjugations. China is the only country which has border dispute along its complete borders in all cardinal directions; one can say it is surrounded by number of territorial disputes. The Map below will give you the idea of where the core China is and the proportion of the occupied territories. What has been occupied, China is not going to give up easily.

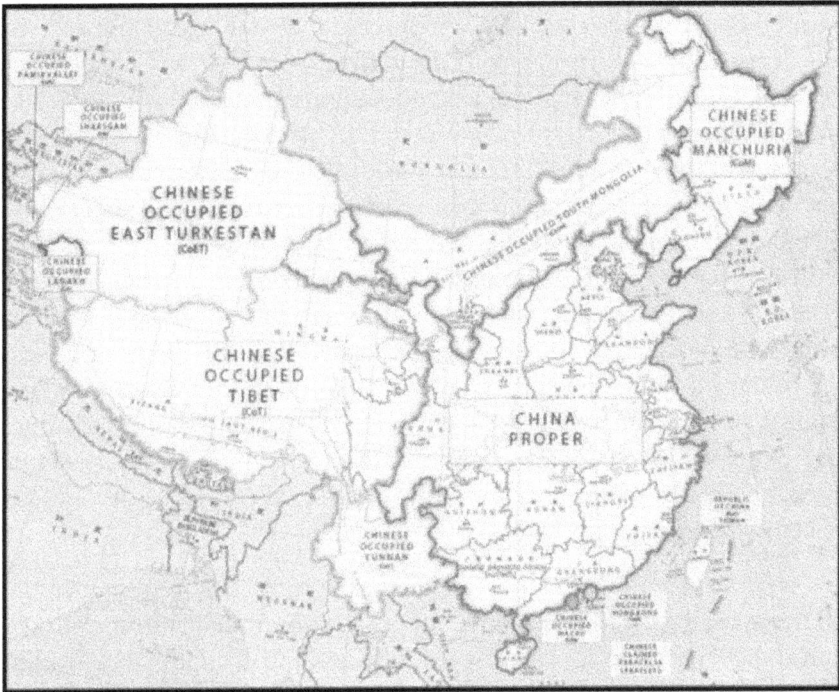

Political Map China

In the Indian context, the occupied territory and ceded territory by Pakistan to China have strategic importance of very high order, any deviation is going to cost very heavy. The link between Central Asia and Main Land China, Blue Waters through Pakistan, Pakistan and Middle East makes Karakoram, Aksai Chin and the Shaksgam Valley important geopolitical and strategic land marks in reference to Xinjiang, Tibet, Pakistan, Himalayan Pass and the associated Chinese geopolitical imperatives and its sensitivities of strategic issues. One has to understand the Chinese psyche of expansionist, in order to make its position strong, it will create situations to establish its domineering superiority and gain grounds to establish its dictates or deny any infringement to the forced status quo, which ever suits its design of arrangements.

In case of China dimensions change, the force proportion is larger and the armed forces potential ratio is more than India. China is having the world's largest Armed Forces and in comparison India is below China, if the power equation is compared in terms of equipments and war machine,

India is low down in order whereas China in comparative table is third world military power after USA and Russia. India taking the initiative in any offensive adventurism, it will be a tough proposition, as China cannot be just set aside in the same way as India is appreciating in case of Pakistan. India which has been very uncertain with its strategic interests, futuristic planning in case of China has been lopsided since 1959, very frankly it is not at all there or is not up to the expectations, reservations are existing on build up of military potential and power, different political parties have varied perception. India being heavily dependent on foreign origin military ware and level of self reliance being rather very low, it will be difficult to do muscle flexing and be part of power block. Yes, if it comes to defend the country it can give befitting reply to China and China also knows that India is no more the same as what it was in 1962. The bully aspect of China will be prevailing factor in any border dispute; China also understands the economic importance of India and will not like to ruffle the feathers beyond a limit.

India therefore cannot think on the lines of Pakistan, as per the strategic analysts, China is a different proposition. India has capability to run-over Pakistan in less than seven days and the occupied areas within a day as claimed by many analyst and defence experts. No analysts has ever predicted such time and space for China. Strategic thinkers in case of China have reserved their opinion and the fact is that India to come to par with China will take more than a decade of consistent efforts and continue to remain so thereafter.

The face off with China at Galwan Valley and the Line of Actual Control was due to factors which has to be understood to understand the Chinese psyche and the motives, India is not going to trust China, as it is the case of 'once bitten, twice shy' and China's attitude of "two steps forward, one step back" part of expansionist military policy, the relation equation is always going to remain apprehensive and of distrust. The point of debate is 'why did not the Indian Congress Government after 1962 Sino-India War ask for the return of the captured territories and why not the intervention of UNO sought before granting UN membership and position of veto in the UN Security Council to China ?

Nearly Sixty years have passed since 1962 and India never made any attempt to reclaim the captured Aksai Chin, as India always remained a vanquished nation since 1962 and this had become the mindset. It was Indian Prime Minister Narendra Modi who after abrogating the Article

370 and 35 A of Indian Constitution with regard to the State of Jammu and Kashmir, reconfiguring the Map of Jammu and Kashmir with subdividing the State into two union territories and claiming return of illegally occupied territories of the State, this has happened for the first time. The Chinese apprehensions has seen an increase, till date China was happy with status quo and did not take much cognisance of the Line of Actual Control(LAC), in between kept the issue of dispute alive with some transgressions and withdrawals. China kept developing the military infrastructure in the Tibet region and up to the LAC. However, of late what has made China sceptical about India are:

❖ The recent development of road communication and infrastructure development near to the LAC. The fear of rapid build up of Indian forces has now become cause of concern. For last sixty years, the under developed status had kept the Chinese happy, any build up of Indian forces was strenuous and time consuming whereas from Chinese side the military build up remained faster. With Indian build up of habitat infrastructure and effective deployment of strategically important key feature has made China think twice before bullying India and threatened the Indian sensitivities.

❖ Making the defended localities on the LAC stronger and better defendable with well linked up roads for logistic support. This has created fear of the under belly of China and its sensitivity to Tibet. With refuge to Dalai Lama and the exiled Tibetan Government in India, the sensitivity factor plays an important role in the Chinese apprehensions and fear of losing Tibet. This has made China to increase the buildup of forces and connectivity with the main land as part of their strategic thinking.

❖ Similarly the ceded Shaksgam Valley and the Karakoram Tract and captured Aksai Chin, Chinese are sensitive to both, as Tibet and Xinjiang from the Ladakh Region becomes vulnerable. The military buildup in this region is the heaviest. Buddhists who are settled in Ladakh has high percentage of Tibetans. Again, the sensitivity of likely breaking of the autonomous regions of Xinjiang and Tibet makes Chinese anxiety, high.

❖ Even though India does not match China in military power equation but it has capability to turn flanks and upset the balance by going in for offensive in the vulnerable areas along the LAC from Ladakh to Arunachal Pradesh. China is aware of Indian capability and nationalism in the Indian Armed Forces; it also knows that all along the front it cannot maintain equilibrium and concentration of forces, there will be gaps which can get exploited and India has capability to exploit it. Chinese understands that full fledge deployment on the LAC (Line of Actual Control) is not possible, as the borders of China are not dormant elsewhere, in any case China cannot take the risk of thinning out or taking the risk of losing the territorial disputed areas to gain hold on the territories across the line of Actual Control with India.

❖ The Chinese attitude and show of arrogance has created a new dimension in the deployment along the LAC and the McMahon Line, India has now been compelled to hold its ground permanently with no scope of withdrawal. This will force China to maintain a very large standing army in the region of Tibet. This eye ball to eye ball contact is going to cost heavy to both India and China. This was forthcoming since long, one cannot keep accepting the bully intrusion time and again over the ages, and threatening the sovereignty of the country with illogical and concocted historical claims.

China declaring war on India on the issue of reclamation of Aksai Chi and Shaksgam Valley, is not likely, it would prefer talks with India or maintain the status quo by show of strength. It will not like to disturb India for it fears the repercussion in the economic front. The Indian dependency on China is heavy and it won't like to lose business. In the economic front China is very apprehensive about India, India is getting into competition with China, some of the fears are:

❖ China and India together contribute more than half of Asia's GDP. India is the only country that can overtake China and hence is giving a scare.

❖ China's foreign exchange flow compared to India is lower. India for the first time in 2015 became the world's leading FDI with $63 billion, overtaking China $56.6 billion and US $59.6 billion.

❖ India's increasing manufacturing competitiveness. Although India is still in its initial stage of developing export-oriented manufacturing industries, but has great potential to emerge as a regional hub for labour-intensive industries.

❖ India, after spread of Corona virus and the international anger against China catching up with many business establishments, those who are shifting out of China. Chinese fear India will capitalise on the international hatred towards China. Also, India has been welcoming these businesses with lucrative propositions. India is providing talent and is having talent pool which China is unable to provide. More and more knowledge based companies are shifting towards India.

❖ Indian launching of satellites and placing the same in orbit successfully has created history. China has grudgingly accepting India's superior technology in space.

❖ Indian software hubs are in demand due to availability of trained talents and India has been consistently doing well in World soft ware market. US-based software firm CA Technologies disbanded its research and development team in China while setting up a team in India with some 2,000 scientific and technical professionals over the past few years.

❖ India and the U.S. signed the Logistics Exchange Memorandum of Agreement (LEMOA), a military pact that facilitates the provision of support, supplies and services between the US and Indian Military. US also has been more than forthcoming in supporting India in the recent skirmish at Galwan Valley and the post Galwan developments, it also has successfully mobilised the support of the entire world. India has become more powerful in diplomatic circle. China though lost more men in Galwan Valley, that is not a worry for them, but India is able to be the 'Being Heard Country' in diplomatic circle, which is worrying China.

❖ India's aggressiveness and checkmating of the Chinese moves of encroachment of Line of Actual Control, has made China apprehensive and increased its level of anxiety. India is no more a pushover as it was in 1962. Uncompromising attitude of India at the Military Level Talks on Line of Actual Control (LAC) and after Galwan incident have put caution on Chinese approach of having their own ways.

One thing is crystal clear, India has to deal with China separately and not in tandem with Pakistan in reclaiming the occupied territories. Whatever is the status of India's military power and level of compatibility with China, addressing dual front will be a difficult proposition. If the front is opened by China, the question will be different, as the war will be thrust upon India, in that case India must not only hold China but also take the war into China, then there is no option left but to increase the military potential to near par with China. Any decision with reference to China has to be very deliberate, with prudency and sagacity. Any war with China, India cannot afford to lose and give up the claim of the captured territories. This will be a challenge to the strategic and military thinkers.

It would be prudent to discuss what all options India have to get back Aksai Chin and the Shaskgam Valley, which rightfully and legally belongs to India:-

❖ The matter has to be internationalised and world opinion to be shaped. Diplomatic initiative has to be initiated with China and rest of the world. The possibilities of international intervention and moderation have to be examined. The case must be brought up in the United Nations

❖ Bilateral relation manifest should contain the issue of return of captured area of Aksai Chin and the border issues. For country like China, it has to be continuously prodded to get the issue into the focus; initiative will never ever be from Chinese side.

❖ Use of force to take back Pakistan Occupied Jammu and Kashmir, this will throw open the Chinese reaction and gauge the response, if it gets committed in a limited way then taking the opportunity to reclaim the captured and the ceded territories becomes better.

❖ In case two fronts get opened and require simultaneous addressing, it would be prudent to hold China in the First Phase and sweep the Pakistan's operations on a faster pace, in the Second Phase take the offensive into China (Tibet and Xinjiang).

❖ After fall of Pakistan, China attacks India. India it this contingency must be ready to fight an all out war, along with the nuclear risk. China must be made aware of Indian Nuclear response and retaliation.

❖ Like 1962, if China declares war, independent to the Indian action against Pakistan under the apprehension of Indian claim of return of captured territory of 1962. The Indian response in that case should be to give prompt and apt reply by not restricting to only reclamation but to resolve the border dispute in totality. Here the support of the world power blocks will be mandatory to contain the might of China.

❖ India proclaiming war with China must be avoided and must be kept as the last resort, where both the expansionist endeavours and adamancy of retaining the captured territory continues. In such a scenario India has all the rights to safe guard its territorial integrity and sovereignty and if warranted, declare war on China. India must not take the Chinese bullying lying down. All will depend on how much strong is the political will.

❖ Last option is to wait for balkanisation of China on the lines of USSR; it will provide opportune moment to reclaim the captured and ceded territories, as also support Tibet and Xigjiang in their liberation. In the new diplomatic ties all issues in relation to China can then be amicably resolved and have peaceful co-existence. The wait in this can be long. In another case China getting into the Third World War and subsequently getting disintegrated, for this India has to be part of the allied forces, this is very hypothetical and surety is very ambiguous.

China will be a different ball game, rhetoric are not going to work. In many TV interviews the retired military personnel have been talking about comparison with China and have been giving advantage to India of having more seasoned and motivated nationalist troops. There is misconception that Chinese military consists of conscripted force where individuals serve only for three years. China has combination of standing Army and conscripted three years of civilians' military service. India must accept that Chinese Army is superior in weapons, equipment and standoff weapon systems/platforms, China is India's number one enemy and it will be really challenging to come to par with China. This can only be offset by joining the anti China lobby, USA the only super power which is clear of its China stance, Russia even though is having border dispute with China but its communist affiliations is concern for India. Without engaging China in other fronts, it will be difficult to take China head-on.

The entire Sino-Indian border (Line of Actual Control and McMahon Line) is 4,056 km long and traverses Indian Union Territory of Ladakh, and four Indian states of Himachal Pradesh, Uttarakhand, Sikkim, and Arunachal Pradesh. One has to understand the topography to deduce the strategic importance of the terrain both sides of the LAC and McMahon Line and what are the tactical imperatives to both the Chinese Army and Indian Forces, the Map below gives the details of the topography:

Map Topography China

The terrain brings out the following imperatives which will have the strategic and tactical implications for both China and India:-

❖ **China.** The mainland China from the Indian Line of Actual Control (LAC) is at a crow flight distance of approximately 3000 kms, it is separated by Greater Himalayas, Tibetan Plateau (Qing Zang Gaoyuan) and the Chengdu – Lanzhou Mountain Ranges. This distance has been reduced by having rail and road connectivity to induct its forces at a shorter time frame:-

➢ In the plateau region, the expanse is very large and to cover approximately 4000 Kms of LAC, the spread of locating the forces is also very large, thus it has to built its military hubs with good connectivity, Over the years it has built laterals and axial all weather roads linking the LAC.

➢ Military infrastructures in echelons have been built to accommodate forces to cover the expansion of the frontage and the depth.

➢ The rail and road link has the vulnerability of bridges and tunnels, which if destroyed will cut off the route from the mainland China. China will be sensitive to its vulnerability.

➢ Plateau is plain and has manoeuvrability for mechanised forces; mechanised warfare thus is possible once it can be inducted either by air or through the mountains. China has as such placed its mechanised forces in the plateau and located it at suitable locations to reduce the time factor.

➢ The terrain is at high altitude, this has restrictions on use of equipments and aerial combat machines. Acclimatisation of troops will be required. The Greater Himalayas on the Chinese side is at lower heights as it merges with the Great Tibetan Plateau, it was for this reason Chinese could build roads up till the LAC.

➢ The area of Aksai Chin is more mountainous as compared to the areas in the North East. The Karakoram Mountain Ranges in the North borders Xingjian Province of China, with proximity of the Karakoram Pass (though under Chinese occupation) China is vulnerable as the connectivity of Xingjian and Aksai Chen will be lost.

➢ The North East Rivers have source in China, in a way China controls the water through series of dams, its major power demand is met from hydro electrical projects. These dams are also sensitive targets which can cause problems for China and floods can create havoc. These rivers are life line for Arunachal Pradesh, Assam and Bangladesh.

❖ **India**. The Indian side of the terrain is more tough and difficult; the LAC is running along the watershed at its utmost height. The major part of Great Himalayas are in the Indian side and due to the difficult accessibility and inhuman living conditions, the areas near and on the LAC has remained remote :-

➢ The Indian side is more mountainous and thus better defendable. In case of any offensive by the Chinese, the troop ratio will be 1: 8 minimum; there Chinese will require eight times more troops than India.

➢ Construction of roads is difficult, thus connectivity is poor. It is of late that India has started construction of roads up to the LAC. This has made China jittery. Earlier China had advantage of faster concentration of forces as compared to India. As on date most of the roads and tracks are of British vintage and same is being used, new roads are rare and lack of government initiative and bureaucratic lethargy, environmentalists and courts putting breaks and delays, had made road construction real problematic and projects being shelved by Boarder Road Organisation. What is important that people of India must realise the strategic importance of the their land and visualise what can happen, this lack of nationalist spirit which only see the present and not bothered for the future, one of the reason which makes India lag behind.

➢ Any offensive through the Indian side of the terrain towards China, the climb is through altitudes for concentration of forces and equipment build up. There is lack of space for deployment and dependency is more on axial deployment along the road alignment. From the single axes in the present time there is requirement of multiple axes for build up, need for improving the road communication network. It was for this very reason the Dragon has been sleeping and keeping quiet, for it knew India can never think of any offensive against China.

➢ Himalayas are great barrier for both sides, thus China has made use of the plateau to locate as forward as possible to the LAC, its military camps and infrastructures. Camps are well furbished and are able to station troops in peak winters also. Indian deployments are on the line of outposts all along the LAC and at places harsh winters compel withdrawal of troops. Terrain has been handicap for India and no effort have been made to improve or develop forward infrastructure by the political parties in power especially Congress. It was BJP which was made to realise that China is enemy number one of India and it is this party which has recognised the importance of building of forward infrastructure, lot is yet to be achieved.

> ➤ In mountains the distances are large and reaching from one location to another is time consuming, thus lateral and axial roads have a major role to play, In case of India as compared to China hardly any laterals or axials are existing, this aspect requires early addressing, it is only then that forces can be switched from one sector to another.

The above analysis of the terrain, it is evident that China is in better position as compared to India, Chinese build up will be faster and it can launch its forces directly from the military establishments on the Tibetan Plateau. For India it has to build up forces in slower time frame, thus it will amount to stationing troops in strength in the inhospitable terrain and weather; one can compare it to Session deployment. Therefore, in case of any war the disadvantage is with India and lot of efforts are required to improve the aggressive and proactive posturing to threaten China. China has worked out its strategy very well in advance and ensured that India remains at disadvantage operationally.

Now the question is how to handle China, it will be prudent to know the facts as obtainable on ground. China is a near world military power and trying to establish itself as the world power. To make its reach world over, it has bases in South East Asia, Indian Subcontinent at Myanmar, Sri Lanka and Pakistan, Middle East at UAE and now making alliance with Iran, Latin America, Argentina, Cuba, Littoral States in Indian Ocean Region and African States, these are the PLA Logistic Military Bases. China wins over a country with Humanitarian Aid, Military Exchanges, Arms Sale and Technology Transfer, the dependency level is increased to an extent that the country is compelled to agree to the terms which is purely business and military. In case of any all out war with China, it may not just stick around LAC and McMahon Line, the blue water threat will also be there. The distance which is a handicap to China, to increase the reach China has gone in for Strategic Missile Forces and aerial capability of long distance hauling of conventional and nuclear weapons by strategic bombers. India on the other hand has the Strategic Force Command for its missile and Air Defence Command which in itself is a challenge to China and Pakistan. India to an extent is somewhat weak in Strategic Air Force capability, except for missiles India does not have bombers in the category of B52 strategic bombers. Still India carries militarily nuclear deterrence based on its missiles, to give at par response to any Chinese misadventures and take the battle into China's sensitivity of Tibet and Xingjian. With these strategic and tactical backdrops, let us see what all options India has for reclamation of its captured and ceded territories of Aksai Chen and Shaksgam Valley respectively.

Option – I

Check Mating Chinese Moves

It was the Indian weakness which China has been playing around, the Indian political 'will' have been lacking and no one was interested to get a solution to end the border dispute and claim back the captured territory in 1962 Sino – India War. Border infringement and encroachment has been the game play of Chinese to keep India on tenterhooks, India has been at the receiving end and actions were reactive by compulsion. Indian Army was kept at a held back position and escalation was avoided.

If the case of Line of Actual Control or the McMahon line the territories held by China is in the Indian side, it is illegal occupation. The Chinese justification are not logical and there is no historical linkage, just saying that Tibetan Monastery link existed thus land automatically becomes part of Tibet (now China) does not stand the geographical map authenticity claim which was globally acceptable and recognised, in case of India British Indian Map, thus Indian claim cannot be denied by China. The other thing is, Tibet was never a part of China, it was takeover by overthrowing the legitimate Tibetan Government, thus it cannot be Chinese who can decide what was India's border with Tibet. On this pretext India has all the rights to reclaim its own territories which are illegally occupied. China was nonexistent when the border agreement was there with Tibet.

In this option India has to first stand face-to-face and challenge China. In the process of reclaiming, India has the rights to retain the areas which it holds and this process must carry on till the actual Line of Actual control is reached. India must not accept pushover stance any more. To achieve this there are certain considerations which India must ponder upon:-

❖ The areas held by the Army, ITBP and SSB must be permanent (no evacuation in winters). This will give permanency to the deployment and deny occupation by Chinese. The locations must be well connected and proper habitat made to keep the troops warm and comfortable. All locations must have drones and monitoring units. Chinese never to be trusted. Such outposts must be capable to relocate and deploy to improve the posture, by occupying dominating heights where there is scope and within the Indian perception of Line of Actual Control. The posturing has to be aggressive. The areas of Aksai Chen and Shaksgam Valley being Indian territories illegally occupied, need here would be of being more aggressive and take advantage of all windows of opportunities to improve the defence posture and where there are gaps these must be occupied. Chanakya said *"Any activity which harms the progress of the enemy engaged in similar undertakings is also a progress"*, for China this is very apt. Important aspect is that the Line of Actual Control (LAC) which was left unattended and under developed now has to be made more approachable.

❖ Wherever China encroach areas on or across LAC (Indian perspective of alignment of LAC), in similar manner same or larger areas elsewhere should be encroached by India with the same arguments. The same policy as Chinese 'two step forward and one step back'. To have this courage, India must be well prepared to maintain its stand and if required face up to the threat of local skirmishes or localised war. To quote Sun Tzu *"The clever combatant imposes his will on the enemy but does not allow the enemy's will to be imposed on him. Remaining one step ahead than your enemies which will cause the enemy to make plans in contrast to yours and there would be no scope where he can out manoeuvre you"*, this must be Indian policy, let India apply the same policy as that of China.

❖ India must think on 'Grab Actions' in the illegally occupied areas of Aksai Chen and Shaksgam Valley, India is well within its right to reclaim the captured and ceded territory. After Galwan, what India is up to is apt and rightful, but it has to stick with it and do not get buckle down under pressure, time has come to see 'eye to eye' with China. American volunteering for mediation in view of the standoff between India and China on the LAC, must be exploited, if the issue is kept bilateral then chances are there that the situation of 'no go' develops with Chinese domineering and show of muscle power.

Such mediation (if it would have been an offer for intervention it would have been a better proposition) offers will put China in cautious approach, moreover the LAC, captured territory return and occupation of illegally ceded territory issue must be brought to international focus. Bullying by China must not be tolerated. It is by grab actions India has to make its posture strong and exploit the incurred position of advantage with firmness and resoluteness. Still such time the political 'will' is there Indian Army must consolidate and face up to Chinese threats

❖ None of the Non Aligned Member Nations have remained so. It is high time, Nehru's philosophies be changed, during his life time he saw the repercussion of so called Non Aligned concept and ultimately had to indirectly get aligned during 1962 Indo – China War. In order to check mate China, India has to get aligned with the Power Block or it becomes world power in itself. Today's world is all on alignment equations, thus in isolation no country cannot fights its way out, China is a power in itself which has created alliance of its own.

❖ In this option resoluteness on Indian part is an important imperatives, the level of preparation on the LOC has to be more and extra than equal in terms of level of forces, surveillance, intelligence and the fire power. In other words the threshold level to be just below the all out war; however the scope should be kept within the levels of localised war. The Indian Government endeavour must be to keep improving the potential of the Armed Forces to bring it at par with China, in the diplomatic front there has to be equal offensive and proactive posturing not to get cowed down into submission. India must try to establish relation with all those countries which have got involved with China and forced to accept its hegemony and give permission to have bases and promise of military support. Indian initiatives on the lines of Sri Lanka, to make realise the Chinese game play and its repercussion, like Sri Lanka realisation and distancing from China, similarly other countries must be brought under the purview of diplomatic offensive to checkmate China.

Option – II

Divide the Chinese Forces And Deny Shift

In this option it is suggested that Line of Actual Control be divided into two parts/Commands, *firstly* From Siachen – Aksai Chen – Nepal West including Shaksgam Valley ceded by Pakistan and *secondly* From Nepal (East Sikkim) – Bhutan – Arunachal Pradesh. The dynamics and the geography is different in both the Commands, moreover the strategic prospective are very different and requires different addressing at various levels. This way the Indian preparedness and development to checkmate China will be prudent and practical approach. The problem had been that the Indian political parties have always considered it as the entire McMahon line and LAC as one front and the approach has been similar, even though the areas fall under Northern, Central and Eastern Command of Indian Army and Air Force Western and Eastern Command. In the North 3 Corps and 14 Corps, Central 6 Mountain Division and in East 3, 4, 33 Corps and 17 Corps as Mountain Strike Corps are deployed, on paper looks to be adequate for the Chinese front. The issue now is, when India will be going for change with Integrated Battle Groups and having Composite Commands on the lines of Strategic Forces and Air Defence Command, the need is to have specific delineated Commands and have these based on geographical and strategic specifics in case of the Chinese front. This must be viewed in terms of China's development of military potential in next ten years, which is going to go leaps and bounds, in its desire to be the world power. China is going to make it nuclear status as the threat and deterrence along with its strategic missile force; this will also change the regional equation. Under such scenario, the checkmating China will be a big bother, having dedicated Commands with par or near par potential of composite forces will matter here, it is not that India does not have dedicated Commands against China front but what is lacking is the matching potential and catering for future geopolitical possibility, the reason why such Command level Force is required must be understood: -

- ❖ **North Eastern Command (can be named as Ladakh- Uttaranchal Command).** The Command's area of operational responsibility will be from Shaksgam Valley – Siachen – Aksai Chen – Nepal West. The area requires specialised forces and capable to operate in all weather conditions. Based on the terrain configuration the

Command's weapon profile have to be determined. The Command will have integrated forces of land and air. Specialized forces for high altitude and snow/glacier warfare, for battle in the Chinese plateau region mechanised warfare, heliborne operation capability, airlift and air assault operational capability, specialised surveillance and communication groups and integrated fire support groups will be main stay of the organisational profile. Now the question why Nepal? Nepal is going to play a very important role in any future war with China and will be used and exploited by China as firm base to take the battle into India. Whatever the Nepalese may say about their independent Hindu Kingdom which never was part of any empire or never succumbed to any invasion, but in case of China, the possibility of taking over Nepal cannot be totally denied, it has already started infiltrating Nepal. On the other hand Nepal can open a second front for India. Nepal thus is and will be a critical issue which India has to handle. This Command therefore has to cater Nepal as part of its strategic planning for both defending as also taking the offensive through Nepal into China. The Command has to have both defensive and strike force integrated battle groups. Equipping this Command will be a challenge to India, in order to get it at par with China. The Command must be having capability to take war into China's Xingjian and Western Tibet.

❖ **Eastern Command (Existing Command).** The area of operations of this Command would be from Nepal East – Sikkim - Bhutan – Arunachal Pradesh. The terrain is similar to the Northern Command in the Himalayan Region it is mountainous and forested at lower altitude and tree line is upto 6000-9000 feet, and towards the plains of Assam and Arunachal Pradesh it is riverine and cultivated. The Indian sensitivity is the Chickens Neck (between Sikkim and Bangladesh called Siliguri corridor) and narrowness of the Indian corridor is cause of concern, if this part is severed then India will lose Seven States of the East of India. The deductions in case of Nepal, same is also applicable for Bhutan. Bhutan for that matter is very small country and will capsize within 24 hours in case of invasion by China. Bhutan is sensitivity of India and is totally dependent on support from India. This Command is different from the North East Command, with its own dynamics. Assam, Sikkim and Arunachal are the front line States which get directly involved in the battle. Myanmar, which is in the East is also liable to be used by China during war and this must not be ruled out totally. The Command has both defensive and offensive capability; however, there is need to enhance its strike capability.

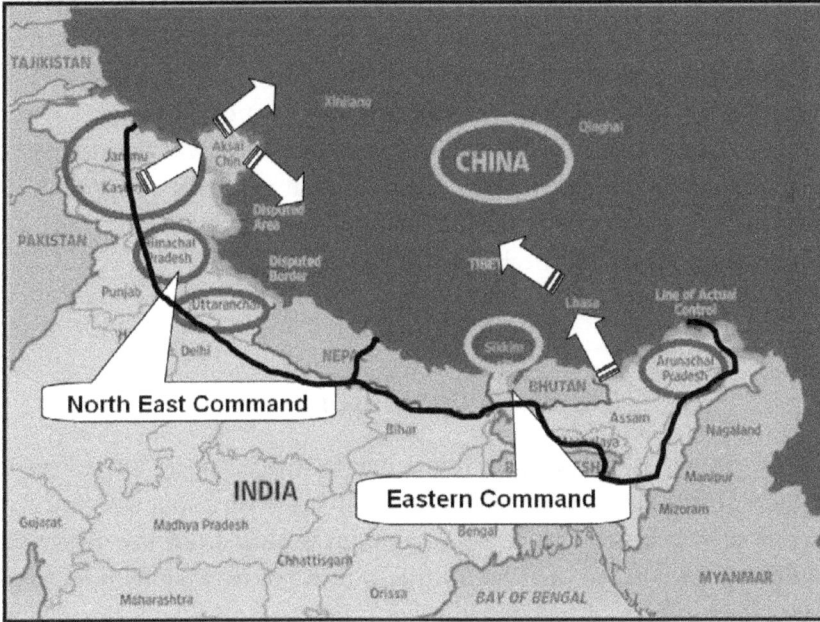

Map: India - China

China is India's enemy number one and India must focus more on China. The battle field is different, and will require separate considerations. India under the presumption that if the Pakistan front is not active then forces can be side stepped to the China front to meet the force ratio equation is possible, but here the issue will be of troops and equipment adapting to the battle field conditions and acclimatisation. If Pakistan front is nonexistent then the China front will have more than matching combat potential, however the question is when Pakistan will be nonexistent. In case dual front opens up then the criticality will come up, India says it can face both fronts with the present resources, this confidence is good but can India withstand double front war, I have my doubts. As suggested India must have two Commands dedicated and each having adequate strike capability to take the war into China, the present force levels are not adequate and more is yet to be done to increase the overall potential inclusive of all operating outfits. Let us not only look at Tibet but also the Xingjian, and the countries like Nepal, Bhutan and Myanmar which can get involved in the war against China. Having two strong Commands will divide the Chinese forces; commit more forces on ground this denuding the reserves, create apprehension and uncertainty thus making it more cautious and keep guessing about the Indian moves. If China feels threatened of Karakoram, Xingjian and Aksai Chen it will be compelled to deploy forces. Moreover in case Uyghur Muslims and Tibetan population stands against China and create unrest or revolt, China will have to deploy its forces to contain the unrest, to exploit such windows of opportunity India must be ready to take the initiative and having such Commands will be advantageous and to checkmate China.

Option – III

If War is Thrust upon India

If the war is thrust upon India, due to own strategic interest or in support of Pakistan by China, in both case it will be an all out war, however in case of war in support it would amount to dual front war for India. China will exploit Pakistan by making it declare war against India to tie down Indian forces, it understand that if Pakistan front is dormant then India will have advantage over China in the force ratio. In case war is thrust upon India the first objective for India will be to capture the occupied territories both in case of dual front war or single front war. In case of single front i.e. China only, the reclamation of Aksai Chen and Shaksgam Valley will make China vulnerable. In this case it would be prudent to fight the war Command wise, in case the North East Command is going for offensive than the Eastern Command should also be offensively poised and as the North East Command offensive progresses and there is shift of Chinese forces from East, this advantage must be taken to launch offensive by the Eastern Command. The Operations of North East Command after reclaiming Aksai Chin must turn into Tibet to outflank Chinese forces thus compelling it to go in for counter offensive in the Eastern Command which can be neutralised giving heavy loss to China, the success must be exploited and no windows of opportunities to be wasted . Similar will be the case for the Eastern Command with Lhasa being the objective. Thus having two strong Commands on the LAC (Line of Actual Control) and McMahon Line will be beneficial and will be to India's advantage, as the time and space is not in favour of India due to the terrain factor and distance, the scope for side stepping or reinforcements between the Commands is not possible, it will be better to have self sufficient independent Commands. In case of single front war, Command wise addressing will be more beneficial and to make this happen, both Commands have to be equal in potential and strike capability:-

❖ The chance of outflanking the Chinese army is more both in the North and East, for threatening the depth to which it is very sensitive, especially in the Tibet region. The depth areas have to be held in strength thus will result in force dispersion; this will denude the front line forces strength. The battle will be in the plateau thus both Commands must be having armoured and mechanised formations.

❖ Gives more than one option to India, this will make Chinese cautious and uncertain, thus will be compelled in having strong reserves and forced to keep them dispersed to reduce the time gaps in the plateau region as long distances are to be covered, moreover as the move will be on the plateau interdiction will be easier to cause delays.

❖ The disadvantage of distance, time and space has to be made up by having independent Commands both having equal potential of holding defences, going for pre-emptive strike and counter offensive capabilities. Commands should be based on integrated battle concept with equal distribution of resources. This will make China also to divide its forces to meet the threat from each Command differently.

❖ In case of localised or restricted war for occupied territory only one Command will then get engaged, the other Command can be on alert if China opens the Arunachal Pradesh front claiming it as own territory occupied by India (which is historically wrong, without factual support and is theory conjured by Communist China after forcible takeover of Tibet) thus the escalation of war gets adequately covered. There will not be any requirement to move forces from the Western front deployment and moreover which cannot be directly inducted into the mountain and high altitude battle due to the acclimatisation factor.

The thrust upon war may become dual front war; in that case it would be prudent on the part of India to tackle China first with full steam and try to take the war into China and in the process plan reclamation of the occupied territories. Pakistan must be made to commit it maximum forces for the Indian offensive, India must go in for full fledge offensive in the Northern Area and Azad Kashmir to reclaim the occupied area in conjunction with Indian offensive into China, checkmate Pakistan in the other fronts and then go in for counter offensive depending on the progress of operations in the Chinese front, however as some of the forces from the Western front may get engaged in the Chinese offensive in the third tier , there may be some delay in completion of operations against Pakistan. To achieve the capability of handling dual front India must develop its potential accordingly. The thrust upon war should not be fought totally on defensive basis but should be on the concept of offensively defensive.

The Chinese build up in Ladakh sector and series of trespassing incidents on the line of Actual Control, among them the Galwan valley episode in July 2020 where 20 Indian soldiers were killed and in retaliation Indian soldiers killed more than 50 Chinese which was not acknowledged by PLA. It was the first time Indian soldiers showed aggressiveness in face to face hand combat. This was followed by occupying tactical heights on the Kailash Range from the south bank of Pangong Tso to Tsaka La that included Helmet, Black Top, Gurung Hill, Magar Hill, Mukhpari, Rezang La and Rechin La. All these areas are on the Indian side of the LAC and were sites of intense battles in China-India War of 1962. China also recognises the alignment of the Line of Actual Control (LAC) in these areas, except in the area of Black Top, which it claims is east of its claim line. The aggressiveness of the Indians have taken China by surprise and made Chinese troops to recoil, since China harps on 1959 claim line and has been at will, moving into un-held areas. The 1993 agreement on Maintenance of Peace and Tranquillity and the subsequent agreements have lost their relevance. Presently the concept of 'grab and hold' has been in practise, though the LAC (Line of Actual Control) is still being maintained for politico - diplomatic purpose and keep the scope of dialogue open. India by holding the heights along the Kailash Range has upset the Chinese calculations. Xi Jinping Chinese President loss of face and tactical defeat of the PLA, will not be tolerated, moreover China is surrounded by problems all round and USA's actions at South China Sea to liberate Chinese hold and domination, to draw out the attention India may be targeted. The question of large scale build up of forces for nothing is not acceptable.

If the war is thrust upon India by China there is no alternative other than being defensively offensive and the issue of Shaksgam Valley and Aksai Chin can be sorted out.

Option – IV

Reclamation Militarily

In this option India declares war to reclaim the occupied territories from China. India in this case must first take the Pakistan occupied Jammu and Kashmir, see the reaction of China. In case China does not get involved it would be suiting India, otherwise it will open the second front as a localised war or go for an all out war. India in order to take the decision on going for reclamation of the occupied territories by use of force have to ensure that all other options have been tried out and it is no go. China's counter claim of whole of Arunachal Pradesh which it claims to be occupied by India, though the argument lacks substance and logic but China is sticking on to it, actually it is bullying India with the issue, can be made the reason of going in for all out war. If India goes for Aksai Chin, China will then go into Arunachal Pradesh, then it will be matter of negotiation and whose interest which part of reclamation serves better.

Any action on the part of India will not remain an local action and definitely escalate to a full fledge war, China will not like to easily accept military action of India in the Aksai Chin or Shaksgam Valley as its strategic interest is involved, neither China will like to accept defeat as its hegemony in the region will get affected. China will bounce back with full power, war will not be with machete, spikes, ramrods and sticks as it happened in the Galwan Valley episode in Ladakh region on 15 Jun 2020 and Helmet Top near Chishul on 30-31 Aug 2020. As per World interpretation of military power goes, India is no match to China, yes in certain localised actions India can achieve upper hand but not in a full fledge war or escalation of skirmishes into all out war. War with China would mean very less scope of any intervention, as China will not that easily succumb to any pressure. Rhetoric by Indian politicians will not make India at par with China; lot has to be done on ground to improve the capability and potentials not only in any single dimensions but all the dimensions, the Government of Bharatiya Janata Party has started the process and this must continue.

In this chapter the reclamation of Indian territories occupied by China has been discussed, the Indian think tanks have to deliberate should China be tackled separately or in conjunction with Pakistan. The possibility of sequential dealings will be the best option, but question is when the realisation of the India's intention in reclamation, then chances of joint remonstration getting manifested in combined actions to denying India the endeavour of reclamation of the occupied and disputed territories cannot be ruled out. Going in for simultaneous or near simultaneous military actions for reclamation will also get contested by dual front war. As the world is seeing change in world order and power lobbies are getting in the forefront, which has only two interests of Nation and Economics which have become the survivability factor, in the years to come there will be many such lobbies with varied interests both based on regional and associational mutual obligatory relationships . It is under pressures from such lobbies, some relief can be obtained without going in for war or India can hope to become the Regional Power having matching military muscle, economy and established position in the world order. China is going to be different ball game and for which India has to be well prepared.

Reclamation by war will amount to all out war, there will be lobbies but war will be one to one. Pakistan will be playing spoil sport here but will not be of much consequence, for by that time it will be busier managing its internal issues and the rough militant s at its own back yards. Full fledge war with the present resources will not be adequate, there has to be dedicated Commands for China as advocated in this Chapter. Integrated battle groups of the command have to be area specific and profiling carried out to deal with any contingencies. The contact battle will be very restricted, more dependency will be on standoff, disruptive, precision and long range munitions assault by the Chinese. Strategic Force weapons drone swarm and cyber warfare will be the key elements. China will not limit its offensive to land only but will try to put pressure from the sea front.

The question is how long will China hold on to the nuclear tolerance and how fast it wants to end the war. China must also realise that any war with India is not without risk. The risk will be:-

❖ Power blocks backing India. The chances of getting the power blocks involved cannot be ignored. The second risk that dual front gets open in North China/ South China Sea and the Himalayan Front. Xinxiang Uyghur Muslim and Tibetan Revolution can be a great cause of concern for China. The Azerbaijan and the Central Asian Countries are not favoring China on Uyghur issues.

❖ War on Himalayas is going to cost heavy and weather will play an important role in progress of operations.

❖ Indian strike capabilities will put caution in the Chinese. War will be matter of who is making use of the terrain to gain position of advantage.

❖ It is not that China is outside the range of Indian Missiles, thus the threat and deterrence is existing. By the time the war takes place, the equations and dynamics would have seen many changes.

India in a way is at an advantage, basically due to its seasoned troops which are acclimatised, with the changed dynamics of the LAC deployment continuous occupation of the areas is going to make the soldiers more robust, the linkup with the LAC by interior roads and bridges will make the logistic support more flexible and forward deployment will facilitate efficient build up and give the war 'cold start' thus retaining the surprise. It has been since very long we have given more than due to China and tolerated its bully, it is time that the Dragon faces the Tiger. National strategy is complex, just being rhetoric and toeing the media sentiments will not serve the purpose, very pragmatic and realistic approach is required, and today's war cannot be fought under whims and fancy. Generals have to study and keep pondering the dynamics, train and be prepared. China can be handled in our terms.

> *"The possession of power and happiness in a greater degree makes a king superior to another; in a less degree, inferior; and in an equal degree, equal. Hence a king shall always endeavour to augment his own power and elevate his happiness"*
>
> *- Chanakya*

Epilogue

The Bharatiya Janata Party and the National Democratic Alliance government, have for the first time claimed the Pakistan and Chinese occupied Jammu and Kashmir, and asked for their return. It is for the first time India has claimed that if required these occupied territories, will be taken forcibly. For last 70 odd years these territories have been used by both the occupiers, for activities against India and have taken it for granted that these areas will not be reclaimed by India. Lack of seriousness on the part of erstwhile governments was taken as Indian weakness and it built so much of confidence that, China and Pakistan went in for the China Pakistan Economic Corridor in the occupied and disputed areas held by Pakistan.

The world after the failure of UNO Resolution of 1948, have left the issue of Jammu and Kashmir to be handled at the bilateral level, even though India is having full rights over Jammu and Kashmir legally. In fact the question of bilateral, was never there but was brought in the ambit by USA to de-escalate the regional tension and for own interest of using Pakistan for its global objectives. The bilateral part is not standing its ground as the attempts were superficial from both the ends. The issue of Kashmir has been kept alive for retaining the occupied Jammu and Kashmir, whereas truth is that just 15 percent of the population comprising Sunni Muslims inhabiting only five Districts of Kashmir Province are fanning the separatist activities, so much of internationalisation of the issue have been made to look upon India as an culprit nation. If one looks realistically the percentage of Muslims who are desirous of joining back India in the occupied territories are more.

Conjuring the fabricated Kashmir issue and making it a Jihad for Azadi was not for the sake of Kashmir or Kashmiri Muslims, Pakistan loss of East Pakistan (now Bangladesh) is the main cause and Pakistani's want of revenge against India is the motivating force. What is occupied will be held in strength and never returned in spite of Indian's rightfully claiming it as the occupied territories being integral part of India. If Kashmiri Muslims are feeling that they will be welcomed with open arms by Pakistan on separating from India, then they are sadly mistaken, for they also will be called Mujahir. The question is why there should be demand of Kashmiri only handful of Sunni Muslims who occupy only 15 percent of the land area under India and are 33 percent of Muslim population of Jammu and Kashmir and out of 22 Districts only 5 anti India Districts and rest being totally pro India, does not make case of any Azadi or Jihad. The grievances are there and partly Kashmiri Muslim is also to be blamed, as they called on the terrorism and Jihadi in their aspirations of separation from India.

The abrogation of the Article 370 and 35 A, has jolted Pakistan as the scope of separation and using the autonomy and independent governance clause to develop the theory of Kashmiri fight for independence, got topsy-turvy. Lot of water has flown under the bridge, over the occupied territory now the case has taken a shape of permanency where both China and Pakistan have taken it for granted that occupied territories will not be forfeited. It was this confidence that occupied territories have been used for military and economic alliances. India's reclamation of the occupied territories is not going to be an easy affair.

Influence of Regional Power equation of India is to be enlarged; India on its own cannot achieve this status. The influence radius will get enlarged only when India starts participating in the world power gambits, it is the reciprocal interest which is going to matter. India's enemies have joined in alliance both militarily and economically, it has become strong bondage, moreover China has relevance in the world economic order and this has to be accepted as it is going to play an important part in the economic businesses. What the Prime Minister Mr Modi is propagating the idea of 'Made in India', 'Make in India' and 'Self Reliance' is of relevance and India has to achieve so that it cannot get throttled or black mailed. India cannot be bystander but has to be part of the lobby of world power. There are good indicators of India going in for agreements with the USA and its lobby on Logistic Military support, participating in the South China Sea front, increasing the military bases in Indian Ocean, Middle East, Central Asia and Littoral States, improving the strategic military reach and building the military potential. Only when a country is recognised of its potential then only it can think about reclamation of its lost territories over which it has sovereign rights.

The grounds are to be prepared for which there will be requirement of time; actually this should have happened immediately after 1971 and 1999, but these windows were wasted and neither there was any interest shown, it was found appropriate to fight back the declared Proxy War and appeasing the Kashmiri Muslims. The first step of integrating Jammu and Kashmir with India and removing the controversial clauses which was being used as an instrument of invoking separatist mindset, abrogation was an essential step, nationalists have appreciated but others have their reservations which are not founded. If development of the State can bring relief to the population grievances which was denied on purpose, this has to show results on ground, if it can make people united, then reclamation will become stronger claim and getting the population on the other side of LOC on board will be easier.

What I have discussed in this book is my perception and I have given out number of hypothetical scenarios, this is only to give impetus of thinking out of the box measures to deal with Pakistan and China. It is not that India is not at it but people are not aware of it. The question is when India is going in for getting back the occupied territories, how much is India prepared to face war because nothing less than war can give the result. The decision has to be taken by Indian politics. Presently there is lack of unison on the issue of reclamation among the various political parties; there is lack of confidence and belief. Propaganda from all fronts are going on in a big way in the media each claiming an upper hand over the other, it is more of rhetoric expression of one's capability. Though every party is apprehensive and uncertain including India, waiting will continue for some time. India has to build its capability and potential in this interim period before taking the bold decision. Indian political power cycle of five years will also matter in respect of continuity, maintaining the tempo and military development, will make lot of difference as the perception may not be matching, in a away both Pakistan and China are waiting for this to happen and looking forward to the next election in India.

"Of war, there is open war, concealed war and silent war. 'Open war' is obvious, and 'concealed war' is what we call guerrilla warfare or insurgency in more relevant terms, but silent war is a kind of fighting that no other thinker one knows of has discussed. 'Silent war' is a kind of warfare with another kingdom in which the king and his ministers—and unknowingly, the people—all act publicly as if they were at peace with the opposing kingdom, but all the while secret agents and spies are assassinating important leaders in the other kingdom, creating divisions among key ministers and classes, and spreading propaganda and disinformation. So as per him today we are witnessing an environment that combines both 'concealed' and 'silent' war, although their attributes varies".

– Chanakya

Index

A

Abbottabad 140, 141

Abdul Ghani Bhat 88

Abdul Ghani Lone 88

Abdul Hameed Khan 144

Aksai Chin ix, 31, 38, 39, 40, 54, 56, 78, 108, 111, 128, 145, 146, 147, 155, 156, 158, 160, 172, 174, 176, 178, 181, 182, 183, 186, 189, 198, 201, 202

All Parties Hurriyat Conference (APHC) 81, 82, 83, 84, 85, 86, 87, 89

Al-Qaida 75, 84, 121, 132

Article 370 vii, viii, ix, x, 5, 7, 8, 9, 10, 11, 12, 13, 15, 16, 17, 18, 19, 20, 21, 22, 23, 25, 46, 50, 51, 52, 54, 56, 58, 59, 60, 61, 63, 64, 67, 68, 74, 81, 83, 90, 92, 94, 95, 99, 100, 101, 102, 110, 121, 145, 157, 182, 206

Azad Kashmir 32, 55, 57, 61, 62, 64, 121, 133, 136, 139, 140, 141, 142, 143, 147, 149, 151, 157, 158, 159, 160, 161, 163, 164, 174, 178, 200

B

Badakhshan Province 43, 44, 45

Bakarwals 60

Bakshi Mohammad 18

Balawaristan National Front 144

Bilafond La 38

Budgam 68

C

Central Asian Republics 55

Chabahar port 42

China Pakistan Economic Corridor (CPEC) 31, 35, 39, 78, 145

D

Dalai Lama 183

F

Financial Action Task Force 63, 79

G

Galwan Valley 178, 182, 185, 202

Geneva Convention 32, 155

Ghazwa-e-Hind 62

Gujjars 57, 60, 81, 96

Gyong La 38

H

Hajipir 141

Hari Singh 2, 3, 4, 10, 17, 19, 48, 108, 109, 130, 143

Hizb-ul-Mujahideen 82

I

Imran Khan 131, 177

Indo-China war 31

Indo–Pak War 1947-48 29

Inter Services Intelligence (ISI) 82, 83

J

Jamat-e-Islami 88

Jamat-ud-Dawa 38

Jammu & Kashmir Liberation Front 88

Junagarh 28, 177

K

Karakoram Ranges 31, 151

Karakorum Tract 38

Kargil war 32

Kashmiri Muslims vii, xi, 7, 8, 13, 15, 18, 19, 20, 22, 23, 27, 37, 51, 52, 54, 57, 60, 75, 76, 92, 96, 100, 110, 205, 206, 207

Khalistan Movement 37, 64

Khyber Pakhtunkhwa 31, 33, 35, 36, 48, 104, 118, 122, 132, 134, 147, 150, 153, 161

Kotli 136

Kulgam 68

L

Lasker-e-Taiba 38

Line of Actual Control (LAC) 50, 188, 193, 200

Line of Control (LOC) 4, 7, 47, 50, 70, 117, 175

Logistics Exchange Memorandum of Agreement (LEMOA) 185

M

Manmohan Singh 69

Mehbooba Mufti 94, 95

Mirwaiz Umar Farooq 88

Mohammad Abbas Ansari 88

Mughal Road alignment 56

Muhammad Ali Jinnah 37

Muslim Conference 88

Muslim United Front (MUF) 81, 82

Muzaffarbad 140

N

Narendra Modi 68, 76, 115, 157, 182

National Conference (NC) 85, 93, 94, 99

Neelum 136, 138

North-West Frontier Province (NWFP) 31

O

Operation Topac vii, 62, 64, 77

Organisation of Islamic Cooperation 79

P

Pakistan Occupied Kashmir (POK) x, 47

Pangong Tso 33, 200

People's Democratic Party (PDP) 85, 93, 94, 95

Phulwama 68

R

Rawalpindi 31, 140, 145, 157

Rezang La 200

Riyasat–e–Sadar 22

S

Saltoro Ridge 31, 38, 40

Sardar Patel 37

Shaksgam Valley ix, 31, 38, 39, 56, 78, 111, 129, 145, 146, 147, 158, 160, 162, 172, 174, 176, 178, 181, 183, 184, 192, 193, 195, 198, 201, 202

Sheikh Abdullah 10, 16, 17, 18, 37, 94

Shekupura 140

Sher-i-Kashmir. *See also* Sheikh Abdullah

Shia Muslim 46, 57, 58, 64

Shopian 68

Shyok Valley 33

Siachen Glacier 31, 33, 38, 39, 40, 146, 177

South Asian Association for Regional Cooperation (SAARC) 112

Sunni Punjabi Muslims 58

Syed Ali Shah Geelani 88, 91, 92

Syed Salahuddin 82

T

Tarek-e-Hurriyat 82

Tarek-e-Taliban 43

Tehreek-e-Insaf 131

Tehrik-i-Taliban Pakistan 119

Tibet Autonomous Region 53, 56

Tukre-Tukre Gang 22

W

Wazir-e-Azam 22

X

Xinjiang Autonomous Region 43

Y

Yasin Malik 88

Z

Zanskar Range 151

Zia-ul-Haq 62

www.ingramcontent.com/pod-product-compliance
Lightning Source LLC
Chambersburg PA
CBHW021703210326
41599CB00013B/1504